Dear Mr. Buffett

Dear Mr. Buffett

What an Investor
Learns 1,269 Miles
from Wall Street

Janet M. Tavakoli

WILEY

John Wiley & Sons, Inc.

Published by John Wiley & Sons, Inc., Hoboken, New Jersey.
Published simultaneously in Canada.

For general information on our other products and services or for technical support, please
contact our Customer Care Department within the United States at (800) 762–2974,
outside the United States at (317) 572–3993 or fax (317) 572–4002.

Wiley also publishes its books in a variety of electronic formats. Some content that appears
in print may not be available in electronic books. For more information about Wiley
products, visit our Web site at www.wiley.com.

Library of Congress Cataloging-in-Publication Data:

Tavakoli, Janet M.
    Dear Mr. Buffet: what an investor learns 1,269 miles from Wall Street / Janet M. Tavakoli.
      p. cm
    Includes bibliographical references and index.
    ISBN 978-0-470-40678-6 (Cloth)
      1. Investments—Decision making. 2. Investment analysis. 3. Financial risk
    management. 4. Value. 5. Buffett, Warren. 6. Berkshire Hathaway Inc. 7. Tavakoli,
    Janet M. I. Title.
    HG4521.T34   2009
    332.6—dc22

                          2008035055

Printed in the United States of America.

10 9 8 7 6 5 4 3 2

Nobody was ever made by him [Claudius Maximus] to feel inferior, yet none could have presumed to challenge his pre-eminence. He was also the possessor of an agreeable sense of humor.

—Marcus Aurelius

Contents

Preface

In 2003, I moved from London to Chicago, my original hometown, and founded a finance consulting firm, Tavakoli Structured Finance, Inc. Sophisticated financial institutions call me when they have trouble understanding complex financial products, and in recent years, the products have exploded in size and complexity. They also call me when they fight with each other over these products. As a result, my firm is a lightning rod for the myriad problems facing the credit markets. My client list is short and elite, and in one way or another, most of my business comes from my former employers.

I created a niche business at the right time. Structured finance birthed a plethora of new products with acronyms such as ABS, MBS, CDO, and CMO, among other alphabet combinations. Reporters and television networks frequently ask me to make sense of market madness. I've made repeat television appearances—CNN, CNBC, BNN (Canada's Business News Network), *CBS Evening News, Bloomberg TV,* and *First Business Morning News*—on where I've frequently predicted problems long before the market or even the Federal Reserve acknowledged them. I've been quoted in major financial publications including the *Wall Street Journal,* the *Financial Times, BusinessWeek, Forbes, Fortune* and *Investors*

Dealers' Digest (among others) in which I was often the first to publicly and specifically challenge major financial institutions, the Federal Reserve Bank, and the major rating agencies: Moody's Corporation (Moody's); Standard & Poor's (S&P), part of the McGraw-Hill Companies, Inc.; and Fitch, owned by France-based Fimalac SA.

Beginning in 1985, I worked for various Wall Street firms in New York and London. These included Salomon Brothers (now part of Citigroup), Bank One and Bear Stearns (both now part of JPMorgan Chase), Goldman Sachs, Merrill Lynch, and others. I chiefly worked on trading floors, and most of my colleagues were men. My career travels took me to New York, Japan, continental Europe, and England. I traded, structured and sold complex financial instruments. Although I often held management jobs, I was chiefly a hired gun; I took the jobs others considered too new or too difficult.

I wrote finance books well known to users of esoteric financial products with tongue-twisting names such as *credit derivatives* and *collateralized debt obligations.* Ten years ago, these products were limited to a small group, but now these products pose hot-button issues for investors ranging from very sophisticated banks to near-retail clients including local governments, small pension funds, and condominium associations. I wrote articles for major financial publications explaining problems in structured finance and warned that it would not end well. I predicted the mortgage meltdown, the global credit bubble, and the collapse of investments backed by unwise mortgage loans. I warned about the risks of hedge funds using leverage including Long-Term Capital Management (LTCM). While the rest of the financial community tripped over themselves to extend LTCM credit (and later regretted it), I recommended cutting their credit. Along the way, I acquired fans and a few groupies. At a Washington D.C. conference, a woman approached me in the ladies room to ask me to sign a blank sheet of paper, just to have my autograph. At a New York conference, an attendee from the Netherlands asked me to sign an extra book he had packed for his absent colleague, a fan who could not make the trip to New York. As I was finalizing paperwork at my doctor's office in Chicago, a man standing at the counter said: "Tavakoli? Are you the lady who wrote the credit derivatives book?"

I stumbled upon a career in finance. My parents met near the end of World War II, during which my mother's brother was killed after parachuting into Normandy. My Wisconsin-born father was chief of surgical services tending wounded soldiers in the Central Europe and Rhineland campaigns. My mother, who hailed from Buffalo, nursed burn victims in England. They met through mutual friends and returned to Chicago to raise a large family. My father had worked his way through medical school at Jesuit-run Loyola University during the first half of the last century, when well-educated adults were expected to be well-read polymaths. He died when I was 12, and during the summers of my teenage years, I read his collection of books, including texts about medicine, mathematics, Greek philosophy, history, and poetry. My father had read the *Wall Street Journal* every day, but after he died, my mother had not kept up the subscription. I was interested in finance, but I did not yet know much about it.

I graduated with a B.S. in chemical engineering from the Illinois Institute of Technology, and got married five days after graduation. I worked as a chemical engineer, and a couple of years later (in 1978), I moved to Iran with my Iranian (and now ex-) husband. Our timing couldn't have been worse. Six months after we arrived, Iranians deposed the Shah, and the Ayatollah Khomeini returned to lead an anti-American, repressive theocratic government. I returned to the United States carrying one suitcase of clothing and $1,000. My husband remained in Iran with his wealthy family. He returned to the United States a few years later to start a business with his father's help, but by then, he was my ex-husband. I had lost my possessions and savings, but my true wealth is portable and remained on my shoulders. I worked as an engineer by day and received an MBA from the University of Chicago's Graduate School of Business night program, where I later taught derivatives part time.

Just because one is an expert in complicated financial products like derivatives, it does not mean one is good at value investing. (But it doesn't mean one is bad at it, either.) Although I had read a lot on the subject of value investing, I had not really absorbed it, and I had not diligently practiced it when making investments for my personal portfolio. Then I took a trip to a city 1,269 miles from Wall Street, and my perspective changed.

Harry Truman once said: "The only thing new is the history you don't know." I thought I knew a lot, until I met Warren Buffett. In June 2005, I received a letter from Warren Buffett inviting me to visit him in Omaha. A few years earlier, I had sent him a copy of a book I wrote on credit derivatives with a letter stuffed between the pages. It was a pleasure to receive his invitation; but I delayed in responding to him, even after learning that lunch with Warren Buffett went for $202,000 in 2004 and $351,000 in 2005 in charity auctions on eBay (the winning bid in 2008 was $2.11 million, and the proceeds benefit the Glide Foundation, a charity dedicated to helping the poor and homeless get back on their feet[1]). I am glad I didn't delay our meeting longer because when I finally met Warren Buffett, I came to realize that I still have a lot to learn. Truman is right that we can learn a lot from history (Buffett's annual letters to Berkshire Hathaway's shareholders), but Warren Buffett also taught me that I can learn new things about evaluating the present to improve the odds that the future will be better.

This book is about my meeting with Warren Buffett on the eve of the greatest market meltdown in history and how meeting him subtly changed the way I look at the global financial markets. I already knew the principles, but meeting Warren encouraged me to think about all financial products in a Benjamin Graham-style framework.

I also changed the way I invest. I have no illusions that I am in the same league with Warren Buffett, but I improved after I met him. Buffett's successful track record spans a half century, so you'll have to check back with me in fifty years to see how well I performed to use him as a benchmark. But you will have to do the measuring. I don't measure myself against benchmarks any more than Buffett does. Instead, I focus on value.

Benjamin Graham was Warren Buffett's mentor. Over time, Buffett applied and interpreted Graham's framework to his own unique investment style. This book is not about Graham's ideas or Buffett's ideas, it is about my reinterpretation of my own ideas about the financial markets as I looked through the lens of the value framework of Benjamin Graham and Warren Buffett.

My ideas and conclusions are my own and may differ somewhat from Warren Buffett's. No two people think exactly alike; *that is what makes a market.* But in areas where we may disagree, I should also point out that Warren Buffett has more experience and a much better track record, and I am still learning. Like him, I consider myself a life-long learner. But unlike Buffett, I have so much more to learn.

Monetary wealth is just one measure of value, however. Steven F. Haward, in writing about Winston Churchill, noted the characteristics that set him apart from other men: "candor and plain speaking, decisiveness, the ability to balance attention to details with a view of the wider scene, and a historical imagination that informed his judgment."[2] I could say the same for Warren Buffett. But I have to add that he has a genuine affection for the human race, and a generous desire for everyone to get as much from life as he does. He shared that with me, and now I am sharing it with you.

In the interest of full disclosure, I own Berkshire Hathaway stock (BRKA).

Acknowledgments

I would like to thank the many people who offered comments, encouragement, and suggestions, especially Arturo Cifuentes, Ph.D., managing director, R.W. Pressprich & Co.; David Kuenzi, head of Risk Management and Quantitative Research at Man Glenwood; Lee Argush, cofounder and executive managing director of Concord Wealth Management; Jim Rogers of Rogers Holdings; Hilary Till, cofounder, Premia Capital Management, LLC; Carl Schuman; Costas Kaplanis; Kenneth Brian Brummel, who made tactful comments on an early draft; Greg Newton, founding publisher, MAR/Hedge; Michael Siconolfi, senior editor at the *Wall Street Journal*; Eric Gleacher, founder and chairman of Gleacher Partners; Stephen Partridge-Hicks, cofounder of Gordian Knot; Suzette Haden Elgin, Ph.D. (for decades-old encouragement—you may have forgotten, but I have not); and Edward Stone, Nancie Poulos, Fred Watson, Julian Tyacke (for the question), Andrew Tobias, Osamu Yamada, J. Allen Meyer, Mary Anna Evans, Allen Salter, Rita Ilse Guhrauer, Teresa Brinati, and Libby Hellmann. I would also like to thank the many people who did not wish to be named but who acted as mutual sounding boards.

My manuscript benefited from constructive comments from the editors of John Wiley & Sons, namely Pamela van Giessen, who took a special interest in this project and gave developmental suggestions; Emilie Herman, who removed many speed bumps; Kate Wood, who facilitated; Todd Tedesco, senior production editor; and James Reidel, who copyedited.

Finally, I would like to thank Warren Buffett, chairman of Berkshire Hathaway, who told me to "keep writing."

No opinions or theories presented in this book necessarily represent those of the people I have thanked. I am responsible for any errors, statements, interpretations, or conclusions.

Dear Mr. Buffett

Chapter 1

An Unanswered Invitation

Be sure to stop by if you are ever in Omaha and want to talk credit derivatives . . .

—Warren Buffett in a letter
to Janet Tavakoli, June 6, 2005

I t was August 1, 2005, and I was rereading a letter in my correspondence file dated June 6, 2005. The letter was from Warren Buffett, the CEO of the gargantuan Berkshire Hathaway conglomerate. I had not yet responded and had no explanation for the delay save for a little awe. For the several years prior, *Fortune* listed Warren Buffett as either the richest or second richest man on the planet. He and Bill Gates annually jousted for the top spot, with the outcome depending on the relative share prices of Berkshire Hathaway and Microsoft.

Several years earlier, I had sent Warren Buffett a copy of my book, *Credit Derivatives & Synthetic Structures*. In his letter Buffett wrote that he had been looking at the book again and had just found a letter I had tucked between the pages, "Please accept my apologies," he continued, "for not replying to you when I first received it."[1] He invited me to stop by if I were ever in Omaha. I looked up. After all this time, I could not remember what I had written in that old letter. I did know that I had not expected a response. But certainly now a response was needed from me, a belated one. "Dear Mr. Buffett," I began.

I am an investor in Berkshire Hathaway "A" shares, but Mr. Buffett would have no way of knowing that since I hold shares in brokerage accounts. Perhaps Mr. Buffett had a bone to pick with me, but I had warned about the risk of credit derivatives and the hidden leverage they created. I was so persistent in exposing the flaws in the financial system that *BusinessWeek* called me the "Cassandra of credit derivatives."[2] But most journalists overlooked a much more important derivatives quote in Mr. Buffett's 2002 shareholder letter. Berkshire Hathaway invests in multinational businesses with a variety of complex operations, and that means that investments have to be hedged or entered into in ways that create tax or accounting advantages. Mr. Buffett had also written: "I sometimes engage in large-scale derivatives transactions."[3] Yet I dithered and had not responded to his letter.

In 1998, Berkshire Hathaway acquired General Reinsurance. Warren Buffett initially called it his "problem child,"[4] and its General Reinsurance (Gen Re) Securities unit was its problem sibling. Even before the acquisition, both Warren Buffett and Berkshire Hathaway vice-chairman Charlie Munger realized that the value of Gen Re Securities derivatives transactions was overstated and vainly tried to sell it. Some of the contracts were for 20-year maturities, and the operation would take years to wind down. Furthermore, the models valuing the derivatives give poor approximations of the true *mark-to-market* value—the price at which the derivative can be bought and sold in the market—of some of Gen Re Securities' esoteric derivatives contracts. There was no real market. Instead, the derivatives contracts were priced or *marked* based on model valuations known as *mark to model*. Buffett wrote that in extreme cases, it was a "mark to myth."[5]

In his 2002 letter to Berkshire Hathaway shareholders, Buffett wrote that it sometimes seemed "madmen"[6] imagined new derivatives contracts. His pique was prompted by the multiyear-long hangover of losses from derivatives, chiefly credit derivatives, in the GenRe Securities unit. It showed a loss of $173 million, partly due to restating faulty, but standard, derivatives accounting from earlier years. The loss inspired Buffett to call derivatives "financial weapons of mass destruction."[7] His viral sound bite quickly circled the globe. After reading Buffett's quote in the financial press, one investment banker joked that my book on credit derivatives is "the manual on how to blow up the world."

Warren Buffett's letter to me arrived in June 2005, a hectic month. One of my clients was a law firm representing a large money center bank as plaintiff in a securities fraud case involving another large money center bank. The defendants' lawyers had hired a former chairman of the U.S. Securities and Exchange Commission (SEC) as their expert witness. Earlier, I had written both my expert opinion report and a report rebutting the former SEC chairman's point of view. I prepared to give a two-day-long deposition to discuss my opinion in the case in which hundreds of millions of dollars had been lost. The defendants had read my work, knew they faced serious trouble, and subsequently changed their strategy. In fact, they sent their most experienced litigator to depose me.

I put Buffett's letter in my purse to remind myself to respond to it. The morning of the deposition's first day, I saw the letter and felt a glow of confidence. I am not a superstitious person, but I couldn't help thinking of the letter as an auspicious sign. I put it in my pending correspondence file and forgot about it again.

The deposition came and went, and the plaintiff's lawyers were delighted. "Everyone gets bloody in a battle, but you slaughtered them." The defendants' arguments fell apart in the face of the facts, and the case never went to trial. Shortly thereafter, the defendants came to a settlement agreement to the plaintiff's satisfaction.

At the end of June, I reviewed my correspondence file and read the letter again. Client business would not take me to Omaha, and I was fairly certain Warren Buffett did not need my help.

July 2005 was another busy month: I had focused so much on the securities fraud case that I had a backlog of business, so I took a much–needed week-long vacation to decompress. At the end of July, I reviewed my pending correspondence file, and it contained only one item: the letter.

After rereading the letter on August 1, I wrote a letter in reply and offered three dates, with August 25, five days before Warren Buffett's 75th birthday, being the earliest of the three:

> It is my turn to apologize for being so late getting back to you. . . . . Business isn't taking me in that direction anytime soon, but I would be happy to fly in for the day—just because I would enjoy doing it . . .

On August 3, I received an e-mail from Warren Buffett through his assistant stating that August 25 would work:

> If you can make it for lunch, I would be glad to take you to a place with no décor but good food.

Everyone in the global financial community knew Warren Buffett by reputation, and his name continually popped up in the financial press, but I operated in specialty niches of the industry, and he was just part of the background noise of my world. I hadn't read any of the books about him, and I hadn't read the many articles about Warren Buffett, the man. But I had read many of Berkshire Hathaway's annual reports including Mr. Buffett's shareholder letters, which I enjoyed very much.

Warren Buffett was already a billionaire at age 60. That in itself was an achievement beyond the reach of all but a miniscule percentage of humans, but his future success dwarfed that accomplishment. Due to the benefits of continued compounded growth off of a greater base of wealth, the bulk of Buffett's wealth accumulated after the age when most men retire to spend their money.

Throughout my career, I worked with people who eventually met or did business with Warren Buffett. It was as if we attended the same university and he were a popular senior and I a freshman. I was well respected in my field, and was a self-made woman; but Warren Buffett was a financial legend *superlatively* good at making money for himself and for his shareholders.

In 1987, Warren Buffett and Charlie Munger rode to the rescue of John Gutfreund, the CEO of Salomon Brothers. Their "white knight" investment of $700 million of Salomon Inc.'s convertible preferred stock enabled Gutfreund to fend off Ronald Perelman's hostile take-over. Perelman, a famous, colorful cigar-loving corporate raider with a reputation for ruthlessness, had already swallowed up Revlon, Sunbeam, Panasonic and other companies in the 1980s. In contrast, Buffett and Munger were not well known, and their lifestyles didn't provide salacious material for the media frenzy that surrounded corporate raiders.

Initially, Salomon's preferred stock was an ideal Berkshire Hathaway investment. Buffett never supplied management; he looked for good honest managers, and he thought he had found one in Gutfreund. Things changed in 1991. Paul Mozer, a trader on the Arbitrage Desk, pleaded guilty to felony charges after a government bond trading scandal. John Meriwether, the head of Salomon's Arbitrage trading desk, told Gutfreund that Mozer had confessed to him. Their failure to immediately come forward compounded the scandal, and neither of them survived the fallout. Buffett was compelled to protect Berkshire Hathaway's investment. In the summer of 1991, he became Salomon's reluctant CEO for 10 months. Mr. Buffett's leadership and reputation for integrity salvaged Salomon's business, which rapidly recovered. The convertible bonds outperformed the fixed income securities that Berkshire Hathaway had sold in their place, but by 1995, the option to convert to common shares of Salomon stock was worthless. In 1997, Buffett off loaded the investment on Sandy Weil, and Salomon eventually became a part of Citigroup.

I had joined Salomon Brothers' summer 1985 training class lampooned by my classmate Michael Lewis in his book, *Liar's Poker*. Unlike Lewis, I was one of the trainees actually paying attention at the front of the class, but by the time Mr. Buffett served his brief time as CEO, I was no longer working at Salomon Brothers.

After almost 20 years working for Wall Street firms in New York and London, I made my living running a Chicago-based consulting business. My clients consider my expertise the product they consume. I had written books on credit derivatives and complex structured finance products, and financial institutions, hedge funds, and sophisticated investors came to me to identify and solve potential problems.

Although I was an experienced finance professional, I did not focus on value investing. The University of Chicago was steeped in the myth of efficient markets and leaned to theories put forth by eminent economists. Warren Buffett had earned his MBA at Columbia Business School. He became a friend and disciple of Benjamin Graham, and later worked for Graham's hedge fund. I had read *Security Analysis* by Graham and David Dodd in 1985, but I had not actively practiced its principles for my own investment portfolio. Around the same time, I read John Burr Williams' *The Theory of Investment Value,* and the fourth edition of *The Intelligent Investor.* My edition includes an introduction by Warren Buffett with a tribute to the late Benjamin Graham as well as Warren Buffett's 1984 commencement address at Columbia University titled "The Superinvestors of Graham-and-Doddsville." I remembered both the tribute and the address and reread them in preparation for meeting Mr. Buffett. My focus was chiefly on derivatives and complex securities. While I applied many of the principles of value investing to my analysis of complicated financial products, I did not yet focus on it for my own investments or as a way of looking at the global markets as a whole.

Derivatives are financial bets that something will or will not happen. Any financial investment involves a bet, but derivatives are *leveraged bets.* For very little money down—sometimes no money down—you can make gobs of money (or lose gobs of money). The part about losing gobs of money is something most investors try hard not to think about. Sometimes investment banks selling the products help investors achieve this goal by putting the part about gobs of losses in very fine print buried in hundreds of pages of documents.

Leveraged bets are so popular that there is more money at risk in derivatives than in stocks or bonds. The problem with leverage-driven binge banking is that everyone tends to disgorge assets at the same time, depressing market prices. Financial leverage sometimes moves global markets, and if allowed to get out of hand, leverage can theoretically trigger a global market Chernobyl.

Warren Buffett disproved the theory of efficient markets that states that prices reflect all known information. His shareholder letters, readily available through Berkshire Hathaway's Web site, told investors everything they needed to know about mortgage loan fraud, mispriced credit derivatives, and overpriced securitizations, yet this information hid in plain "site."

I knew the financial markets were at great risk—like children playing with matches in a parched forest—but those thoughts were far from my mind on that hot summer morning in 2005 as I boarded the plane for Omaha. I was about to meet a financial legend, the greatest investor who ever lived.

Chapter 2

Lunch with Warren

Thanks for sending along the . . . link, which I had not seen. The next guy will probably name his company Buffett, Bernanke and Tavakoli.
—Warren Buffett
to Janet Tavakoli, August 27, 2007

The day was sunny and clear, and the flight from Chicago only takes a little over an hour. I wondered how a man with Warren Buffett's enormous wealth would behave. The late Howard Hughes suffered from paranoid schizophrenia attributed to brain damage suffered during self-piloted plane crashes. According to popular legend, he once roared: "I am not a paranoid deranged millionaire. Godammit . . . I'm a *billionaire*." A sense of humor is indispensable if one is *insanely* rich.

My flight got into Omaha two hours before my appointment. I wanted to be on time for lunch. When I told the cab driver the address, he looked confused. I assumed that every taxi driver in Omaha would know the location of Mr. Buffett's office, but I was wrong. He asked another cab driver for directions, and we were on our way. It was a short ride.

The taxi dropped me off at an unremarkable buff-colored office building. I opened the door and entered what appeared to be a hallway instead of a lobby. A lone security guard sat at a small desk. He seemed to be expecting me, telling me to go right on up to the 14th floor. An elevator was already on the ground floor, and there was no one else in the lobby. I rode up alone.

The elevator doors opened to a vacant hallway. As I stepped off the elevator, I was startled to hear a friendly female voice say: "Janet, make a right and then another right, and go straight ahead." I quickly looked around. There was no one there, and I didn't see a camera or a speaker. I did a quick mental review of my actions since entering the building and was relieved I hadn't adjusted my skirt on the elevator. The voice repeated the instructions, and this time I followed them.

One of Warren Buffett's assistants sat to the right of the small reception area. There was no one else there. I told her I had arrived early, but I planned to read Paul Erdman's book *Tug of War* about the global currency crisis in the mid-1990s. She offered me beverages, and I accepted a glass of water. I had barely taken a sip, when Warren Buffett appeared. He gave me a quick look and said energetically: "Oh, Janet's here. Show her right in."

🍭 🍭 🍭

Warren Buffett was taller and trimmer than I expected. He later told me he works out with a trainer three times per week. His famous eyebrows were trimmed—unlike an old Internet photo—and his skin glowed as if freshly scrubbed. He wore a light gray suit and looked as if he dressed for comfort and appropriateness rather than to impress.

He invited me to sit on a sofa while he took a neighboring chair. Plump beads of sweat rolled down my water glass, and I looked around his coffee table in consternation for a coaster or an ash tray. I didn't want to be known as the person who left a blistering water ring on the smooth surface. *Oh that? A calling card from Janet Tavakoli.* Noticing my hesitation, Warren retrieved the *Wall Street Journal* from his desk. He set it down, and said I could put my glass on his paper. I looked down at the paper knowing I was about to make a mess of it. It looked so smooth. Warren Buffett had worked as a paper boy for the *Buffalo News* and identified the *Washington Post* as one of the great bargains of the twentieth century for Berkshire Hathaway's investors. Warren's love of newspapers is well known, and for more than half a century he has been a loyal reader of the *Wall Street Journal*. My heart sank at the thought of making a mess of his paper. *Had he finished reading it?* I looked up, and to my complete surprise, Warren Buffett appeared nervous. He wouldn't feel comfortable until I accepted his offer of hospitality; he couldn't relax until I relaxed. I rested my glass and sat down, smiling inwardly.

Then I blundered. In an awkward attempt to lighten the moment, I said: "Some days that is all the *Wall Street Journal* is good for."

His head snapped around and he gave me a sharp look. A few seconds passed. "I agree," he finally said.

But I knew he didn't mean his comment, and I hadn't meant mine. What's more, he knew I didn't mean it, and I suspected he knew that I knew he didn't mean his. Judith Martin, the *Washington Post's* etiquette columnist, maintains etiquette has been given a bad name by strangers using fake familiarity to make demands on our time, our privacy, and our resources. Genuine etiquette is a useful social tool designed to make others comfortable without sacrificing one's own rights. Months later, Warren wrote me that he didn't think he had "studied her advice sufficiently," but I thought he graduated *summa cum laude*.

The *Wall Street Journal* sparked a discussion of how the news media has changed. Stock price quotations are almost instantaneous. There is more financial news today than ever before originating from a wider variety of sources including the Internet.

Warren loves newspapers, recognizing that newspaper ownership confers status and influence out of proportion with economic gain, yet run properly there is also a lot of economic gain to be had. As he talked, Warren mentioned Kay. *Kay?* My mind raced. *Who is Kay?* Fortunately, I quickly realized that Warren meant the late Katherine Graham, president and publisher of the *Washington Post*. Warren said she was "great lady," a "remarkable woman," and recommended I read *Personal History*, her Pulitzer Prize–winning autobiography.

With Kay's sponsorship and his substantial ownership position, Warren became a board member of the iconic *Washington Post*. He said she was the least confident person he had ever met, a curious fact given her privileged life, social standing, and accomplishments. In *Personal History*, Katherine Graham expresses admiration for Warren and expresses her gratitude to him for the tutelage he gave her in financial matters. She relied on him for both professional and personal support, and his mentorship was a source of strength, giving her confidence. The otherwise all-male board was initially wary of their friendship and she noticed some sexism: "Tom Murphy [another member of the *Washington Post*'s Board of Directors] could consult Warren and no one questioned him, but if I consulted him, it seemed to be something threatening and sinister."[1] Often, when men and women have a close business relationship, it is characterized as a Mephistophelean bargain, but when men form a close business relationship, it is just business. Ms. Graham also noticed: "As Warren and I started to spend more and more time together, people's eyebrows shot up, and I was young enough then for our relationship to become quite an issue."[2] Even a woman of Katherine Graham's stature and maturity—she was 13 years older than Warren—could not escape petty innuendo; but she did not let it deter her from taking advantage of Warren's expertise or spoil her appreciation of their friendship.

I could well imagine Warren's companionable appeal to Katherine Graham, and Warren lights up when he reminisces about Ms. Graham. He seems to enjoy women without enjoying them too much. It is the difference between spending time with an art connoisseur and a cat burglar. One makes you feel as if you are a national treasure; the other makes you feel as if you are about to be snatched and stuffed in a bag, never to be heard from again. For his part, Warren says he admired Kay's courage and persistence.

Warren recognizes that the news business had changed. He said the *Wall Street Journal* threw away a golden opportunity to dominate Internet business news. Internet financial news is both instantaneous and less reliable. Newspaper and magazines—even the online versions of legacy print media—often lag behind blogs and certain specialty new services. There are a handful of Internet financial journalists who are every bit as good as the best reporters in the print media, but they are scattered all over the Internet.

Matthew Currier Burden wrote a book about this phenomenon: *The Blog of War*. The military is having difficulty containing sensitive information as soldiers pour out their stories over the Internet. The day after our lunch, I sent Warren an article written by John Hockenberry, "In Iraq for 365," from *Wired.com*. Warren wrote back that he found the blogs on Iraq particularly interesting along with "the potential that it has for changing journalism."

The blogs of soldiers in Iraq are much more informative than any state-side news media, including television, radio, newspapers, magazines, and other Internet news sources. Warren is keenly interested in that. Traditional channels of information are being bypassed and passed up by direct information from the front lines, something that had never happened before the Internet Age. The accounts from soldiers are more compelling and informed than the so-called "professional" reportage from mainstream media.

I mentioned that Comedy Central's *The Daily Show with Jon Stewart* often has better news analysis than what tries to pass as news shows on other channels. Warren hadn't watched the program, but asked if he should. I said Stewart's interviews of leading world figures might be of interest, and later occasionally sent a link. Warren had not yet gotten around to getting a TiVO. Neither had I.

Warren displays an open mind to all new ideas. Warren and I both love our newspapers, but we love *news* more, wherever we find it. The challenge is to find *reliable* news. I was about to discover that some of the information I had read about Warren Buffett was incorrect, and the coming years would reveal more inaccuracies.

Dustin Hoffman once remarked on a story he read about how he and Tom Cruise were holding up shooting because they were a couple of prima donnas. The story was fabricated: "but if I wasn't making a movie with him and I just picked up the paper, I'd believe it. That's interesting, isn't it?"[3] There is a reason we call it the "Information Age," not the "Age of Wisdom."

Financial research often ends where the Internet begins. Articles are frequently incorrect, urban legend is sometimes presented as fact, and trivial errors sometimes become viral financial lore. Benjamin Graham, Warren Buffett's Columbia School professor and mentor, founded a hedge fund in the 1920s. Warren says that Graham's hedge fund was the earliest as far as he knows, though there may have been another before it. Yet, most media report that the first hedge fund founded in the United States was done so in 1949 by A. W. Jones.[4] Financial journalists rarely mention Benjamin Graham's fund. Apparently there are no Google references to the 1920s.

On a televised talk show, Ben Bradlee, vice president and managing editor of the *Washington Post*, held that he didn't think newspapers would ever be supplanted by the Internet. Some Internet sources are excellent, but it is still unclear if they can make enough revenue to continue putting out quality information, and new competitors keep popping up on the Web. He is probably correct that there will always be a demand for newspapers; but newspaper revenues are already being partially supplanted as they lose chunks of lucrative classified ad revenues to the Internet.

Unlike Bradlee, Warren does not let nostalgia get in the way of a good business strategy. On November 21, 2005, Cathy Baron Tamraz, the founder of Business Wire, a San Francisco–based distributor of online press releases, sent Warren a letter in which she told him, "We run a tight ship and keep spending under wraps . . ." She describes a business with no secretaries or management layers, and they invest most of what they have to stay abreast of technology. By the time he finished reading the letter, Warren had decided to acquire a business perfect for his investment style: it has dedicated management, eliminates unnecessary overhead, produces a product people need and has huge potential for revenue growth. By March 2006, Warren had closed the deal, making Business Wire, an Internet phenomenon, a wholly owned subsidiary of Berkshire Hathaway.

An assistant handles Warren's e-mail. This is because Warren molds technology to his lifestyle rather than letting it mold him. He joked that Bill Gates offered to send him an attractive young female computer expert to show him the ropes. Warren, however, is quite comfortable with the computer. He plays hours of online bridge, and he asked me about my bridge-playing skills: "Do you play online?" Warren encouraged me to, but I like to see the other players. I responded: "Audrey Grant, a master bridge player I met, says bridge is about luck, skill, and your relationship with your partner. I like to hear the bidding with all the inflections."

At the mention of Audrey Grant, Warren's eyes twinkled with delight; he knows her. I had already told him "Tavakoli" is my ex-husband's name, and Warren asked: "Have you read Audrey's nonbridge book, *Ex Etiquette?*" No? He jumped up and called out to his assistant: "Let's buy Janet that book!" We walked to his assistant's desk and she searched

Amazon. The book had been published in 1988 and was out of print. Undeterred, Warren had his assistant order it from the used books option to be delivered to me at a later date. (I saw Audrey again in July 2006, when she came to Chicago to give a bridge lesson. After I handed her the book to sign, she flipped it over in confusion, having completely forgotten it. She no longer even had a copy of her own and was astonished that Warren remembered it.)

I was not prepared for Warren. I am accustomed to a business world in which most of the men are not "nice kids," and I have long been used to prudently dealing with disrespect by lesser men (not twice). If Warren had simply avoided overt rudeness, it would have been an upgrade from most finance professionals, and it would have given me bragging rights: *I met Warren Buffett, and he was civil!*

It is hard to explain how Mr. Buffett managed to thoroughly win me over. He seemed to look away for an instant and then looked back with an almost imperceptible nod. It was as if he considered the totality of his impressive experience, and then concentrated on me with a compelling bias in my favor—as if he had exactly the impression of me, that at my personal best, I hoped to impart. In that moment, Mr. Buffett became *Warren* and seemed to convey that I should believe in myself the way he believed in me.

It seemed as if our conversation up until now had been a test drive. Warren trotted out his well-worn clichés reported over the years in magazine articles. Now he picked up the pace and asked a lot of questions. We must have covered over one hundred topics.

I lived in Iran for a year? Warren met Farah Diba, the late shah of Iran's third wife, at a Washington dinner party. I am grateful to be back, grateful for the opportunities, and relieved to again enjoy my rights as a woman born in the United States? So was Rosa Blumkin, the Jewish Russian emigrant furniture sales entrepreneur who sold her business to Warren and died at the age of 104. Inspired by his late wife, Susie, Warren is a major supporter of Planned Parenthood and a woman's right to choose. I do most of my work out of my home office? Warren likes the idea of keeping overhead low, especially since I rent conference offices when needed—he had worked out of his home office for years running his first highly successful investment partnership. I wear casual clothes to work unless I am meeting clients? Warren had considered that, too, but in his position as CEO of Berkshire Hathaway, it isn't practical. I attended a fundraiser in Chicago and met Ted Kennedy? Warren knows Ted Kennedy, but on a much different plane. I read *Forbes*? Warren knew the late Malcolm Forbes, son of the magazine's founder, B. C. Forbes. California housing and politics? Warren had advised Arnold Schwarzenegger, and another of Warren's personal friends was throwing him a birthday party in California, where Warren has a house. I had worked my way through my MBA as a chemical engineer? A chemical engineer and his wife, Donald and Mildred Othmer, had invested $50,000 with Warren in the 1960s and it was worth $750 million when Mr. Othmer died in 1995 (Mildred Othmer died in 1998. Today their holdings would be worth more than $3 billion). I was born in Chicago? Warren had owned and later sold retail stores in parts of town I probably didn't visit. I think the rating agencies' opinions are unreliable? Warren doesn't rely on them either for his investment decisions. Derivatives sometimes present opportunities? Warren had taken on a large derivative position on the dollar weakening (and later reduced it and put on another). I know large business owners? Warren is looking for good foreign businesses—preferably family owned—of $1 billion or more in size.

When Matteo Ricci studied at the Jesuit College in Rome in the late 1500s, he created a memory palace in his mind. Each item in the palace represents a series of concepts. The rooms and locations within the palace serve as directories and files do on a computer. Ricci later rose to elevated status in Ming dynasty society, because he was able to instantaneously learn, retain, and retrieve hundreds of new Chinese kanji to the astonished delight of the Chinese nobles. I felt as if Warren were giving me a private tour of his memory palace.

As we conversed, Warren seemed to find new knickknacks to place on a memory mantelpiece. Aristotle believed a trained memory is essential for developing logical thought processes. Warren does not rely on finance nursery rhymes like "diversification reduces risk," in fact, he often rejects them in favor of logic. Renowned professors like Yale's Benoit Mandelbrot urge investors to broadly diversify as a way around the fear and greed driven fluctuations of what Benjamin Graham called the manic depressive "Mr. Market."[5] Mandelbrot, who popularized fractals, seems resigned: "It is, in my view, premature to be hoping for serious gains from fractal finance. There is still too much we do not know."[6] Mandelbrot is correct about fractal finance, but he might be surprised to

of $4.6 billion." Another winning feature of this trade is that Berkshire Hathaway has zero credit risk. In the unlikely event that a payment is made 20 years from now, the put buyer is relying on Berkshire Hathaway to make a payment. Berkshire Hathaway is not depending upon an investment bank to make him a payment if the market is so troubled that stock index level is below today's level; an investment bank would probably be wiped out. Berkshire Hathaway, on the other hand, is likely to be doing much better than other companies in that scenario. Even the required payment on the put option in 20 years will be buffered by the fact that it is only a small part of Berkshire Hathaway's portfolio and it is partially offset by the value of the premiums in 20 years.

Warren also noticed that credit derivatives are often mispriced. When this occurs, he earns upfront premiums for taking default risk on baskets of high-yield (junk) bonds. When junk bond yields are very high and most investors avoid them, Warren will enter the market when he can be handsomely compensated to take the risk of carefully chosen companies. Warren invests when the prices are right; but he is happy to do nothing for years when the price for the risk is not right.

Warren is aided by the fact that most investment banks use sophisticated Monte Carlo models that misprice the transactions. Some of the models rely on rating agency inputs, and the rating agencies do a poor job of rating junk debt. Ratings guru Arturo Cifuentes, a managing director at R.W. Pressprich & Co., is one of the original developers of Moody's *collateralized debt obligations* (CDO) model. Among other serious problems, he notes that Moody's released a report in 2005 (and again in 2006) that shows that when judged by impairment rate, there is no difference in performance between CDO tranches with a junk rating of BB– and those with an investment-grade rating of BBB.[10] Other models rely on the relationships between historical market prices or on historical yield spread data.

If you play with coins or dice, you can learn a lot about the outcomes by flipping and throwing them thousands of times and recording the results. A Monte Carlo simulation uses a computer to throw a whole lot of random inputs into a model. It is like shaking a newly made chair to see how stable it is. Financial firms use correlation models to look at what happens when corporations default. The model tries to determine if other companies will behave similarly when one company strengthens or weakens. The models are highly unstable. They are like a chair that collapses beneath you as soon as you sit on it. Small changes to model inputs result in huge changes to the results.

If you play with coins or dice, you know exactly what your inputs are and you can model all potential outcomes. You can examine the coins (heads or tails per coin), and you can model all of the possible outcomes. You can examine dice (one to six dots on each face of each cube), and again, a mathematical model can describe all potential outcomes. We do not have to guess at the inputs for dice and cards; they are known in advance and the relationship between the inputs does not change, even though we may use a Monte Carlo model to randomize the inputs (the flips and tosses).

The inputs to credit models are a bit of a guess, since we rely on data approximations to come up with the inputs in the first place. Furthermore, the relationships between the inputs can change. Most of the data describing how one corporation behaves in relationship to another is based on market prices such as stock prices or the prices of credit default swaps based on corporate debt. Moreover, there is very little of this already-suspect data to work with. The results are guesses about relative price or yield spread movements, which result in a guess about the correlations. When a credit upset occurs in a financial sector, correlations that were previously fractional numbers tend to converge to one. Everything seems to fall apart at once. A model will calculate the wrong answer to nine decimal places, but it cannot tell you it is the wrong answer.

The biggest problem with the models is that even if they temporarily get the correct answer, they do not tell you what you need to know. Wall Street estimates *asset* correlations instead of the necessary *default* correlations. Furthermore, the overwhelming flaw in the methodology is that if you want to make up a default correlation between two companies, you must make the false assumption that *default probability* does not vary, but of course it does. Even if the models measured the default probability of individual companies—and they do not—if a company defaults, you still have to guess the *recovery rate,* the amount left over, if any, after all obligations are paid. You cannot solve for two independent items of information from a single piece of information such as a letter grade or a price. You cannot get both the probability that a company will default *and* the amount of money you will have left if it does default.

Warren warns Wall Street it is about to get into a fight it cannot win, and Wall Street comes anyway. The models are incapable of generating the information Warren has in his head. Warren says he doesn't use a model, but he does. Warren himself is the model. He has spent so much time reading annual reports that he has a good idea of whether or not a company will default, and if it does, how much will be leftover after everyone else is paid off. Moreover, he knows how businesses affect each other and how the impact may change in a variety of scenarios. He is much faster and much more accurate than a misguided computer model. *Warren does not rely on a price since that is what you pay. He relies on value because that is what you get.* Unlike the computer models, Warren does not guess at the inputs. He does not use a potentially irrational price as his input. Warren sizes up each business and relies on his rational assessment of value.

A couple of years before I met Warren, a Wall Street firm paid Berkshire Hathaway to take the risk of the first corporation to default in a basket of junk debt. Warren only considers deals he knows are mispriced, and he has a couple of conditions. *He chooses the specific corporate names; he refuses "diversified" portfolios containing a large number of corporations. He does trades in massive size—$100 million or more, if possible.*

The following is a simplified example. If one of a handful of prechosen corporations defaults, Berkshire Hathaway pays the original full amount for the debt, which is 100 percent of the first corporate name to default. Berkshire Hathaway then gets the recovery value—the market price of the debt. This price will depend on the remaining value of the company. Warren happily enters this type of credit derivative trade, when he can create a margin of safety—when Wall Street pays him so handsomely in an upfront premium that it exceeds anything he might lose if one of the companies defaults.

When Collins & Aikman defaulted and filed for bankruptcy in June 2005, Berkshire Hathaway recovered 35¢ on the dollar, or put another way, it "lost" 65¢ on the dollar. David Stockman, the director of the Office of Management and Budget during President Ronald Reagan's administration, was Collins & Aikman's CEO and stepped down the week before the bankruptcy was announced. In March 2007, he and other top officers were charged by a New York federal grand jury with conspiracy, several counts of fraud, and obstruction of justice. Allegations are that, among other things, loans were disguised as revenues and revenue was booked before it was earned. U.S. Attorney Michael Garcia said: "They resorted to lies, tricks and fraud."[11] Warren's margin of safety greatly increases the likelihood he will make money, even when an unexpected event like this occurs.

It is more important to have a margin of safety to protect oneself against a Black Bart—someone fancying himself to be an offspring of the famous Wells Fargo stagecoach robber—than a rare Black Swan type market event. Berkshire's "loss," given that the Collins & Aikman default occurred, was 65¢ on the dollar, but Berkshire had received *much more* than 65¢ on the dollar in upfront premiums. On average, Berkshire Hathaway had taken in around *75¢ on the dollar* in upfront premiums.

Warren does these trades in very large size. For example for every $1 billion of transactions, Berkshire stands to lock in $100 million (or more), *if* there is a default. Meanwhile, it has the use of $750 million in premium money it puts to good use. In 2005, Warren had $1.5 billion in premiums to put to work. *Isn't that adorable?*

Normally, first to default trades are viewed as the riskiest trades, and junk debt is viewed as the riskiest kind of asset; but Warren builds in a margin of safety that makes this a wise investment as long as Wall Street misprices the risk. Warren Buffett has figured out the safest way to take junk risk in the history of junk debt.

Investment banks could put on the same trades if they did fundamental analysis of the underlying companies, but they are too busy playing with correlation models. Banks and investment banks have become invisible hedge funds putting risk on their balance sheets that they cannot quantify. Meanwhile, Warren Buffett models the risk in his head and profits.

Warren has another advantage: Wall Street underestimates him.

In the fall of 2006, I was talking to a friend in New York, and I mentioned that Warren Buffett and I have similar views on credit derivatives, and—now comes the bragging part—I had *met* Warren Buffett. The problem with bragging is that it often backfires. This was one of those times. My former colleague, a Wall Street structured products "correlation" trader, wrinkled his nose and sniffed: "*That old guy?* He *hates* derivatives."

opportunity in a company that meets his criteria—$1 billion or more in size—to bring it to him. He also asked me to call him.

The flipside of that coin is knowing what *not* to buy. Another feature of Berkshire Hathaway is that, unlike hedge funds, Warren Buffett and Charlie Munger eschew leverage, avoiding companies burdened with debt. If you are not leveraged, and your businesses generate enough cash to meet your expenses, you do not have to worry about what anyone else thinks of your financial situation. You never have to sell assets into a distressed market to raise money, and if the stock market closes for years, you do not need to worry, since your assets keep growing and generating value. Warren and Charlie know they could have had higher historical returns had they used leverage, but in a distressed market, one can obliterate a great track record by destroying shareholder capital.

When calculating compounded returns, the game is over and your track record is irrelevant if you multiply by zero. We both knew the market was overleveraged, rating agencies misrated debt, and investment banking models were incorrect, but neither Warren nor I was aware that day that our interests would become more closely aligned as the largest financial debacle in the history of the capital markets began to unfold.

Both Warren and I knew the financial markets were overleveraged and credit derivatives contributed to the excessive leverage. Things were still relatively calm as I boarded the plane home in August 2005, but financial warning lights flashed bright red. Archimedes, the ancient Greek inventor and scientist, had said that if you gave him enough leverage, he could move the world. The global markets had combined high leverage with bad lending practices, and the financial world would soon feel the negative force.

Chapter 3

The Prairie Princes versus the Princes of Darkness

Bravo! Your Golden Fleece Award is a gem.

—Warren Buffett
to Janet Tavakoli, October 2, 2006

Both Warren Buffett and I advocate treating employee stock options as a cost of doing business. Warren operates in a competitive marketplace, and he has no problem compensating employees well. This cost of doing business should be calculated correctly and it should be expensed. Stock options are not an issue when Berkshire Hathaway finds a well-run family-owned business to purchase; if Berkshire Hathaway buys shares of stock in the marketplace, however, stock options are difficult to avoid. For example, Berkshire Hathaway has owned shares of Coca-Cola since 1988 (8.6 percent of Coca-Cola shares as of the end of 2007)[1], but Coca-Cola did not start expensing employee stock options until 2002.[2]

In his 1985 letter to Berkshire Hathaway shareholders, Buffett challenged the CEOs of corporate America. He offered to pay a substantial cash sum to any executive granted a restricted stock option in exchange for the right to any future gain the executive might realize. *Stock options are a real cost of doing business. You say you cannot value them? Great! I'll pay cash for them. Now try to explain to your shareholders how this cash didn't just come out of their pocket and move into yours.* Warren's challenge, which he continually reissues, remains unanswered.

Many corporate executives resist expensing the value of employee stock options, complaining there is ambiguity in how one values them. But accounting practices are rife with ambiguities. As long as the rules are understood, accounting helps paint a picture of corporate value with a semblance of consistency. For example, corporations depreciate expensive factory equipment according to accounting rules. While depreciation does not precisely capture the exact cost and timing of equipment replacements, it highlights the fact that there is a significant cost to stay in business. The rules of depreciation create some ambiguities; but one cannot use this as an excuse to ignore a real cost of doing business. Treating all employee stock options as an expense clarifies whether the hit to reported earnings is justified by the projected increase in shareholder wealth needed to compensate shareholders for the cost. No wonder some CEOs did not want to expense them.

The intent of stock options is benign, but the execution is flawed. In a rational world, options have a realistic strike price reflecting the true business value after building in carrying costs and retained earnings. If employees increase the value of the company beyond that, they can exercise the options, buy the stock at a reduced price to the future higher price due to employee value creation, and participate in the gain. It is theoretically possible to come up with a fair and rational strike price, but it is rarely attempted.

Stock options, which are *call* options, are a moral hazard inviting unnecessary risk taking because corporate officers get leveraged rewards for any success—and suffer no consequences if they fail. Officers of

weren't buying back company stock at some of the price dips. This would have increased shareholder value. Instead, some executives used their lowest stock price to dilute shareholder equity in order to enrich themselves. Backdating executives and their sycophants twisted financial logic with flexibility that rivals the gymnastics of Cirque du Soleil. There should be some sort of reward for executives that used backdating to increase the probability of their realizing upside without taking additional risk. They demonstrated calculating "creativity."

U.S. lawmakers blamed themselves in the ensuing scandal. They cited a tax law passed by Congress in 1993 exempting employee stock options from the $1 million tax deduction limit for senior executives. Executives have an incentive to award themselves stock options, and backdating may have been an unintended consequence of the law. Honest executives use stock options as they were intended, by both setting rational strike prices and securing the tax deduction, thus benefiting stockholders. Backdating, a perverted twist on employee stock options, is a separate problem. Shareholders and U.S. lawmakers alike were ambushed. Backdating directly benefits the option holders; greedy executives would probably have backdated with or without the tax deduction.

The late William Proxmire, while serving in the U.S. Senate, created the Golden Fleece Award for congressmen who waste taxpayer money. The Wisconsin Democrat named it after the mythological Golden Fleece swiped by the creatively *deceptive* Jason. Following Proxmire's example, I wrote a commentary in October 2006 bestowing the Golden Fleece Award for Optional Integrity on corporate executives who backdated their own stock options and failed to specifically disclose this material information to their board of directors and shareholders.[11,12] I nominated Harry Markowitz, the surviving Nobel Prize winner who supports not expensing stock options, to bestow the award. Warren called the idea a "gem."[13]

Had I not met Warren Buffett, I do not know if I would have ever published such an article pushing against famous names in finance. Meeting him encouraged me to put my own views forward and not to concern myself with what everyone else was doing, however many titles or awards they may have accumulated.

Warren wrote a memo the previous week to Berkshire Hathaway managers partly because of the option-backdating scandal that already embroiled more than 100 companies, and partly in reaction to Hewlett-Packard's headline-making *pretexting* scandal. Warren sent me a copy of his memo the day after I sent him my commentary.

Former Hewlett Packard chairwoman Patricia Dunn stepped down and, along with four others, faced criminal charges after allegedly using pretexting—a nice way of saying investigators pretended to be someone else to dupe phone companies—to obtain the phone records of staff, board members, and journalists. It seems that in trying to track down a boardroom leak, they became bigger rats.[14]

At the time Warren wrote this memo to the "All Stars"[15] (his managers), Berkshire Hathaway employed over 200,000 people. It is impossible to totally eliminate bad behavior in a conglomerate that size. Nevertheless, Buffett asked his top managers to increase their efforts especially when there was even a hint of a problem. He especially admonished his managers not to excuse potential problems because other corporations were doing something problematic:

> The five most dangerous words in business may be "Everybody else is doing it.". . . [L]et's start with what is legal, but always go on to what we would feel comfortable about being printed on the front page of our local paper . . . Your attitude . . . expressed by behavior as well as words, will be the most important factor in how the culture of your business develops.[16]

On October 8, 2006, I sent Warren an e-mail about a segment I had watched the previous evening on television:

> I found it ironic that Patricia Dunn of HP defended her actions during her *60 Minutes* interview by claiming everyone was doing it while you lead your memo by debunking that excuse. I especially liked: *And culture, more than rule books, determines how an organization behaves.*

Warren agreed that I should share the memo with others, and I sent it to several people, including Richard Beales, at the time a reporter at the *Financial Times,* who was looking for news. The paper posted the entire letter on its Web site.

Jamie Dimon, CEO of JPMorgan Chase, wrote me that he agreed with Warren. When people justify their actions with the excuse that everyone else is doing the same thing, it is a red flag.

Warren walks his talk. When he took his stance in the 1980s that stock options should be expensed, it was an unpopular viewpoint. The SEC and U.S. politicians pressured to continue the practice. On Christmas Day 1994, the *New York Times'* Floyd Norris handed out a "Consumer Deception Award" to Arthur Levitt, then chairman of the Securities and Exchange Commission. Levitt praised the Financial Accounting Standards Board for "great courage" when—*after succumbing to political pressure*—FASB backed down from requiring that executive stock options be expensed.[17] Even though the FASB, politicians, corporate executives and the SEC supported the opposite view, Warren Buffett never wavered.

Neither Warren Buffett nor Charlie Munger takes stock options, restricted stock, or huge cash payouts as part of their compensation packages. Berkshire Hathaway is run more like a partnership than a typical U.S. corporation. The annual report includes "An Owner's Manual" outlining the partnership commitment. Warren Buffett's and Charlie Munger's net worth is due to their Berkshire Hathaway stock holdings, and the other board directors are heavy investors in the company, too. Their own gains and losses are in direct proportion to that of other shareholders.

Buffett and Munger draw a salary of only around $100,000. Their wealth grows as they create value for others. Successful value investing is not a get-rich-quick scheme, it is a way to get rich and stay rich.

Benjamin Graham wrote that a speculator "wants to make his profit in a hurry."[18] The global capital markets suffered because people with access to *other people's money* wanted to get rich in a hurry, and "investing" seemed to be the last thing on their minds. Backdating executives put their own compensation ahead of investors' interests. But stock option backdaters are not alone in seeking extraordinarily compensation. Investment bankers that ended up subtracting value from the global capital markets earned millions of dollars for a single year of bad work. Many hedge fund managers create much less value than the prairie princes (Buffett and Munger), yet they rack up compensation in the hundreds of millions of dollars.

Russian phone system was poor. Even a bandwidth sharing arrangement using excess Soviet military communication lines resulted in numerous communication breaks. (Imagine if there was a real need during the Cold War!) Argush installed Sprint and traded the currency arbitrage.

Since a true arbitrage is so hard to find, I focus on value investing for my personal portfolio in the Benjamin Graham and Warren Buffett tradition.

WhileWarren Buffett continues to look for value opportunities, all over the globe new money gushes into hedge funds and leveraged investments.We do not care if rich people want to speculate knowing they may lose their money. Unfortunately, many public pension funds and other "safe" investors allocate some of their money to hedge funds.

In 1990 there were a few hundred hedge funds with less than $50 billion in total assets under management. By the summer of 2008, there were around 8,000 hedge funds (depending on who was counting) with $1.87 trillion in assets under management.[8] Since hedge funds can only be sold to wealthy investors, they are mostly unregulated based on the flimsy theory that rich investors are sophisticated investors.

Only accredited investors are allowed to invest in hedge funds, but they are pretty easy to find. Regulation D of the Securities Act of 1933 defines an accredited investor as anyone with a net worth—including the value of real estate—in excess of $1 million. If your net worth is not that high, but you have income greater than $200,000 for the past two years—make that $300,000 if you are married—and expected the same this year, you qualify as an accredited investor.

A mere million dollars makes you a high-net-worth individual, but that may not be enough to get you access to the elite hedge funds. Some require a minimum investment of $5 million. Others court the "carriage trade" (old money) and the "caviar crowd" (new money), seeking out ultra-high-net-worth investors worth more than $30 million. In the estimated $1.87 trillion global hedge fund business, fewer than 10 percent of the funds control more than 85 percent of the money.

Banks, savings and loans, and most investment companies qualify as accredited investors. Most trusts with more than $5 million in assets and partnerships also qualify. Many retirement plans, including Employee Benefit Plans, Keogh Plans, and IRAs meet the test. *Now there is a happy thought.* A pension fund manager can gamble away your retirement money for you, and sometimes they do, especially if their fees are based on "performance." Money has flooded into hedge funds. High management fees, combined with little regulation of hedge fund managers, is like throwing gasoline on a lit fire.

The easiest way for a hedge fund investor to make a small fortune is to start with a large one. If you are an accredited investor and you are bound and determined to ignore *caveat emptor,* no one will stop you. Besides, it can be thrilling. But the thrill you experience when you detect a glint of mica—fool's gold—feels as real as if you had actually struck gold. In the world of hedge funds, there is much mica and little gold.

Theoretically, a hedge fund allows investors to invest in ways that would be difficult on their own. It can amass the funds to make a run at the equity of an undervalued company and take the inevitable regulatory heat. It can study thousands of technical charts to look for a market anomaly and perhaps find an "arbitrage" opportunity. It can take large loan positions in interesting ventures. Theory rarely works out in practice.

When I met Warren in 2005, six of the top 25 highest paid fund managers achieved only single-digit returns, and these are the "successful" hedge fund managers. Yet Edward Lampert of ESL, one of the "sickly six," earned $425 million in 2005. The top two earners, James Simons of Renaissance Technologies Corp and T. Boone Pickens of BP Capital Management, respectively, earned $1.5 billion and $1.4 billion. Renaissance's chief fund charges a 5 percent annual management fee, and the managers take 44 percent of the upside, if any exists. In 2007, Jim Simons, Steven Cohen, and Kenneth Griffin each earned over $1 billion.[9] Warren Buffett and Charlie Munger each earn a salary of about $100,000 per year, yet their long-term track record has topped these hedge fund managers.[10]

Many hedge fund managers got into the business because of the incredible success of the legendary Paul Tudor Jones. Tudor Investment

Corporation's $5.7 billion Raptor Global Fund, managed by James Pallotta, had 19.2 percent annual returns since 1993, but when it stumbled a little on U.S. equity investments dropping 8.5 percent by the beginning of December 2007, investors pulled out $1 billion. It is unrealistic to expect that any investment, particularly a hedge fund, will always have a positive return relative to the market. Paul Tudor Jones has had a very successful investment run since 1980 with never a down year until 2007.[11] Yet even he does not represent that his funds are safer than the market. Every new hedge fund manager wants to be the next Paul Tudor Jones, George Soros, Jim Rogers, or Ken Griffin. Like Warren, there are true stars who outperform the hedge fund averages, but Warren may sleep better at night.

There is nothing wrong with making a big bet, but one cannot be lulled into thinking that investing in hedge funds is safer than the market. The strategies are so variable that some funds pose much more risk than others. The best can give high performance with few stumbles. Investors may find, however, that at best they have paid high fees to invest with a pale imitation of greatness or a clueless rookie. At worst, they may invest with a crook. Hedge funds have the potential not only to have a zero return—no increase in your capital—for a year, they have the potential to completely wipe out your capital. When you are trying to compound returns, it is fatal to multiply your capital by zero.

I run a hedge fund. My strategy? It's a proprietary secret. Domicile? It is located onshore in the United States, but the investments are global. There is no lock-up or waiting period for withdrawing an investment from my fund. At the moment it is not leveraged, but sorry, you are not entitled to even that much information.

You won't find my fund's returns reported as part of a hedge fund index. Hedge funds do not have to report their returns. You won't find my fund covered in the financial press, either. What I refer to are not financial products that I market to outside investors. I refer to my personal investment portfolio. Given the low barriers to entry, almost any portfolio of $1 million or more in discretionary investments can call itself a hedge fund.

What does a good hedge fund make? It is supposed to make alpha, excess return—adjusted for risk—above and beyond a passive investment in the overall market, or beta. Alpha is supposed to be your reward for accepting extra risk. Hedge fund investors should expect nothing less from a hedge fund than from any other well-managed company. Just like actual hedge fund, I have no obligation to disclose my portfolio's return, and I don't. But my returns after all expenses and taxes are enviable by any hedge fund standard, and actual hedge funds have not given me much competition. Very few hedge funds achieve great returns, and if they do, they are not doing it consistently.

Part of the reason my personal returns are so healthy is that, unlike actual hedge funds, I do not withdraw fees ranging from 2 percent to 5 percent of the value of my portfolios each year, nor do I liquidate assets to pay myself 20 percent to 44 percent of the upside. My portfolios are tax efficient. I don't charge myself administrative fees of around 0.5 percent per annum, and I don't pay for research using "soft dollars" paid to investment banks by marking up trades at the expense of my investment portfolio. I don't lend myself money from my investment portfolio. I don't let brokers commingle my funds with theirs to potentially expose me to their credit risk, either. Unfortunately for their investors, traditional hedge funds usually do the opposite of what I do when it comes to fees and efficiency.

Finding the right hedge fund is like truffle hunting—and you need a good pig. Investors may find that fund of funds managers are no help in sniffing out truffles; they are often mere fee hogs. A large Chicago-based fund of funds manager recently observed that out of the universe of hedge funds, only about 25 met his standard for investment. He looks for a critical mass of employees, comprehensible strategies, and well-developed back-office operations. But he is having his own infrastructure problems since his staff cannot keep up with the new structured credit products that the hedge funds embraced. This lack of expertise comes at a high price: on top of hedge fund fees, many funds of funds charge a 2.5 percent load, more than 3 percent in annual expenses, and ask for 25 percent of the upside. Instead of compound interest, you get compound fees.

I reinvest my fees. If I would not take out fees for my own use, why would I pay them to a manager who has a mediocre track record? Yet many investors allow mediocre managers to suck the life blood out of their portfolios.

Do you want to know the fastest way to become rich in hedge funds? *Run one.*

Financial journalists deify hedge fund managers, who boast of elite sports abilities and savant-like mental powers. A money manager may show off his ability to play multiple chess games simultaneously instead of showing off verifiable weighted average returns. This is especially useful when managers do not have a long, reliable, credibly audited track record to boast about.

Blackjack card counting is offered as evidence of a hedge fund manager's genius. I have played blackjack, I have counted cards, and I have won doing it. Unfortunately, playing blackjack will not make you a better money manager. The cards in the deck are known in advance. Even when casinos reduce the edge of a card counter by adding more decks, the cards are still known in advance. Real world finance is not as dependable. Not only does reality add more decks; it removes cards, and adds wild cards (fraudsters). Probability-based models fall apart. Besides, as Warren Buffett knows, the real action is in insurance companies, not casinos.

Warren Buffett plays bridge. What does this have to do with his ability to make lucrative investments? Nothing. It may help keep you sharp, but so would a lot of other mental (or even physical) activities. I also play bridge but I have never played with Buffett. Would I become a better investor if I played bridge with him? Not unless he gave me investment tips at the bridge table.

One reads about hedge fund squash champions, marathon runners, hang gliders, bikers, and triatheletes. That has nothing to do with whether a money manager will be successful. But I shouldn't sell sports short. After running a marathon, I had shin splints for three months. It gave me more time to read annual reports, and *that* is useful when one is managing money.

It seems that hedge fund managers spring up out of nowhere. Many have addresses in New York, London, Chicago, Los Angeles, and other locations, but sometimes these managers are using the addresses of virtual offices in office buildings that provide a telephone number from which

calls are forwarded to the "manager's" cell phone. It is very easy to create
the illusion of a global corporate presence in the age of the Internet. It is
even easy to create the illusion of a network of legitimate people.

Last summer I returned a cell phone call from a "hedge fund manager" who said a professor I know from the University of Chicago's
Graduate School of Business was on his advisory board and the professor suggested he call me. The fellow's story sounded odd, so I declined
to meet with him. I called the professor and asked him how well he
knew the man. He admitted to being on the man's advisory board; but
he was about to meet him for the very first time. When I asked the
professor why he would lend his name to someone that appeared to
operate from a cell phone, he said the man dropped *other names* and
said he had raised $10 million. I told the professor: "I raised $50 million. See how easy it is to say that?" It is also easy to drop names and
numbers! While the fellow may be legitimate, the professor had no way
of knowing that. It is dangerous to lend one's name to a total stranger.
Warren likes to look people in the eye.

In June 2005, I was surprised to get an e-mail from Chris Sugrue,
then chairman of Plus Funds. He invited me to some hedge fund events
organized in concert with the development office at the University of
Chicago:

> The University and alumni in the hedge fund industry are
> working together to provide additional networking and edu-
> cational events in the future. We've put together several hedge
> fund events over the past two years. . . . Starting July 1, 2005,
> future hedge fund events will only be open to those who are
> $2,500+ annual fund [of the University of Chicago] donors.

Sugrue had an undergraduate degree from the University of Chicago,
but did not have an MBA, and somehow had gotten names of Graduate
School of Business alumni to solicit. I wrote back to Sugrue asking for
an explanation. I said that I found his e-mail solicitation "pretty shame-
less." My firm and nine others had already contributed funds to the
Finance Roundtable so that students and alumni could attend for free.
We gave hedge fund seminars usually discussing the risks; I had given
one myself; they were open—and would remain open—to everyone.

The alarming part was Sugrue's Plus Funds' association with Refco, where Sugrue had once been an executive. Plus Funds' investor money had been commingled with Refco's in an unregulated account. When Refco filed for Chapter 11 bankruptcy protection on October 17, 2005, Sugrue demanded that the money be moved to segregated accounts, and the money was moved to accounts at Lehman Brothers Holding Inc. Refco creditors naturally wanted the money back. One wonders why the money was not in segregated accounts in the first place. Refco had lent money to Sugrue for various purposes including $50 million, of which $19.4 million went to an entity controlled solely by Sugrue.[12]

Court documents state that "Upon information and belief, Sugrue has fled the United States and currently resides in Angola."[13] Angola is a lousy venue for hedge fund conferences. Greg Newton pointed out in his blog, *Naked Shorts,* that the bad news is Angola does not have an extradition treaty with the United States. The good news is that "[f]oreign nationals, especially independent entrepreneurs, are subject to arbitrary detention and/or deportation by immigration and police authorities."[14] Warren's Omaha isn't a grand enough address to feed some hedge fund managers' ravenous egos. How's Angola for a swanky address?

Robert Cialdini, Ph.D., wrote about confidence men in his book, *Influence.* Grifters know that glitz, honorific titles, and seeming sponsorship of well-known institutions have a powerful influential effect on us, and they do so without any conscious effort on our part. Investment banks tend to lend money just because another investment bank has lent money due to *pluralistic ignorance.* The second bank to lend will assume the first bank checked out the borrower, and it will skimp on its due diligence. We look around to see what the other guy is doing, and if everyone else is doing it, we go ahead. As Warren Buffett admonished in his letter to his All-Stars, don't do something just because "everybody else is doing it."[15]

Fortunately, Dr. Cialdini points out that all we have to do to avoid being fooled is to make a conscious decision to look for counterfeit social evidence. People can rent virtual offices, expensive homes, flashy cars, and eye-popping jewelry. They can infiltrate the alumni list of a prestigious business school. Question everything. By the way, Robert Cialdini got his Ph.D. in psychology. Did you even question me? But if Cialdini's Ph.D had been in art history, you would be right to be upset with me for citing him as an expert in psychology.

Irrational hype should make an investor skeptical as should any claim of intellectual superiority or mystical abilities. Some men seem driven to self aggrandizement. When Father W. Meissner's psychobiography of St. Ignatius was published in the 1990s, shock waves reverberated through the Catholic Jesuit community. Ignatius was born to a noble Spanish family and aspired to become the paragon of hidalgos; he was a soldier, courtier, and seducer. After a canon ball shattered his leg, Ignatius devoted his energies to founding the Society of Jesus. Meissner claimed he displayed the symptoms of a phallic narcissist: exhibitionism, self aggrandizement, arrogance, unwillingness to accept defeat, and a need for power and prestige. Phallic narcissists can have "counterphobic competitiveness and a willingness to take risks or court danger in the service of self-display." This "ruthless drive" may give them the "appearance of strength of character and resourcefulness."[16]

In other words, the biography of the saint read like the profile of many a hedge fund manager.

Alfred Borden, a magician played by Christian Bale in *The Prestige,* counsels a small boy on the art of illusion: "Never show anyone anything. No one is impressed by the secret. It is what you use it for that impresses." Borden offers this advice right after showing the lad a cheesy coin trick.

Just as a private investment portfolio can maintain secrecy, hedge fund strategies can remain a proprietary secret. Hedge funds that have a "patented" investment strategy or that feel they have a "proprietary" model that only they, "the smartest guys in the room," have discovered, are probably bad bets. The usual excuse for secrecy is that they do not want someone else to copy their trades or manipulate the market and damage their profits. That was Long-Term Capital Management's excuse, until it blew up and had to disclose its positions to its creditors. Sometimes there is no strategy other than to employ as much leverage as possible with the hope to get lucky.

What if the secret strategy means your hedge fund manager invests in a diversified stock index fund portfolio and pays fees of only about

0.1 percent per year while charging you much more? How would you know? Suppose your hedge fund manager thinks the stock market is going to tank. When a hedge fund manager has more than $1 billion in funds under management, he can invest in virtually risk-free T-bills and do well for himself with a 2 percent management fee. In a down market, he can claim victory with even a small positive performance. How long would it take investors to figure it out they are paying hedge fund fees for T-bill performance and pull out? Remember, the strategy must stay secret.

Warren does his best to create transparency. His shareholder letters try to explain everything, even anomalies created by accounting and conventional reporting. He even explains his derivatives positions and educates investors on potential volatility of earnings. His investors can find him at the annual meeting, and he and Charlie Munger entertain detailed questions for hours on end.

The offshore location of many hedge funds makes it easier to keep investors from second guessing managers. Moreover, managers do not even have to tell you when they change strategies, as long as the documents you signed allow them to do it. There is usually a waiting period for withdrawing your investment from a fund, so in the meantime, you just have to take a manager's word for how well they are doing.

A hedge fund manager usually has an anecdote, an *after-the-fact* anecdote, about how he made a small fortune on a prescient bet on, say, the renminbi. He will leave out the part about the large euro trade in which he lost a large fortune. The manager is rarely able to tell you about his *current* trades; he will claim he doesn't want other managers to know his strategy.

Hedge funds do not create new asset classes or new investments, and investing in them does not necessarily make you more diversified. You cannot be more diversified than the market portfolio, and hedge funds trade in the global markets. If you go long and short market assets, as traditional hedge funds used to do, the mix does not become more diversified. The stock market offers a simple way to look at this. Together, passive and active investors own 100 percent of the global stock market. The average return of all passive and active investors together is exactly equal to the average return of the global market. The average return of passive investors, the indexers, is also equal to the average return of the global stock market.

This means that active investing is a zero-sum game. Given that passive investors' return is the average, active investors must also have the same average return as the global market, before fees, before expenses, and before taxes. If some hedge funds wildly outperform the market, as some claim to do, other hedge funds must spectacularly underperform. Fees, expenses, and taxes just make the spectacular underperformance even worse. *Tavakoli's Law states that if some hedge funds soar, some must crash and burn.*

Hedge funds protest that active investors also include some small individual active investors, and they say they are making money off of those people. But there is no evidence that is true. I do not buy the argument that, on average, individual active investors underperform hedge funds. It is probable that individual active investors *outperform* hedge funds after one adjusts for creation bias, survivorship bias, fraud, other misleading methods of reporting returns, and high fees.

Taken as a whole, active managers in the market will underperform the market average by an amount equal to their cost of trading (their trading commissions plus their total fees). This is true for hedge funds, mutual funds, and an individual investors' stock portfolio. Unless you can consistently improve your assets by trading, the less one trades and the lower one's fees and commissions, the better off an active investor will be.

*   *   *

Investors are only human, and human beings are not good at assessing probabilities (and therefore risk) without formal training. Even experts sometimes have trouble. *Scientific American's* Martin Gardner authored a section on mathematical games and asserted that in probability theory it is "easy for experts to blunder."[17]

One study suggests that people with injuries to the frontal lobe might be better investors, even though this type of brain damage results in poorer overall decision-making ability. Studies showed individuals would take a 50–50 bet in which they could win 1.5 times more than they would lose, but people with sound minds would not take the bet unless they had a 50–50 chance of winning *twice* as much as they might lose. A few business school professors suggested that the brain-damaged people would make better investors. For example, brain-damaged hedge fund managers might accept a 50–50 chance of winning $3 billion versus losing $2 billion, whereas a hedge fund manager of sound mind might not accept the bet unless he had a 50–50 chance of winning $4 billion versus losing $2 billion.

The problem with that reasoning, as hedge fund after hedge fund has discovered, is that the market has uncertain outcomes and the probabilities are unknown in advance. In such circumstances, making riskier bets does not show superior decision-making ability, it just means the fund manager is happy to accept a lower margin of safety.

Even the hedge fund manager of "sound mind" can be wiped out on a series of bets that have a 50–50 chance of winning $4 billion versus losing $2 billion. John Maynard Keynes warned: "The market can stay irrational longer than you can stay solvent."[18] Warren Buffett is even more risk averse than the hedge fund manager of "sound mind." Yet he is the best investor in the last century—perhaps in the history of mankind—disproving the theory of efficient markets, a pet theory of many business school professors. "You can occasionally find markets that are ridiculously inefficient," Warren points out, or "…you can find them anywhere except at the finance departments of some leading business schools."[19]

In his book *Innumeracy,* mathematician John Allen Paulos gives many examples showing human beings are not good at assessing probabilities without formal training. We like to explain random events after-the-fact as if we predicted the outcomes. Many hedge funds are successful simply because of lucky bets. If the bets randomly pay off and the fund has a great year, the lucky fund manager takes credit for being a genius. When Nassim Nicholas Taleb, a risk theorist, discusses Buffett's success, he seems to damn it with faint praise: "I am not saying that Warren Buffett is not skilled; only that a large population of random investors will *almost necessarily* produce someone with his track records *just by luck.*"[20] If Taleb needed an example of success due to random luck, he did not choose well; he could have chosen from any number of hedge funds instead. Taleb fails to mention *conditional* probabilities (in this context), and it is remiss to describe Warren's success without bringing that up. Certainty is not possible, and luck is always a part of the equation, but Warren works hard to uncover a margin of safety whenever possible.

What is the probability of a successful investment, given that one has a sound methodology for analyzing a business? It is much better than the probability of success without the sound methodology, and the probability of disaster is very low. In contrast, a one-sided leveraged bet presents an altogether different conditional probability. What is the probability of a disaster, given that one has merely leveraged a market bet? If one is lucky one will do well, but if one is unlucky—or simply flat out wrong from not doing one's homework—the probability of disaster is about 100 percent.

I sent Warren a client note in September 2006 in which I made a similar point after the Amaranth hedge fund imploded after losing its shirt on natural gas contracts. The hedge fund leveraged up a bet and the bet (on natural gas spreads) went against them. It was a classic Dead Man's Curve trade: "The last thing I remember, Doc, the market started to swerve."[21] Unlike Warren Buffett, Amaranth had no margin of safety. Warren wrote back: "You both think and write well."[22] Since meeting Warren, I've found myself comparing every trade against value investing.

A man once asked the late Richard Feynman, a Nobel Prize–winning physicist, how he would design an anti-gravity machine. When Feynman replied he could not, the man pointed out that it would solve the world's problems. Feynman said it didn't matter, he didn't know how to do it. Many investors seem to hope that hedge fund managers have designed a strategy that uses leverage to create profits that will forever defy gravity. Yet Warren Buffett will be the first to admit that even he cannot design the financial equivalent of the anti-gravity machine.

Most hedge fund managers happily load up on risk to stay in the game. Hedge fund wisdom is "heads I win, tails you lose, and I *still* win—just not as big." There is one other possibility: The coin can stand on edge—the hedge fund manager gets bailed out, and you give back your winnings, but we will get to that later. For now, winning means that a hedge fund's returns are up, managers collect hefty fees while attracting new money, and investors get a reasonable return on their money. Losing means that hedge fund managers still make hefty fees and investors have a negative return or perhaps even lose all of their money. The hedge fund manager hates to lose, since he will not be able to attract new money and the money, upon which he gorges, will shrink, thus decreasing his payday.

Nobel Prize–winner Daniel Kahneman and Amos Tversky, a Stanford psychology professor, studied the financial psychology of judgment and decision making. They found that people feel more strongly about the pain that comes with loss than they do about the pleasure that comes with an equal gain. In fact, most people feel about twice as strongly about the pain of loss according to their study. If you really hate to lose, you may feel even more strongly about it than that. Surprisingly, people will take much more risk to avoid a loss than they will to earn a gain, even when the economic results are the same.

If you don't believe it, try the following game. Imagine that I have given you $100,000, and I have also given you two choices. I will either guarantee you an additional $50,000 or I will allow you to flip a coin. If it's heads you get another $100,000; if it's tails you get nothing additional. If you choose to take my guarantee, you are certain to walk away with $150,000. If you choose to flip the coin, you get either $100,000 or $200,000. Which option do you choose? Most people choose to take my guarantee and walk away with the certain $150,000.

Now suppose instead I have given you $200,000, and I have given you the following two choices. I will either take away—guarantee you lose—$50,000, or you can flip a coin and try for a different outcome. If the coin comes up heads, you lose $100,000; if it's tails you lose nothing. Now which option do you choose? Most people will choose to flip the coin to try to avoid the certain loss of $50,000 even if it means they might lose $100,000.

In both situations, you wind up with $150,000 if you choose my guarantee. In both cases if you choose the coin flip, you have a 50–50 chance of ending up with either $200,000 or $100,000. Most people choose the sure $150,000 when they stand to gain. It is a very different story when they stand to lose. Most people will choose to flip the coin because they will take more risk to avoid losing money, even if that means they will potentially be worse off than if they just took their loss. The feeling seems to be that they should at least try to avoid the loss. They shouldn't stand by, do nothing and just let it happen to them.

I prefer Warren's conditional probabilities to any of these choices. The odds of a favorable outcome appear much higher to me.

Now imagine you were running a hedge fund earning 2 percent on all of the funds you have under management and earning 20 percent of the upside. Better yet, if you can get away with it, take 5 percent as a fee on the assets under management, and take 44 percent of any potential upside. If your bet loses, your investors will withdraw all of their lovely money and you will get no fees at all. How much will you hate losing now? Enough to risk doubling your investors' losses?

If you were the hedge fund manager, would you hate losing enough to make it appear you were making money when you were not?

In New York State Court, the trustee for the Lipper Convertibles Investment Partnership filed suit to get money back from a trust fund of Henry Kravis's children, Sylvester Stallone, John Cusack, and the former New York City Mayor Ed Koch. They had all invested in the partnership, and each of them withdrew their investment and thought they made money. Other investors in the partnership lost money in an alleged fraud. It seems the trustee wanted all investors, even *former* investors, to share in the pain, claiming the gains were "unjust enrichment."[23]

The estate manager for the Bayou Group LLC was even more aggressive. Bayou had only about $100 million remaining of more than $300 million in original investments. Now Bayou's past investors are being told they should have known that fraud had occurred, and they had no right to withdraw their money, even if they had withdrawn the money as much as three years before the fund collapsed. The estate manager is seeking not just their gains but even their original investments, so that presumably the pain will be shared on a pro rata basis. The coin is standing on end.

Bayou's principals, Samuel Israel III and Daniel Marino, pleaded guilty to fraud charges after the fund suddenly closed in 2005. Lawsuits alleged Bayou operated a Ponzi scheme using money from new investors to pay old investors. When Israel received his 20-year prison sentence and was ordered to disgorge $300 million, he said: "I lied to you and I cheated you and I cannot put into words how sorry I am."[24] So, if he had not been caught, would he have put even the admission of his guilt into words? We may never know, but it seems he really hates to lose. Israel wanted a reduced sentence claiming infirmities, but the judge ruled: "He suffered from these ailments while he did the crime. He can deal with them while he does the time."[25]

I learned that Samuel Israel III has a tattoo on his right hip, was born July 29, 1959, his Social Security number is 438–68–0727. It said so on the Wanted by U.S. Marshals notice issued by the U.S. Department of Justice.[26] In June 2008, after Israel failed to report to serve his 20-year sentence, his abandoned car was found on the Bear

Mountain Bridge (despite its name, the bridge is not in the vicinity of Dead Man's Curve). The car contained what appeared to be a rambling suicide note or the first draft of a new hedge fund document. Scrawled on his car's hood dust were the words "suicide is painless" from the *M*A*S*H* theme song, which probably doesn't sound funny to the investors whose cash was mashed by Israel.[27]

Israel's partner, Dan Marino, had earlier left a suicide note saying that he, Israel, and James Marquez, another partner, had "defrauded" investors. But Marino had not committed suicide, and many believed Israel did not either. Lee Hennessee, head of the Hennessee Group, said: "I believe he's dead as far as I can throw him."[28] Greg Newton's blog titled his review of "Scammy's" disappearance: "Show Me the Corpse!"[29] Twenty-three days after he faked his suicide, Samuel Israel turned himself in, faced an additional bail-jumping charge, and the $500,000 bail was forfeit.[30]

Hedge fund managers seeking fast money sometimes find their exit of the business is quick and final. Kirk Wright, the Harvard-educated 37-year-old founder and CEO of International Management Associates, (IMA) committed suicide by hanging himself in his jail cell, after being found guilty in May 2008 of securities fraud, money laundering, and other charges. Since 2001, he had allegedly inflated balances in investors' accounts and lied to investors about the performance of the $150 million fund, which collapsed in 2006. He spent lavishly and drained the fund's cash accounts as it collapsed. When taken into custody, he was using an alias and was arrested poolside at the Hilton in Miami Beach, Florida.[31]

If Wright had invested his clients' money in T-bills and taken $3 million in management fees (2 percent of assets under management) per year, the clients would still have been misled, but they would have been better off since at least they would have their principal plus a little extra. It appears he neither played it safe nor legitimately bet the ranch; he simply bought the farm.

In finance, the good do not die young and they do not go on the lam. Like Warren Buffett, the good are usually long-term investors and live to a contented ripe old age.

Hedge fund managers may invest their own money in their funds thereby claiming their interests are aligned with their investors. Yet are they really aligned? Many managers and employees of smaller hedge funds are not as wealthy as the investors, but they would very much like to be. After all, they reason, if they are taking the risk of working for a hedge fund, they should get paid for it.

How much should hedge fund employees get paid? Senior risk managers at investment banks get paid in the high six figures. A well-known bank hired a second-tier compliance officer for $800,000 per year. Structured credit researchers got paid anywhere from the high six figures to $2 million per year. A mediocre senior investment banker will earn around $2 million per year, and a good one can earn much more. But many beginning hedge fund managers can only aspire to this compensation.

Many hedge funds are small, undercapitalized shops that have an "investors only" Web site. If a fund rents offices, purchases computers, phone systems, reporting systems, trading systems, hires staff and retains accountants, it may not break even on the 2 percent annual fee unless it has several hundred million dollars under management. The trouble is, if a manager's results are not good, investors will run for the exits.

The strategy reminds me of a bridge saying I sent Warren about having a 50–50 chance your play will win while expecting it to work out 9 times out of 10.

The temptation is to lever up just for the sake of making a lucky bet so that the 20 percent fee on the upside kicks in to keep the fund solvent and keep investors happy. But can you trust that leverage is employed for the right reasons when the fund is feeling a cash crunch? Is it any wonder they want a waiting period to return your money?

Overcrowding makes most hedge fund strategies look very unattractive. Many hedge funds are merely shorting (selling) volatility to earn risk premiums, selling options in a low implied volatility environment and selling credit default protection in a skinny credit spread environment, or using investment banks' financing to make a bet on the market. *In other words, underperforming hedge funds often resort to leverage in a gamble to inflate returns.*

It is as if they are the young boy in D. H. Lawrence's story "The Rocking-Horse Winner," who gets visions of the winners of Ascot's horse races while madly riding his rocking horse. At first he wins enough money to pay off the family debts, but that is not enough, the household goes mad with greed and he must keep riding to produce winners until he dies of exhaustion. "Although they lived in style, they felt always an anxiety in the house. There was never enough money." After the boy's initial bet wins, the house seems to say: "There must be more money, there must be more money." When the boy wins even bigger, the voices become louder and more urgent: "There must be more money! There must be more money!" The boy asks his emotionally bankrupt yet greedy mother about luck and she responds: "I don't know. Nobody ever knows why one person is lucky and another unlucky." The boy manically rides the rocking horse "Now! Now take me to where there is luck! Now take me!" The voices in the house rise to a frantic pitch: "There must be more money! Oh-h-h; there must be more money. Oh, now, now-w! Now-w-w—there must be more money!—more than ever! More than ever!" The boy eventually dies of nervous exhaustion and his uncle mourns: "eighty-odd thousand to the good . . . But, poor devil, poor devil, he's best gone out of a life where he rides his rocking-horse to find a winner."[32]

Warren avoids leverage. While it is true that Berkshire Hathaway's returns would have been much higher on average, both Buffett and Munger feel that it is their responsibility to shelter shareholders from leverage's swift and painful downside. Benjamin Graham counseled: "It should be remembered that a decline of 50 percent fully offsets a preceding advance of 100 percent."[33]

Some hedge funds are betting on leverage and luck as if they are rocking horses. Instead of relying on rocking horses, they look to their prime brokers, their investment banking and bank creditors. The hedge funds not only gain access to leveraged financing—there must be more money!—the investment banks also provide trading strategies.

Richard Heckinger ran into many hedge fund managers during his multiyear stay as managing director at Deutsche Boerse. He believes that many of them have no financial savvy:

> I am amazed at how many of them don't understand the nuts and bolts of what they're trading. I've met . . . several dozen over the last several years who are not too clear even on the concept

of an "exchange" . . . most deal with their prime brokers and
order up their strategies much like calling Domino's and order-
ing a pizza.[34]

The barriers to entry into the hedge fund world are low, and there
seems to be a philosophy in the global hedge world that "anyone can
do it." It seems all it takes to go from zero to hero is swagger and loudly
trumpeted self-reported claims.

In the late 1990s, there were only a few hundred hedge funds. By
the summer of 2008, the number was estimated at around 8,000 globally,
and hedge fund management had become a $1.87 trillion industry. Most
of the money is concentrated in large funds. Funds that manage more
than $5 billion have 60 percent of the market share; funds that manage
$1 billion to $5 billion have another 26.7 percent of the market share. Put
another way, less than 3 percent of hedge funds control 60 percent of the
money, and somewhere between 6 percent to 9 percent of the funds control around 87 percent of the money. That means more than 90 percent of
hedge funds are chasing the remaining 13 percent of market share.[35]

Hedge fund managers often claim they can beat the S&P 500,
mutual funds, and just about any other investment available to individual investors. Some hedge funds state that their goal is to achieve
positive returns in both bull and bear markets. Others claim to speculate with the (usually elusive) goal of highly volatile but ultimately high
returns. Quantitative funds or "quant" funds like LTCM claim their
models help them outperform the market.

Survivorship bias distorts returns reported by hedge fund indexes
since the low returns of failed hedge funds drop out of the equation.
If anemic returns and total wipeouts disappear forever, then reported
returns have a greater chance of creating an illusion of better performance than other investments.

Creation bias is an even bigger problem. In military terms, it is the
strategy of rapid dominance through shock and awe. Only "successful"
funds that show a track record of outperforming the market are sold
to investors, while failed attempts to create a successful track record are

never reported. The initial outperformance has a halo effect on later years since the long-term record will continue to carry its swelling effect, even if subsequent returns are mediocre. As more money flows in, the funds often cannot replicate outperformance, devolving into under-performers. Multiyear returns are rarely dollar weighted, so returns are overstated, because large slugs of new money are earning lower returns. As the funds grow, it is harder to make excess market returns, since it is harder to find those incrementally attractive new ideas and assets.

Size has its disadvantages. Warren Buffett and Charlie Munger project they can achieve a tax-efficient average annual return of around 10 percent to 15 percent for the next five years—a very respectable return—but it isn't likely they will match the tax-efficient 27 percent plus average annual return of the past 30 years. Their strategy and pro-jections are disclosed for anyone to read in annual reports.

In first quarter 2008, hedge funds reported their worst performance in nearly two decades according to Hedge Fund Research, Inc.[36] Even those numbers may not represent reality because the lack of reporting controls tempt hedge fund managers to inflate their performance. Some academic studies "suggest hedge funds have been routinely dishonest, or at least economical with the truth."[37] Investment banks tightened credit terms for hedge funds. By the beginning of August 2008, year-to-date hedge fund performance was down 3.5 percent. Hans Hufschmid, a first-hand witness to LTCM's financing crisis, observed it was "much worse" than in 1998 when LTCM collapsed, because "hedge funds live on credit and leverage and the ability to finance esoteric positions for a long time."[38] I would have added that some hedge funds seem to extend their lives because of the ability to set the prices on their own esoteric positions.

Academics seem late to wake up to this. Warren Buffett and Charlie Munger have publicly criticized (mis)representations of hedge funds for decades. *Forbes* has published article after article about hedge fund prob-lems. Some hedge funds simply make things up. Even "legitimate" report-ing is often materially misleading. In 2004, *Forbes* said: "Fakery aside, hedge funds have returned less than stocks and bonds."[39] If you took away various ways of plumping up performance such as creation bias (and a variety of other shenanigans) a Reality Check study showed: "TASS [the largest hedge fund tracking service] net returns drop from 10.7 percent to 6.4 percent annually for the six years through 2002. That compares with a 6.9 percent annual return for the S&P 500 and 7.5 percent for Lehman Brothers' intermediate bond index."[40] Yet, poor relative average perform-ance did not deter investors. Money continued to pour into hedge funds.

Most hedge funds rely on borrowed money. Goldman Sachs, Credit Suisse First Boston, Merrill Lynch, Morgan Stanley and others lend money through hedge fund umbilical cords called prime brokers. Then they trade with the hedge funds and often supply research and other helpful information. Most of the time, the information sharing is legal.

If a hedge fund uses borrowed money to buy securities, it backs the loan with the assets it "bought" *plus collateral* (margin). For example, if a prime broker lends $100 million to a hedge fund to buy securities that the prime broker's investment bank is selling, it may ask a hedge fund to put up $10 million or 10 percent as additional collateral against the $100 million loan (so the assets plus margin are $110 million or 110 percent of the amount the hedge fund owes). That way, if the price of the secu-rities falls a little (not more than 10 percent), the investment bank will have a cushion to make sure it gets back its money. If the price of the securities drops by 5 percent, or $5 million, the investment bank will ask the hedge fund to put up more money (approximately $5 million) to keep the percentage of margin roughly constant. When the invest-ment bank calls for more collateral, it is known as a *margin call*. One would think that investment banks only accepted cash or a cash equiva-lent such as a T-bill as margin (collateral). But sometimes they accept something very illiquid (while asking for a bit more of the illiquid stuff). Investment banks try not to think about the possibility that the value of the securities will drop by say, 50 percent, or that the hedge fund will not be able come up with the margin when asked (perhaps because *eve-ryone* is asking at the same time). That would probably mean the hedge fund is going bust. Prime brokers (affiliates of banks and investment banks) avoid thinking about this horrific scenario by comforting them-selves with the thought of the high fees they charge the hedge funds.

Investment bank prime brokers will even help spawn hedge funds. Typical of most investment banks, Bear Stearns Asset Management

(BSAM) offered a "turnkey" program, essentially a 50–50 economic split after expenses. BSAM became the general partner. In exchange for that, the hedge fund manager would get office space, back office clearance, accounting, legal support, and marketing support, all of which is a top line expense. If BSAM accepted someone onto the platform they also invested seed capital of up to $25 million.[41]

Prime brokers provide hedge funds with a variety of services: They provide financing for leverage; they set up custody accounts for their assets; they act as a settlement agent; and they prepare account statements for customers. Smaller hedge funds often rely on their prime brokers for risk management and trade ideas. These smaller hedge funds also tend to drastically underestimate the cost of doing business. Fortunately for hedge fund managers, the fees fund managers charge can add up faster than the miscellaneous charges on a phone bill. If the hedge fund documents allow loans to management, the lowest returning asset in the hedge fund portfolio may be an invisible low-cost loan to management.

The investment bank symbiosis did not stop with hedge funds. Investment banks also provided loans, assistance, and even management staff to *structured investment vehicles* (SIVs), and *collateralized debt obligation* (CDO) managers, some of which also manage hedge funds.

Undercapitalized managers are easily influenced by an investment bank that set them up in business and trades with them. If an investment bank has a large inventory of overrated and overpriced mortgage loan or leveraged loan-backed securities that it needs to get off of its books, it is very convenient to have symbiotic relationships with structured investment vehicles, collateralized debt obligation managers, and hedge funds. As investment banks needed to get bad loans off of their balance sheets, institutional investors became the prey of both hedge funds and investment banks.

As General George S. Patton observed: "A pint of sweat saves a gallon of blood." Warren Buffett and Charlie Munger would not tolerate the kind of risk that would wipe out a lifetime of hard work, and look for a margin of safety when they make a purchase. Their decades-long track record beats all of the top hedge fund managers. Berkshire Hathaway does not promise to do well in both up and down markets. There are years when the value of the stock decreased or underperformed the S&P; but long-term value investors do not concern themselves with chasing a market return. Warren looks for value and for companies that he is happy to own even if the market closed for five years and he couldn't trade any of the shares.

As a disciple of Benjamin Graham, Warren Buffett does not distinguish between value and growth companies, since the concepts are Siamese twins. Why would you buy a fair company at a good price instead of a good company at a fair price? If possible, try to buy a good company at a good (cheap) price, and a good company has good growth potential.

Berkshire Hathaway defines value companies as those selling at or below a fair price—book value combined with earnings—that have high earnings growth potential relative to alternatives. The price has to make sense and the fundamental economics have to be good. A company (or hedge fund) could produce steadily rising earnings by investing in T-bills, and passive compounding would cause capital earnings to steadily rise even if the company did nothing to generate additional shareholder value. Yet Warren would not consider this to be a value company.

Returns are not kept secret. They are available to the general public on Berkshire Hathaway's Web site. From 1965 to 2007, the S&P 500 (including dividends) has had a compound annual gain of 10.3 percent and an overall gain of 6,840 percent. For the same period, Berkshire Hathaway has shown adorable alpha; it had a compounded annual gain of 21.1 percent and an overall gain of 400,863 percent.[42]

In June 2008, Warren Buffett issued a challenge to hedge funds. He has bet Protégé Partners LLC, a fund of hedge funds, that five hedge funds of its choosing will not produce averaged returns net of fees over the next 10 years above the S&P 500. Buffett and Protégé each staked $320,000 to purchase a $640,000 treasury zero that will be worth $1 million in 10 years when the results are in (around a 4.56 percent annualized return—perhaps a better performance return than the hedge funds), and the $1 million will go the winner's charity. Warren chose Girls Inc. of Omaha, and I am sure they will be delighted when they receive the money.[43]

Chapter 5

MAD Mortgages—
The "Great" Against
the Powerless

The manufactured housing industry's business model centered on the ability . . . to unload terrible loans on naïve lenders . . . The consequence has been huge numbers of repossessions and pitifully low recoverie[s].
—Warren Buffett,
Berkshire Hathaway 2003 Annual Report

Berkshire Hathaway's 2003 annual report arrived in my mailbox in April 2004. Reading it, I learned that Berkshire Hathaway had acquired Clayton Homes, the largest U.S. manufacturer and marketer of manufactured homes. Unlike Oakwood Homes, a Berkshire Hathaway investment that lost money in 2002, Clayton Homes is well managed and practices sound lending through its Vanderbilt Mortgage and Finance Inc. affiliate. Clayton Homes is noted for the good character of its management in an industry rife with corrupt practices where buyers who could not afford homes were steered into fee-bloated loans created by lenders who should not have lent to them. Warren had learned about those practices the hard way after purchasing the distressed debt of Oakwood Homes, another manufactured housing company, which went bankrupt in 2002. Warren wrote: "Oakwood participated fully in the insanity."[1]

Oakwood Homes (Oakwood) designed and manufactured modular homes and sold them either directly to home buyers or to independent retailers. Oakwood provided loans to buyers of its homes. On its own, Oakwood did not have money to lend. Oakwood got money through a line of credit from Credit Suisse First Boston (Credit Suisse). The credit line was similar to a credit card except that Oakwood had to put up the home loans as collateral. Credit Suisse earned fees for the loans and further fees when it packaged (securitized) Oakwood's loans. Credit Suisse (the "old investor") bought the securitized loans and then sold them to so-called sophisticated private and institutional investors (the "new" investors).

Many of Oakwood's "home buyers" had not actually bought a home; they had assumed a mortgage loan they could not pay back. Sales declined. Loan delinquencies (late payments) and repossessions rose. Oakwood Homes had crushing debt and falling income for at least three years before it filed for bankruptcy in November 2002.

Oakwood and Credit Suisse sued each other. These nice kids found each other in a dangerous playground; and they courted each other for years, long after the affection had gone. The court issued an opinion in June 2008. The documents said Oakwood's aggressive lending practices led to the high number of repossessions and a debt load that Oakwood could not support; Oakwood's liquidator called the transactions it did with Credit Suisse "value destroying."[2] The court said that Oakwood's own alleged wrongful conduct prevented it from recovering any money from Credit Suisse; there was equal fault. Basically, the court shrugged at the liquidator's claim: *lay down with dogs, wake up with fleas.* An exception to this would have been if Credit Suisse were a corporate insider (say, if Credit Suisse had an officer on Oakwood's board—which it did not), but Oakwood's board and management made its own decisions.

Warren Buffett learned that the manufactured housing industry's consumer financing practices were "atrocious," and securitization made the situation much worse. Investors in the securitizations supplied money to investment banks who lent to manufacturers and retailers, who then lent money to home "buyers" in the form of mortgage loans or real estate investment contracts. Since the ultimate so-called sophisticated investors, the buyers of the securitized loans, were so far removed from the source of action, they often failed to thoroughly check on what they were buying. Warren learned about the Ponzi-like business models in mortgage lending and securitization market fairly early on. He wrote shareholders (in the annual letter) about his disastrous experience and what he learned from it; then he posted the information on the Berkshire Hathaway Web site for the world to see. The financial industry had not behaved well. The problem was fueled by "buyers who shouldn't have bought, financed by lenders who shouldn't have lent."[3] If Wall Street read Warren's shareholder letter, it either missed his message or walked away with an idea of how to expand on a bad theme.

No matter what hedge fund or investment bank one works for, no matter how lofty the title, no matter how successful the investor, they are all subject to My Theory of Everything in Finance:

The value of any financial transaction is based on the timing of cash flows, the frequency of the cash flows, the magnitude of cash flows, and the probability of receipt of those cash flows.

In finance, we make up a lot of fancy and difficult to pronounce names and create complicated models to erect a barrier to entry that keeps out lay people. High barriers tend to protect high pay. I've written books about some of the esoteric products: credit derivatives, CDOs, and more, but before I look at the latest hot label dreamt up, I look at the cash to find out what is really going on. I also ask a lot of questions.

Everything trades off the next most certain financial instrument, usually starting with U.S. treasuries as the risk-free benchmark. The price will fluctuate, going up as interest rates fall and going down as interest rates rise. U.S. Treasuries have the virtue of usually having a known coupon that will be paid on known dates and a known maturity date. If we all agree on how to discount those cash flows, the entire market will come up with the same price. With every other security, I will have an opinion about when and whether I will get my cash back. To form that opinion, I need to know if the company, consumer, hedge fund, investment bank, or other entity is good for the money.

Why would any diligent financial professional hand over money without asking tough questions of strangers in the marketplace? If a flaky brother-in-law who you wanted to help asked you for a large loan, you would probably grill him before you forked over thousands of dollars. There would be no point in letting him get in over his head since that wouldn't be a loan, it would be something else: When will you pay me back? How much interest are you promising to pay? How often and when will those payments occur? Do you have any collateral? Do you have any other debts? What is the probability you will hang onto your job this time, so that you will have the money to pay me when it is due? You would probably come up with even more questions, and this is for someone you know. You know how to find him if he doesn't pay, and you both have an interest in keeping the relationship going.

If it looks as if there will be a problem getting money back from a borrower, *walk away*. The most important part of My Theory of Everything in Finance is the Buffett Rule: *Do not lend money to people who cannot pay you back*.

♟ ♟ ♟

During the South American debt crisis in the 1980s, U.S. banks warned it would be disastrous for South American governments if they did not pay back their debts. The banks got it partly right. If you are owed billions of dollars by a third world country, and it cannot pay you back, the third-world country is not in trouble, *you are*.

Investment bankers are astute worldly people, and they keep their fingers on the pulse of the global financial markets. However, they tend to run with the herd. After getting badly burned by making unsecured loans to those who couldn't pay back the money, loans backed by assets were marketed as being a safe alternative. Loans backed by collateral such as homes and commercial property were viewed as particularly safe because one could seize the property and sell it if the borrower could not pay.

After the late 1980s thrift crisis, during which savings and loans that made mortgage loans throughout the United States went bankrupt, the government took a more aggressive role in the U.S. housing market. A network of Federal Home Loan Banks makes low-cost loans to banks and financial institutions so that they can lend money to mortgage borrowers. The Federal Housing Administration, FHA, part of the United States Department of Housing and Urban Development, or HUD, insures mortgage loans made by FHA approved lenders. These FHA loans are then sold to GNMA (or Ginnie Mae) a government agency that packages (securitizes) the loans for investors. Ginnie Mae "packages," known as agency passthroughs (they pass through interest and principal payments to investors), are backed by the full faith and credit of the U.S. government, meaning U.S. taxpayers. Fannie Mae (FNMA) and Freddie Mac (FHLMC) were privately chartered United States mortgage giants regulated by HUD. While Fannie and Freddie were private and their securitizations were not guaranteed, the overall sense was that they were (1) too big to fail; and (2) had the implied moral obligation of the U.S. government (that would be you, the taxpayer). Freddie Mac and Fannie Mae are now so huge that many believed a default by either of them would cause a crisis of confidence and the global markets would collapse—they are too big to fail. *Too big to fail means American taxpayers will pay for a bailout.* It turns out this thinking was correct. In September 2008, both Fannie Mae and Freddie Mac were placed in conservatorship. A new regulator, the Federal Housing Finance Agency (FHFA) fired (and replaced) the CEOs, fired the former boards of directors, and took control in a form of nationalization. With so much at stake—meaning U.S. government funds obtained from taxpayer dollars—one would think that HUD, the FHA, Fannie Mae, Freddie Mac, and the 12 Federal Home Loan banks (plus the army of regulators that oversee them) would make sure that the lending is prudent, because if it is not, the U.S. government will have to pay. Sadly, that has not been the case, perhaps because the government feels it is dealing with other people's money—the money of the U.S. taxpayer. Mortgage lending practices in the United States are tightening up, but there is still a long way to go to get back to prudent lending. As for the new regulator, it is headed by James B. Lockhart, who also oversaw the old regulator (the Office of Federal Housing Enterprise

Oversight or OFHEO). It seems to me that the new sheriff looks a lot like the old sheriff.

Fannie Mae and Freddie Mac purchase mortgage loans from mortgage lenders and earn fees for guaranteeing payments on other mortgage loans. To prevent losses, Fannie Mae and Freddie Mac have requirements for the types of loans they will buy. But, they came under pressure to relax those standards, and their risk increased as a result. Fannie Mae and Freddie Mac package up these loans and create securitizations known as conventional passthroughs. Some mortgage lenders cannot keep going if Fannie Mae and Freddie Mac refuse to buy their mortgage loans. In this way, Fannie Mae and Freddie Mac are *indirect mortgage lenders.*

Fannie Mae and Freddie Mac are highly leveraged, and they were extremely vulnerable to failure. If you are highly leveraged, you must keep the quality of the mortgage loans very high, because a small decrease in value is amplified by leverage. But if you have it in the back of your mind that you can have a colossal screw-up and someone will bail you out, it almost guarantees you will make lousy financial decisions. *It is a crazy way for any investor to think.* It is the antithesis of Benjamin Graham's philosophy. Warren told me that, as an investor, everyone makes mistakes, but you don't have to do a lot right as long as you *avoid big mistakes.*

Fannie Mae and Freddie Mac appeared to be careful back in the day. Loans had to "conform" by meeting lending guidelines so the borrower had a good chance of paying off the loan: the borrower's income had to be verified and documented; total housing cost including insurance and fees—no more than 28 percent of borrower's gross income; total debt (including credit cards, auto loans, etc.) less than 36 percent of borrower's gross income; the borrower's payment history could not include too many late payments. The borrower's money for the down payments and closing costs should come from his own savings, not from, say, a "gift" (which may in reality be a loan) from a relative. The borrower should have a steady job for at least two years, and enough extra cash to cover at least two months of all living expenses and other obligations. This is called *prudent lending,* and it protects both the lender and the borrower. Prudent lending practices protect the United States economy from mischief makers whose actions, intended or otherwise, could upset the *entire* U.S. housing market. But as prudence gave way to politics born out of greed, HUD stopped being part of the solution and became part of the problem.

For more than a decade, prudent lending seemed to assuage the fear of losses; but "creative" investment banking ruined even that supposedly safe scenario. If you set up a countrywide system where you overstate the value of an illiquid asset and then lend to borrowers who will have a hard time paying you back, you create bad loans on a massive scale. Cheap money available for loans pushes the prices of homes well above the price of the underlying land and cost to build plus reasonable profit; the prices keep getting pushed upward based on imaginary value and paid for with loans for which few questions are asked. It is as if you created your own third-world country in a bubble.

In contrast, Warren Buffett's Clayton Homes (through Vanderbilt Mortgage) maintains prudent lending standards—that require a certain down payment, proof of income and employment, a reasonable debt to income ratio—the kind of standards that keep people in their homes and paying their mortgage.

Suppose there is an unemployed man with no source of other income other than his representation that he is a successful Internet day trader. Up until now, he has not been very successful at anything. He has a poor credit history, and he wants to buy a home he could not previously afford. Fortunately, he says he has a flair for gambling—I mean—day trading, on the Internet. He does not wish to provide documents verifying his success, because the key to his successful formula is that is must remain confidential. Furthermore, he does not want to make a down payment on a home since his capital is tied up in his successful Internet day trading strategy, which he says is more profitable than the housing bubble— I mean housing investment. Why tie up money in a down payment when he can use that money to gamble—I mean—increase his fortune?

Fortunately, a mortgage broker, who is completely objective, since his income depends solely on the fees he generates by making mortgage loans, is willing to overlook the absence of documentation. The Internet day trader can state his income, and that is good enough for the mortgage broker. The mortgage lender helpfully informs the day trader that there have been mortgages made to people who apparently cannot afford them other than the fact that they are willing to state an income which suggests they can make the payments—so climb on board. Warren Buffett would likely have asked whether or not the trader can pay him back. He would undoubtedly ask for documentation.

After a few months, the mortgage broker calls the day trader with good news. The appraised value of homes in the day trader's area has gone up, so the day trader has equity in his home. The mortgage broker asks if the day trader would like to take out a home equity line of credit, which can then be used to make the payments on the mortgage of another home, an investment property. Yes? Great! (In contrast, Warren Buffett avoids investing in any business [in this case the loan from a shaky borrower] that has excessive leverage, that is, no equity left in the home.)

The way the loans were made was bad enough, but some of the new risky loan products made it difficult for homeowners to pay back the loan, even if their house increased in value, and if the value of the home stayed the same or declined, the homeowner would have a huge incentive to default.

These dodgy loans were so laughable that the risk was an open secret. The market made up pet names with catchy tags for this trash. *NINJA* loan: no income, no credit, no job, no documentation, no down payment, no problem. Get a loan and get in over your head. *Liar loans* will let us take your homes. You will choke your credit trying to pay back *strangulation* loans. *Vampire* loans will suck your blood dry.

In 2002, when Warren Buffett took losses due to Oakwood Homes' bankruptcy and was coming to grips with the credit derivatives losses in his Gen Re unit, President George W. Bush announced his intention to increase minority homeownership by 5.5 million by 2010. It sounded like a great idea—who isn't for home ownership? He lacked a sound plan to achieve it, and the regulatory policies of his administration enabled fraud fueled by greed. It sounded great to say in 2004 that homeownership had substantially increased. But by the beginning of 2008, homeownership was back down to 2002 levels, and minorities are most at risk for losing their homes—and their creditworthiness potentially ruined for years.[4] Furthermore, the population is still growing as homeownership declined, so we have lost ground. Wealth transferred to the wealthy from the poor, and what cannot be wrung out of distressed borrowers is ultimately being subsidized by tax dollars as the Fed bails out investment banks, banks, and thrifts.

The national tragedy is that the Bush administration apparently neither read Berkshire Hathaway's shareholder letters nor sought Warren Buffett's advice.

In 2003, while Warren Buffett was acquiring ethically run Clayton Homes after having taken the lesson of Oakwood to heart, the Office of the Comptroller of the Currency, the OCC, subverted the states' ability to defend the rights of mortgage borrowers against predatory lenders. The OCC examines national bank books and inquires about risk management practices in their capital markets areas. In an unprecedented move, it exercised an obscure power in the 1862 National Bank Act countermanding states' predatory lending laws over the unanimous objection of all 50 states.[5]

Ameriquest was alleged to be among the worst of predatory lending offenders. Forty-nine state regulators and the District of Columbia claimed it ran a boiler-room operation slamming borrowers with loans they could not pay back, hidden fees, and undisclosed escalating interest rates. The U.S. Senate delayed Ameriquest founder, Roland E. Arnall's, confirmation to the post of U.S. Ambassador to the Netherlands, but approved it in February 2006, after Ameriquest paid a $325 million settlement.[6]

Fair Isaac Corporation developed a scoring system (FICO) as a rough guideline of consumers' ability to pay debts. Subprime borrowers have low credit scores; typically FICO scores are below 650. Lending problems were not limited to subprime borrowers, however. Risky mortgage products combined with overleveraging created problems for borrowers at all income levels, but subprime borrowers were hit the hardest. Subprime borrowers tend to be less sophisticated and include a higher percentage of minorities. Unscrupulous lenders prey on the relative naiveté of these borrowers.

In the United States in the last part of the twentieth century, an illegal practice called *redlining* denied sound mortgage products to eligible minorities. As we entered the twenty-first century, redlining was replaced with a perverse spin called *reverse redlining*. This was supposed to help minorities buy homes, but instead Reverse Robin Hoods stole from the poor and gave to the rich. Since many subprime loans do not meet the standards of Fannie Mae and Freddie Mac, mortgage lenders borrowed most of the money from a handful of investment banks that packaged the loans and sold them to investors around the world (banks, mutual funds, insurance companies and more). The subprime loan disaster would have been headed off if sophisticated investment banks had stopped supplying money (through packaging and selling the ridiculous loans) to shaky mortgage lenders.

CNN's personal finance editor, Gerri Willis, exposed despicable lending practices. She told *The Daily Show's* Jon Stewart that in 2007, "*two million* people (in the United States) went into foreclosure,"[7] and in a CNN segment in which she and I both appeared, she asserted "the cards were exactly stacked against [the borrowers]."[8] I told her that some borrowers were "actively misled" and these loans on aggressively appraised homes: "were presented as gifts, but they were Trojan Horses you could ride to your financial ruin."[9] Many minorities are stuck with an insurmountable mountain of debt and many have declared bankruptcy.

The net effect is a huge wealth transfer from minorities to builders, fee-earning mortgage lenders, and bonus seeking investment bankers.

Warren Buffett promoted affordable housing and sound lending practices; he runs a well-managed corporation that has increased in value thus benefiting shareholders; he has bequeathed most of his wealth to benefit those less fortunate. Meanwhile, mortgage lenders and the investment banks that enabled them stole from naïve borrowers—and investors (such as municipal governments).

Many people did not understand what they signed. Stretching funds to participate in what appears to be a rising housing market is merely speculation. No one is entitled to credit for speculation, and credit was pushed on people with the promise of refinancing before interest payments rose, and low-money-down loans were touted as a way to wealth in an unsustainable market in which housing prices were propped up by temporarily cheap borrowing rates. *Sign here, you want to own your dream house and get rich, don't you?*

The idea that minority homeownership would increase was used as a justification for a lot of bad lending. Predatory lending practices were cloaked in a mantle of moral self-righteousness, as if steering borrowers into risky mortgage products was a public service instead of an act of malicious mischief by savvy financiers.

It is true that some borrowers knowingly overreached, but many were duped by confusing and risky loan products. More pain will come due to mortgage loans originated in 2005, 2006, and 2007. Mortgage brokers offered 40-year or 45-year adjustable rate mortgages (ARMs) in which homeowners built up virtually no equity in their homes in the early years of the mortgages. Approximately 80 percent of 2006 loan originations were ARMs of varying maturities with interest payments that reset sharply upward in two, three, or five years. For example, a 2/28 hybrid ARM has a fixed interest payment amount for the first two years, and then resets to an adjustable rate for the remaining 28 years. For a typical subprime 2/28 ARM, after low "teaser" rates of around 8 percent, many loans will reset to LIBOR plus 600 basis points, which as of summer 2008 would be around 8.46 percent. This borrowing rate, however, may be much higher by the time the actual reset occurs, particularly since the Fed will likely have to raise interest rates to head off inflation to avoid further depression of the dollar. For example, using June 2007's LIBOR rate, the interest payment would have been 11.32 percent. And here is the conundrum facing the Fed: If it raises rates, more bad loans will default and prolong a recession. But low rates fuel inflation, which leads to rising costs such as for gas and food, and the United States may slump into stagflation.

Some mortgage loans are *interest-only* (IO), meaning that the homeowner does not accumulate equity by paying down principal; the only way the home owner can build equity is if housing prices rise, but as a result of profligate lending, housing prices are falling. Some of these loans were made with very low (or no) down payment, so the homeowner would now lose money if the house were to be sold.

Option ARMs allow *negative amortization,* meaning a homeowner's principal balance—the amount you'd pay if you pay off your loan right away—can potentially rise. Borrowers may have initial payments so low that the payments do not even cover interest costs. Unpaid interest increases the principal amount, the loan balance, resulting in *negative amortization.* What if you bought a home with no money down (no down payment), and home prices fall? You are in an "upside-down" mortgage. *You owe more than the house is worth, and the amount you owe grows bigger every day.* As the song goes, you get "another day older and deeper in debt," and if you sell the house, all you have left is debt. *You never bought a home, you simply signed for a loan that you cannot pay off. You are much worse off than you started.* These loans are *vampire loans* because mortgage lenders who keep these loans in their portfolio find that they look better dead than alive. The principal balance increases; the loan value appears higher; but the reality is that the borrower may be about to default on a payment (or may have already defaulted on one or more payments). Sophisticated investment bankers knew this, but they bought these loans from shaky mortgage lenders, packaged them up, and sold them anyway.

As Warren Buffett points out, if you lend money to people who cannot pay you back, it will not end well (and it hasn't).

Homeowners with equity in their homes are encouraged to refinance with "no-cost" loans. In my opinion, this term should be made illegal. There is no such thing as a no-cost loan, albeit this type of loan may make sense for homeowners planning to move in a year or two. Fees are buried deep in the mortgage documents as a *yield spread premium.* Usually a borrower pays around 2 percent of the loan amount in closing costs. On a $100,000 loan there are about $2,000 in closing costs. With a no-cost loan, the mortgage lender builds fees into the interest rate, and the borrower pays the fees over time. Since the lender sells the loan to an investment bank, the lender makes money because the loan paying a higher interest rate sells for a higher price, so the lender gets his money right away. Lenders *are not required* to tell a borrower how much this is worth, and most borrowers—even educated, intelligent, otherwise savvy homeowners—do not know where to find the yield spread premium in their loan documents, which seems like pages of boring jargon, much less calculate what it is worth. *Warren counsels that you should not invest in something you do not understand, and that would also apply when taking out a loan to "invest" in a home.*

The borrower may be getting a loan with a higher interest rate than he or she could get through another broker or through a traditional bank. Brokers doing this often raise the rate by 0.5 percent over and above the closing costs and what the borrower would otherwise pay elsewhere. For a $100,000 30-year fixed-rate loan, the extra charges mean additional interest payments of $11,500 above the closing costs already built into the interest rates. Honest brokers will run the math for a homeowner, show the borrower all of the fees, and calculate the breakeven ownership time period where the borrower will be indifferent between paying the closing costs upfront or paying the closing costs over time embedded in the monthly payments. Honest brokers will not fee slam by stuffing an extra 0.5 percent into the yield spread premium above and beyond the closing costs. *There is no such thing as a no-cost loan.*

Some brokers of no-cost mortgages will only pay appraisers at closing (when borrowers sign documents to buy the home). They claim the appraiser will otherwise not work as hard to fairly value the property, but the opposite is more likely. A higher appraisal makes it more likely the deal will close, and the appraiser only gets paid at closing. It creates a conflict of interest for the appraiser. The appraiser has an incentive to come up with a higher number to ensure there is additional value for the seller or for a homeowner refinancing a loan.

Mortgage brokers are responsible for about 70 percent of subprime loans. Many brokers make prudent loans, but a lot did not. According to Aaron Krowne's Internet-based Implode-o-Meter, from late 2006 to June 2008, 262 major U.S. mortgage lenders had gone "kaput."[10] The number continues to climb. This is an unprecedented failure rate.

The Alt-A mortgage market includes borrowers that have higher credit scores, but not high enough to qualify as "prime" borrowers. In both the Alt-A and prime markets, borrowers have purchased multiple dwellings with little or no money down. As housing prices drop, these borrowers find they have to sell property at a loss if the debt burden becomes too much for them.

Fraud on borrowers is a problem, but so is fraud on lenders. Borrowers, often in collusion with unscrupulous brokers, supplied phony documentation or engage in identity theft. Lenders have a right to complain about this type of fraud, but their own due diligence standards should certainly be tightened.

Investment banks funneled money to mortgage lenders by purchasing the mortgage loans and storing them in special purpose companies known as warehouses. Once there were enough loans, thousands of loans, in the warehouse, they packaged up the loans into *residential mortgage-backed securities* (RMBS) and sold them to investors. As long as the banks could keep stuffing the loans into securitization packages and selling them, they did not have to keep the risk themselves. If you are ethically challenged and have reason to know you are building airplanes with defective parts, you will sell the airplanes as quickly as possible. That way, when the parts give out, someone else will fall out of the sky. Unfortunately for investment banks (and mortgage lenders that sold them the loans), they got stuck, and their earnings crashed.

Mortgage lenders were obliged to take back loans that did not meet certain standards. Some of the loans made in 2006 and 2007 were so bad that they began defaulting before an investment bank could get rid of the risk (by selling packaged loans to investors like mutual funds and others). Shaky mortgage lenders could not buy back the bad loans without borrowing money from *another* investment bank. When things got bad enough, investment banks stopped lending and the shaky mortgage lenders went bankrupt. Many investment banks were stuck with mortgage lenders' unpaid loans and with a warehouse full of bad subprime loans.

One really can't say this enough: Warren advises that you shouldn't lend money to people who cannot pay you back. Investment banks—acting as *indirect* mortgage lenders, bought up the mortgage loans and supplied money to shaky mortgage lenders. They kept the "party" going.

Before the party ended, mortgage lenders siphoned off fees and dividends. When everything unraveled, many mortgage lenders had no value to their shareholders and could not pay back their loans from investment banks ("old investors"), without the money provided by the "new investors," to whom investment banks sold the packaged dodgy loans. *Perhaps your mutual fund.* The only thing that kept the money train moving was the fact that money from "new investors" was used to generate the illusion of high returns for "old investors." That is a *Ponzi scheme.* A Ponzi scheme raises money from "new investors" so "old investors" can be paid a return on their money even though the business model is a failure. When Ponzi schemes unravel, even "old investors" lose some of their money, and the "new investors" lose much more. Only "old investors," who get out very early, escape unscathed.

In late 2006, I saw a prospectus for RMBS that took hundreds of mortgage loans, put them into a portfolio, and sold the risk to investors. The deal seemed targeted for foreign investors and showed a portfolio including first and second lien (piggyback) mortgages. Some were adjustable rate, some not. The portfolio included negative amortizing product and interest-only product. The loans were purchased from various mortgage lenders. More than 60 percent of the loans were purchased from New Century Capital, which in turn acquired them from New Century Mortgage Corporation, a subsidiary of New Century Financial Corporation, which filed a news release in February 2007[11] that it would have to restate its financials and filed for bankruptcy on April 2, 2007, under a cloud of fraud allegations.[12] Investment banks had a responsibility to perform rigorous investigations into the quality of loans coming from mortgage lenders.

One would expect investment banks that are obliged to perform due diligence appropriate to the circumstances to yell: *Stop the money printing presses!*

For example, Merrill Lynch (the previously mentioned deal was not a Merrill Lynch deal) was a part owner of California-based Ownit Mortgage Solutions. Mike Blum, Merrill Lynch's head of global asset-backed finance, sat on the board of Ownit Mortgage Solutions. Revenue was up around 33 percent in the first three quarters of 2006, but Ownit was losing money. In November 2006, JPMorgan Chase told Ownit that its $500 million credit line would disappear on December 13. When Ownit imploded, Blum faxed in his resignation. Ownit made second-lien mortgages, issued 45-year ARMs, and originated no-income-verification loans. In the words of William D. Dallas, its founder and CEO: "The market is paying me to do a no-income-verification loan more than it is paying me to do the full documentation loans."[13] In this post Sarbanes-Oxley world, one might have expected Merrill's Mike Blum to insist on a fraud audit of Ownit instead of faxing in his resignation. Warren Buffett points out, "[T]here are worse things than Sarbanes Oxley."[14] *This is one of them.*

Based on public information like this, the SEC should have taken immediate action and asked Merrill and other investment banks why they did not write down losses on mortgage loans and their securitization businesses. If the SEC was not alarmed by the newspapers, they should have been alarmed by an article that I wrote for risk professionals in first quarter 2007. There I emphatically stated that investment bank risk managers involved in securitizing subprime mortgages should get out and short the product, because the predators' fall was in full swing. It was career suicide to be in a position of supposedly overseeing risk if one did not have the authority to stop the insanity. If, however, one did have the authority to do something about it, the time for action was past due. The SEC may not care about my views, but it ignored many voices from the business media and from investment professionals.

Tom Hudson and Beejal Patel of *First Business Morning News* (*FBMN*) broadcasting out of Chicago documented the troubles of subprime mortgage lenders. They were ahead of the pack in predicting massive write-downs at investment banks. With a shoestring budget and a half-hour broadcast, they presented the best overall coverage of the role of the Fed, mortgage lending, investment banks, and lax sophisticated investors. In fact, they presented great overall coverage on all aspects of finance. The show airs at 5:00 A.M. Chicago, and many Chicago traders—the largest volume of exchange traded derivatives in the world changes hand in Chicago—get up to watch *FBMN*'s financial coverage.

In March 2007, Tom Hudson noted that "banks, brokers and auto companies" were writing down exposures to subprime lenders. In Chicago, Corus Bankshares, Inc. took a write-down on its shares of Freemont General, a large subprime lender. New Century was being sued in several states to stop it from giving new loans. Hudson noted that the Fed regulates banks and could have pushed to stop inflating the subprime market by allowing them to offer "teaser rates that weren't explained to the borrowers." I agreed, "The Fed seemed complacent about the risk." I added that U.S. pension funds and mutual funds owned some of these risky products. "I don't know anyone I hate enough to want to have a negative amortizing ARM (also called a *pay option ARM*). It is just a bad product." Your loan amount increases and then the interest rate shoots up, "it is like the levies breaking."[15]

Yet, investment banks and sophisticated investors did not take huge write-downs on their inventory backed by dodgy loans in first quarter 2007. Dodgy mortgage loans (and securities backed by dodgy mortgage loans) were priced using a *mark-to-model*. Investment banks with an incentive to use rosy assumptions controlled the models, and the result reminded me of Warren's comment about the value of derivatives often being a *mark-to-myth*.

The SEC as regulator of the investment banks had the power, but it did nothing to halt securitization activity. Instead, investment banks *accelerated* securitization activity in the first part of 2007.

A typical residential mortgage-backed security, backed by a pool of subprime and other mortgage loans, has several levels of risk known as *tranches*. The risk of the first few loans to default in the portfolio is borne by the equity investor sometimes called the preference share investor, and so on up the line. In a typical deal, the lowest-rated BB tranche is protected by the equity investor, who absorbs the first 3.25 percent of the losses in the portfolio, if any. This is also known as 3.25 percent subordination. An investment-grade tranche rated BBB is protected by investors taking the first 5.5 percent of the loans to default, if any. In other words, it is protected by the combined losses absorbed by the first loss investor and the BB investor. An investor in the A rated tranche is protected by other investors taking the risk of the first 10 percent of the loans to default, and an investor in the AA rated tranche is protected by other investors taking the first 16 percent to default. The lowest AAA tranche is protected by 24 percent subordination, and the highest AAA rated tranche is protected by 70 percent subordination.

Investors might have felt safe with that much "protection" under the AAA rated tranche, but by December 2007, loans that were 60 days or more late in payments or in foreclosure had climbed to 22 percent (according to LoanPerformance) and recovery rates for subprime loans were very low and varied from pennies on the dollar to 50 percent or so for a first mortgage. Second mortgage loans were often worthless. Collateral rapidly vaporized. Deals made up of piggyback (second lien) loans had principal losses eating through tranches rated "AAA." Investors with deals backed by first lien loans found that losses ate corrosively right through AA tranches, the higher tranches required massive and multilevel downgrades, and that was for deals that did not include a high concentration of loans from mortgage lenders with allegations of fraud. Based on past experience with unsound lending practices like in the manufactured housing market, these problems were foreseeable, and many professionals, including Whitney Tilson (of T2 Partners LLC and the Tilson Funds) and William Ackman (of Pershing Capital) sounded the alarm.

After his bad experience with the Oakwood investment, Warren had warned that securitization distanced the supplier of funds (the investment banks) from the lending transaction (mortgage lenders using mortgage brokers) and "the industry's conduct went from bad to worse."[16] Human nature has not changed.

As for Merrill, it continued its securitization activity in 2007, despite red flags from failing mortgage lenders, including Ownit. For example, in early 2007, it created a package of loans including piggy-back loans issued by Ownit.[17] Around 70 percent of the borrowers had not provided full documentation of either their income or assets. Most of the loans were for the full appraised value (no down payment), and home prices were already showing weakness if not outright falling. In the deal documents, Merrill mentioned that Ownit went bankrupt, but did not mention it was Ownit's largest creditor. *Can Merrill say it did an "arms-length" transaction with Ownit when a Merrill officer sat on Ownit's board?* In early 2008, both Moody's and Standard and Poor's downgraded the AAA rated tranche (an investment they had rated as "super safe" with almost no possibility of loss) to B (junk status *meaning you are likely to lose your shirt*). Moody's forecast that *60 percent of the original portfolio value could eventually be lost.*[18]

MAD is the military term for *mutually assured destruction,* and unsound mortgage lending practices guaranteed that the housing market would be damaged along with the balance sheets of investors that participated by ignoring the risk or by being suckered into unknowingly taking excessive risk. By turning a blind eye to the massive rape of the mortgage loan market, investment bankers assured damage to the U.S. housing market and to their own balance sheet when they were stuck with enormous exposure to their own mischief.

Most of the "early post-signing" defaults in loans, originated through the early months of 2007, had been on "stated income loans," (also known as *liar loans*) especially with loan-to-value ratios approaching 100 percent, whether they were subprime or not. This suggested stated income was overstated. Future defaults would kick in as resets on coupons occurred in a soft housing market.

Throughout most of 2007, the Federal Reserve seemed to be in denial, using reverse moral suasion by minimizing estimates of potential damage. On August 3, 2007, I told CNBC's Joe Kernen: "The market is nervous because everyone feels like they are being lied to. Chairman Ben Bernanke seems to have been doing his homework on Wall Street." Earlier Bernanke reported subprime loss estimates of only $50 to $100 billion. Credit Suisse First Boston had been projecting $50 billion and Citigroup projected $100 billion for subprime losses. I felt every one underestimated ultimate default rates and equally important "they are grossly *overestimating recovery rates* in subprime. . . . Wall Street really screwed Main Street." I had projected $270 billion to $340 billion in subprime losses and around $450 billion to $560 billion for all risky mortgage loan products including Alt-A and prime mortgages.[19] My estimates represented only principal losses, and predatory securitization of predatory loans would amplify these losses.

The day the segment aired, a client asked, "Are you saying Bernanke is incompetent, or are you saying he's a lying coward?"

"Can't you think of any other possibilities?" I asked in reply.

"What else could there be?"

"He may be brave in support of the wrong cause."

My client later reminded me of those words when Associate Justice of the Supreme Court, Antonin Scalia, told *60 Minutes* that torture (such as waterboarding) is not "punishment,"[20] implying that the constitutional prohibition against cruel and unusual punishment wouldn't apply to torture. My client joked that investment banks would like to waterboard me to *prevent* me from talking.

My loss projections were higher than anything coming out of the U.S. government or Wall Street. It turns out I was predicting the greatest losses, and I was too optimistic. Housing speculators and overreaching homeowners took risk, seemingly with "eyes wide shut." Many others were lured with the promise of homeownership. Predatory lenders targeted minorities and lower-income people who were intellectually and financially mugged, then dumped on the side of the road. The motto of predatory lenders is "every minority left behind."

Before meeting Warren, I wrote about industry problems, but only in a general way. Warren's subtle encouragement helped me find my voice. Now I specifically challenged the Federal Reserve Bank and major investment banks on national television.

I told CNBC's Joe Kernen that I advocated a temporary moratorium on subprime foreclosures, followed by mortgage restructurings. That meant *first* reappraising to lower values reflecting the devastation caused by predatory lending and *then* restructuring mortgages to an affordable fixed rate. In some areas, the reappraised values will be drastically lower and the mortgage terms radically different. This protects misled homeowners. Borrowers complicit in fraud, or who willfully overleveraged, should not be given the same protection but could unintentionally benefit. Helping fraudsters is not anyone's idea of a solution but having a few of them slip through the cracks was preferable to the ruination of entire neighborhoods. The devastation was already well underway and needed to be halted.

In some parts of the Midwest every third home is vacant in minority neighborhoods. Housing prices have plummeted. Fixing the problem for innocent homeowners will mean losses must be born by lenders, including subprime mortgage bankers, investment banks that provided financing to the mortgage bankers, and the investors in subprime mortgages and securitizations backed with subprime mortgages. There is no reason for U.S. taxpayers to bail out the sophisticated financiers.

It is counterintuitive, but limiting losses by reappraising and rewriting mortgages would result in a higher recovery rate that would be good for everyone and limit overall losses.

Servicers collect and record loan payments and credit loan accounts. In the summer of 2007, a major Midwest-based servicer of mortgage loans told me the rating agencies' subprime recovery rates were much too optimistic. The servicer said modifying a mortgage was highly preferable to recovering zero or *negative value* after foreclosure fees and depressed asset prices took their toll on recovery of relatively low loan balances. These were geographically diverse U.S. subprime loans, but they were alike in risk characteristics. The servicer's staff worked frantic 13-hour days to salvage value. The servicer underreported delinquencies, overdue payments, which were usually reported one month behind prime mortgages already. The day a homeowner missed a payment, the servicer got on the phone trying to work out a new deal. The servicer allowed skipped payments and did not report them as delinquencies. The servicer discovered that if homeowners missed two payments, the loan was virtually doomed to default because most homeowners gave up after that. It aggressively "re-aged" mortgages—ignoring missed payments urging borrowers to make even one payment so the loan could appear alive. If this practice was typical, the scope of the subprime problem was underreported. The servicer restructured loans doomed to fail in the future. It sold loans for pennies (3 cents to 6 cents) on the dollar. Some of the loans had negative equity (the homeowner owed more than the home was worth) at the time of delinquency. The servicer avoided foreclosure, because legal costs relative to low loan balances and long delays ate up more money than it recovered. Assets included trailers, mobile homes, and homes in areas with depressed prices.

If this sounds odd, consider that in 2008 a plethora of banks started reclassifying loans on their balance sheets (Astoria Financial, Wells Fargo & Co., and others) or began using more optimistic data (Wachovia Corp. and Washington Mutual). *If you don't like the numbers, just change the definition.* In July 2008, Wells Fargo stock price jumped 33 percent when its losses were less than expected, but it announced that, as of April 2008, it would wait an additional two months before writing off a loan (180 days instead of 120 days) saying it did not affect its earnings announcement. At the time Wells Fargo's portfolio of home equity loans was $83.6 billion and it was showing signs of stress.[21, 22]

JPMorgan Chase's CEO Jamie Dimon is a master at balancing the short game of earnings announcements with the long game of running a bank. He steered away from most of the mortgage madness, but announced that "jumbo" mortgages (large balance mortgages to good credits) showed increasing losses. Dimon announced that these prime mortgages to the bank's best customers had losses of 0.95 percent (up from 0.05 percent the prior year), and the losses could triple. For example in California, housing prices had collapsed leading to higher loan losses even for prime (good credit) borrowers. He said JPMorgan may have waded back into the mortgage market early: "We were wrong. We obviously wish we hadn't done it."[23]

♟ ♟ ♟

The Federal Reserve kept interest rates low for years seemingly complacent in light of consumer lending problems in the late 1990s and the early part of the twenty-first century. In April 2005, then Fed Chairman Alan Greenspan said mortgage lenders efficiently judged the risk.[24] Instead, Greenspan should have raised the alarm about foolish mortgage lending. The Fed compounded its errors when it bailed out Countrywide, the second largest subprime lender in the United States, which is regulated by the Office of Thrift Supervision. Countrywide is also a primary dealer, authorized to trade U.S. government and other select securities with the Federal Reserve System. The Fed should have revoked Countrywide's primary dealer status and let it fend for itself.

Countrywide posted its expanded interest-only programs on its Web site in September 2003 (and appeared to remove it in 2007). Few borrowers are savvy enough for interest-only loans, since mortgage borrowers paid no principal on loans, just interest. Many hoped housing prices would rise so they could refinance or take a profit. The program included NINA (no documentation: no income verification, no asset verification), No Ratio (no income information, so no debt to income ratio is calculated allowing the borrower to assume a greater debt load than would be allowed with a traditional mortgage), and SISA (stated income, stated assets) loans. The FHA guaranteed some Countrywide loans, and presumably they conformed to FHA's requirements. But FNMA and FHLMC were the chief buyers of Countrywide's loans, and many of these loans were problematic.

On August 5, 2007, I told CBS's Thalia Assuras that the mortgage lending relationship with investment banks is one of the largest "Ponzi schemes in financial history" and "risky mortgage products were made to people who couldn't afford them."[25] I misspoke. I meant to say it is *the largest Ponzi scheme in the history of the capital markets.*

By the end of 2006, Countrywide's loans showed signs of trouble. The week of August 6, 2007, rumors hit the market that Countrywide was looking for a "white knight," a deep pocket investor to either take it over or to provide a liquidity injection, but it had no success. On August 7, 2007, the Federal Open Market Committee issued an economic outlook statement saying that inflation, not the mortgage market problems, were the chief concern, and it would not cut the federal funds rate (the borrowing rate) to inject more liquidity into the market. But just two days later, on August 9, the European Central Bank injected around $130 billion into the European banking system, and the Federal Reserve pumped $24 billion into the U.S. banking system through the Federal Reserve's Open Market Trading Desk.

On August 10, 2007, Warren and I spoke on a different topic, and—without naming names—he mentioned that two large companies had come to him hat in hand needing billions. There would be a couple of major blow-ups since they were running out of options. I independently guessed that Countrywide was one of the beggars.

One of the ways Countrywide got money was by issuing commercial paper (*asset-backed commercial paper* or ABCP) backed by its loans. The week of August 13, 2007, investors shunned Countrywide's debt. Nervous investors demanded higher interest rates. Countrywide told its creditors (investment banks) it wanted to borrow money (by drawing on its credit card-like credit lines). Countrywide wanted to borrow $11.5 billion from a 40-bank syndicate. Countrywide was in a desperate situation. Market rumors were that the banks refused to lend the money, and asked the Fed for concessions.

On August 15, 2007, I wrote Warren that investors were nervous because Canadian money market funds found their investments (not necessarily related to Countrywide) were backed by risky leveraged subprime products. Prices plummeted as investors realized they would lose principal on AAA rated products.[26]

The banks got their concessions, and lent to Countrywide. On Thursday, August 16, 2007, the stock market (Dow) fell more than 340 points as Countrywide borrowed $11.5 billion. It seemed to me that on Thursday, one or more of the banks leaked the news ahead of the Fed's announcement on Friday because, near the end of trading on Thursday, the market rebounded from the 340 point nosedive to finish down only 15 points. On Friday, August 17, 2007, the Fed announced its concessions—a cut of 50 basis points (bps) in the discount rate to 5.75 percent from 6.25 percent along with news of relaxed borrowing terms. The Fed agreed to accept investments backed with (Countrywide's) mortgage loans as long as they had the now-suspect AAA rating. The Fed also extended the "overnight" discount window borrowings to 30 days. On Friday, August 17, 2007, the stock market marched upward.

The Fed's terms mirrored those that nervous investors refused when they stopped buying Countrywide's debt. The Fed bailed Countrywide out of its liquidity problems by lending to the banks who lent to Countrywide using Countrywide's collateral to back the loans. This massive liquidity bailout was the first Fed bailout related to the sub-prime mortgage lending crisis (as far as I know). The Federal Reserve Bank could have exercised its authority to demand Countrywide mod-ify mortgage loans. The Fed was a pushover. Ben Bernanke had dangled raw meat in the face of hungry wolves. More bailouts were coming.

Investors felt pressure from all angles. Quant funds reported losses. I told CNBC's Carl Quintanilla that quant funds put on Dead Man's Curve trades, and "model masturbation makes quants go blind." Warren Buffett and Charlie Munger warned this would happen. They talk about value and price; they don't talk about betas, correlations, and volatilities. Steve Forbes of *Forbes* magazine opposed any bailouts. He noted the Fed had kept rates low, fueling the problem. He cautioned that we should "resist the temptation to bail these people out," and spe-cifically referred to the Fed's bailout of Long-Term Capital.[27]

On August 17, 2007, CNBC aired a series of stories that Warren Buffett might be eyeing Countrywide, but they were all incorrect sto-ries.[28] "It is better to be a bad manager of a good business," Warren always says, "than a good manager of a bad business."[29] He seeks good managers of good businesses. I told the *Journal Inquirer* that the Fed should have asked Countrywide for a quid pro quo in exchange for the bailout: "Given Countrywide's contribution to the problems in the mortgage loan market, and given company head Angelo Mozilo's denial of that role, the Fed should have pressured Countrywide's board to replace him."[30] Warren wrote me that he agreed with my comments.

Less than a year after the August 2007 bailout, Daniel Bailey Jr. got a surprise email reply after asking Countrywide to modify the terms of his adjustable rate mortgage. Bailey Jr. wrote he had not understood how the loan worked; he had been told he could refinance after a year; and now he cannot deal with the payments. Mozilo apparently hit "reply" rather than "forward" when emailing. Mozilo wrote it is unbe-lievable that most of the letters Countrywide receives seem like form letters. "Obviously they are being counseled by some other person or by the Internet. Disgusting."[31]

I can understand the email SNAFU. One Saturday, I sent my nephew, Kenneth, a link to a cheesy but oddly entertaining David Hasselhoff video. Three hours later, Kenneth C. Griffin, CEO of Citadel Investment Group, replied, "Did you hit my address by accident?"

I know Ken Griffin is a gentleman. He promised not to embarrass me by revealing my mistake. I now also know we are both fans of KITT (Knight Industries Two Thousand), the talking car in *Knight Rider.* KITT protected Michael Knight, Hasselhoff's character, but no one seems to protect borrowers from predatory lenders. I understand how easy it is to miss-send an email. But I cannot understand why Mozilo was still CEO of Countrywide and in a position to send it. Mozilo stayed on as Countrywide's CEO until the week after its acquisition by Bank of America was approved by Countrywide's shareholders on June 25, 2008.[32] Warren is a fan of buying large positions in good stocks, and he is also a fan of Mae West, who once said: "Too much of a good thing can be wonderful." I am pretty sure Mozilo's delayed retirement is not what either of them had in mind.

By the spring of 2008, it was painfully clear that mortgage loan losses would be much higher than the Fed's earlier highest projections, and my numbers were closer to reality. The overall size of the U.S. residential mortgage loan market is around $11.5 trillion, of which a little more than 11 percent is subprime and more than 10.4 percent is Alt-A (with credit scores in between subprime and the higher prime borrowers). John Paulson of Paulson & Co. compiled data from LoanPerformance and the Mortgage Bankers Association in a public presentation showing that between March 2007 and March 2008, subprime delinquencies had soared to 27.2 percent in the $1.3 trillion subprime market, an increase of around 163 percent, and in the $1.2 trillion Alt-A market, delinquencies soared to 9.1 percent, a year over year change of around 380 percent. Prime mortgage delinquencies were up to 3.2 percent, a 2.1 percent increase from fourth quarter of 2006 to 2007.

Given the gravity of the loan problems, investment banks should have been reporting large losses much earlier. For example, on October 8, 2007, I told clients that Merrill's *mal de MER* was just beginning. At the time a friend asked me where Merrill stock would be in six months. I responded: "In someone else's portfolio." *Not mine and not Warren Buffett's.* Jeff Edwards, Merrill's CFO had made rosy statements in July 2007. Astute shareholders, not to mention the SEC and Merrill's board, might have wondered why the massive losses reported in third quarter had not shown up much earlier. Stan O'Neal, the CEO, appeared to have a big problem.

On October 10, 2007, I reminded David Wighton of the *Financial Times* that Merrill was one of the lenders to the mortgage-backed securities hedge funds managed by Bear Stearns Asset Management that collapsed in August 2007. Creditors had challenged BSAM's mark-to-market valuations in April, and that is what got the ball rolling for the downfall of the funds: "Merrill was not so finicky when it came to marking its own books."[33]

Merrill began reporting massive losses, but in my view, they were *quarters* late. I was amazed O'Neal was still in his CEO chair. On October 24, CNBC's Joe Kernen, with GE's former CEO, Jack Welch, covered Merrill's earnings report. I appeared on a segment with Charlie Gasparino, CNBC's online editor.

I led off: "Way back in first quarter" I had called this and said Merrill's risk managers should "*get out and short*. Short Merrill's positions."[34]

Gasparino asserted: "When *we* were reporting this about three weeks ago, ahead of everybody . . . we reported there was going to be a larger third quarter loss."

I countered that O'Neal has a big problem: "They were not hedging properly in *first quarter*." I added: "I laughed in disbelief" when I saw second quarter earnings. "It is an *Enronesque* kind of problem, it is a business management problem, not a risk management problem."

Gasparino said he wouldn't go that far and focused on the CFO (Jeff Edwards) and the potential ouster of a risk manager instead of picking up on my assertion about O'Neal. He said the problem with getting rid of Ahmass Fakahany: "Fakahany (the risk manager) and Stan O'Neal are very close."

"I don't think O'Neal survives this," I responded. There is no problem getting rid of O'Neal's friends if he is gone, and O'Neal will have to answer to shareholders and the board about failure to report losses in second quarter. Within a few days, O'Neal resigned. I added that the rest of Wall Street had underestimated how horrific the losses due to low recovery rates would be in subprime.[35]

After the collapse of the stock market technology bubble and the outing of Enron's and Worldcom's problems, Stan O'Neal wrote an opinion piece for the *Wall Street Journal* saying, "In any system predicated on risk-taking, there are failures, sometimes spectacular failures. But for every failure to be viewed as fraudulent or even criminal bodes ill for our economic system."[36]

I agree with O'Neal's words on the face of it. It's great to have an open mind, but don't leave it so open that your brains fall out. O'Neal might have added that taking foolish risks and then failing to examine risk in one's own portfolio makes for poor financial management. CEOs can read the newspapers just like anyone else, and the implosion of mortgage lender after mortgage lender was well publicized. Warren Buffett is a voracious analytical reader, and he told me that he considers risk management one of his key responsibilities as CEO of Berkshire Hathaway.

If O'Neal did not have time to read the papers, he might have asked a few more questions of his managers about Merrill's involvement with failed mortgage lenders like Ownit. How could Merrill resell or securitize those loans and earn the same profits healthy loans produce?

The Department of Justice and the Federal Bureau of Investigation (FBI) issued a press release on June 19, 2008: "From March 1 to June 18, 2008, Operation Malicious Mortgage resulted in 144 mortgage fraud cases in which 406 defendants were charged." Cases have been brought across the United States with losses of approximately $1 billion induced by alleged fraud.[37]

When Bank of America Corp agreed to buy Countrywide in January 2008, the all-stock transaction was valued at $4 billion. By the time Countrywide's shareholders approved the sale on June 25, 2008, the shares of Bank of America had slumped and the value was around $2.8 billion. But Bank of America may not have gotten a bargain. Also on that day, Illinois, California, and Washington State Department of Financial Institutions filed lawsuits against Countrywide, and other states soon followed.[38, 39] Illinois Attorney General Lisa Madigan was the first to file, and the Illinois suit named Angelo Mozilo in addition to Countrywide. She noted that Mozilo has assets. She alleged there was a "pattern of deception." Countywide had the "worst practices" and the "highest volume" of troubled mortgage loans in Illinois, and the "most toxic product (option ARMS), which she said makes up one-third of Countrywide's portfolio. "Countrywide broke the law. Homeowners did not."[40]

Eric Mozilo, the CEO's son, blamed the media, protesting, "All we try to do is put people in homes."[41] He may be correct. That may be *all* Countrywide did for many borrowers. But if that is all Mozilo was trying to do, he would have served many borrowers better by inviting them to stay overnight at his place. Giving someone a bad mortgage loan only puts someone in a home temporarily, and, left many borrowers worse off than before they ever heard of Countrywide.

Countrywide set up IndyMac (Independent National Mortgage) in 1985. The two thrifts split in 1997 and became competitors. In July 2008, IndyMac became the third largest bank to fail in the history of the United States, and in September 2008, $307 billion Washington Mutual (Sold to J.P. Morgan) became the largest to fail. The Federal Deposit Insurance Corporation (FDIC) is drawing on its $53 billion deposit-insurance fund.

Thrifts are regulated by the Office of Thrift Supervision (OTS). John Reich, head of the OTS, seemed to think U.S. Senator Charles E. Schumer bore some responsibility for IndyMac's failure because the senator wrote a letter to the OTS with concerns about IndyMac's solvency. He also made it public, which in my opinion is like yelling "*Fire!*" in a crowded theater. In my mind, it also begged the question as to why Senator Schumer did not seem compelled to speak up earlier about predatory lending and problems at other institutions—say, Fannie Mae, Freddie Mac, or Countrywide. Senator Schumer countered that if the OTS had reigned in Indy Mac's "poor and loose lending practices," the thrift would not have failed, and that the regulator should "start doing its job."[42] Instead of acting like a sheriff of Mortgage Lenders, the Office of Thrift Supervision behaved like the sheriff of Nottingham.

The Office of Thrift Supervision had reason to intervene long before mortgage lenders started dropping like flies. If they did not read Berkshire Hathaway's annual reports, they could read a report from the St. Louis Federal Reserve Bank. It noted in 2005 that *all* loans (subprime,

Alt-A, and prime) have a higher default rate when the homeowner has little to lose—a low or zero down payment, for example. The report suggested that subprime loans with no down payment are an especially bad idea: "Serious delinquency (60 and 90 days) is especially sensitive to homeowner equity and origination."[43] Loosely translated, that meant that thrifts would have a much harder time getting paid back if they offered risky mortgage loans to people with no down payment and low credit scores. *So where was the OTS when no (or low) down payment subprime loans combined with other risky features were being made?*

As of 2008, although subprime loans are only $1.3 trillion (over 11–13 percent depending on how you define subprime) of the $11.5 trillion U.S. residential market, they are the most troubled. In May 2008, Standard & Poor's announced that subprime loans originated in 2005–2007 looked awful, and loans made in 2007 were the worst of the bunch. *Where was the OTS?* Delinquencies for 2005 vintage subprime loans were 37.1 percent and had increased 2 percent from the previous month; 37.1 percent of 2006 vintage subprime loans were delinquent, a rise of 4 percent from March; 25.9 percent of subprime loans originated in 2007 were delinquent, a 6 percent jump from March to April 2008. The 2007 loans were "unseasoned" or young but were already at least a couple of months late in payments.[44, 45] In the second quarter of 2008, a Mortgage Banking Association survey revealed that 9.2 percent of mortgages for single family to four-family homes were a month or more overdue or in foreclosure.[46] It was the worst result in the 39-year history of the survey. In the month of August 2008, foreclosure filings in the U.S. rose to a record high of more than 303,000 properties as the continued drop in home prices, combined with tighter lending standards, made it harder for homeowners to refinance their mortgages, with and an estimated supply of unsold homes of 11 months.[47]

The direct and indirect costs to the U.S. taxpayer will be difficult to assess because of creative accounting that delays the recognition of the true problem. For example, banks and thrifts announced they were delaying their recognition of losses by allowing delinquencies of up to 180 days before taking a writedown on loans, and Fannie Mae and Freddie Mac said that in the past they wrote down loans when they were 90 days past due, but sometime in 2008 they decided to wait *two years.*[48] On July 16, 2002, Alan Greenspan commented on the corporate shenanigans after the tech-bubble burst saying "infectious greed seemed to grip much of the business community," and it was a once-in-a-generation frenzy of speculation."[49] That was after the mini-frenzies of Drexel Burnham Lambert, Long-Term Capital Management, charged-off credit card receivables, manufactured housing loans, and more. Perhaps Alan Greenspan has found a way to accelerate the human lifecycle.

Fortunately for Berkshire Hathaway shareholders, Warren Buffett is the CEO. At year-end 1999, Berkshire Hathaway was Freddie Mac's largest shareholder; it owned around 8.6 percent.[50] Warren Buffett may prefer to hold onto stocks forever but only if he finds an investment that can go the distance with him. In his 2000 shareholder letter he wrote: "we sold nearly all of our Freddie Mac and Fannie Mae shares."[51] Warren later told me that Fannie Mae and Freddie Mac began emphasizing revenue targets of around 15 percent per year. He did not feel this double digit growth was sustainable just based on operating earnings alone. More than that, value investors are not impressed by revenues alone. Anyone can use leverage to inflate revenues. The *quality* of the revenues is paramount, since that is what will sustain profitability.

Berkshire Hathaway's Clayton Homes seems to have avoided the contagion. I toured one of the manufactured homes at the Berkshire Hathaway annual meeting in 2006. Potential homeowners are not encouraged to buy a palace. Clayton Homes offers affordable housing at lending terms designed to help ensure the borrower will be able to pay off the loan. It is the chance for people to live a decent life, and there is dignity in being able to live within one's means while bettering one's circumstances. Most of Clayton's earnings come not from its manufactured housing, but from its loan portfolio. Warren reports its results in the finance section of the Berkshire Hathaway annual report. At the end of 2007, Clayton had an "$11 billion loan portfolio, covering 300,000 borrowers."[52] Berkshire Hathaway provides the financing (instead of, say, an investment bank that would buy the loans, package them up, and resell them). In contrast to the rest of the mortgage loan market, "[d]elinquencies, foreclosures and losses" have stayed constant and the "Clayton portfolio is performing well."[53]

Unfortunately, for many others in the global financial markets, false promises and broken dreams were part of many investment portfolios. The MADness spread across the globe as if it were a hypercontagious flu virus.

Chapter 6

Shell Games (Beware of Geeks Bearing Grifts)

I've looked at the prospectuses, and they are not easy to read. If you want to understand the deal you'd have to read around 750,000 pages of documents.

—Warren Buffett to Janet Tavakoli,
January 10, 2008

On August 5, 2005, two days after Warren and I set up our meeting, Matthew ("Matt") Goldstein, at the time a senior writer for *TheStreet.com,* wrote about problems with mortgage-backed CDOs. Eliot Spitzer, then New York Attorney General, had just sent Bear Stearns Co. (Bear Stearns) a subpoena. Hudson United, a small New Jersey bank, had tried to sell mortgage-backed CDOs it bought in 2002 back to Bear Stearns, the underwriter and seller of the CDOs.

Hudson discovered its CDO investments were worth only a small fraction of the "market prices" that Bear Stearns had supplied Hudson up until it tried to sell them back.

In April 2005, I addressed the International Monetary Fund in Washington about the hidden risks of off-balance-sheet vehicles, securitizations, and the failure of the rating agencies to reflect these risks in their ratings. Sophisticated investors are baffled by the complexity; even multistrategy hedge funds such as Chicago-based Citadel had contacted me about securitizations. I told Goldstein that investors seemed to rely on ratings and rarely ask how the underlying assets are priced or whether they will get full price if they need to sell the investment: "There are huge transparency issues. In some cases, investors have been taken in by hype."[1]

The U.S. Securities and Exchange Commission (SEC) launched a separate investigation into Bear Stearns' CDO activities. Like the New York Attorney General's office, it wanted to know if Bear Stearns had mispriced mortgage-backed CDOs and harmed investors. Bear Stearns subsequently disclosed in a regulatory filing that the SEC intended to recommend action. Many financial professionals believed Bear Stearns would be charged for alleged improper pricing of CDOs it had sold to both a bank and an institutional investor.[2]

Yet, despite increasing attention in the financial press, the New York Attorney General's office dropped its case. The SEC's rumored civil enforcement action involving Bear Stearns' CDO pricing practices fizzled, and the investigation was closed.[3] The Slumbering Esquires Club rolled over and went back to sleep.

The SEC's new head struck me as the Antichrist of investor advocacy. On July 26, 2005, just a few days before Goldstein's article and my first reply to Warren Buffett, Christopher Cox attended a Congressional coffee klatch—commonly known as his confirmation hearing—for the post of chairman of the SEC. One of Cox's former clients pleaded guilty and got a 10-year sentence in a case involving defrauded funds.[4] Cox had worked on a separate public offering that was not implicated in the case. Among other things, Cox wrote a letter for his client saying it "would unfairly and unreasonably harm the investors' rate of return"[5] to appraise pools of mortgages. Cox also wrote that suitability—a standard meant to ensure that naïve investors did not get saddled with risky product—should not apply: "Because all of the trust fund loans are secured and overcollateralized, there is relatively low risk."[6] Cox wrote his letter in 1985, and unbeknownst to Cox, his client's fraud involving separate vehicles began in 1982 and continued until 1994. Appraisals may have stopped the fraud earlier. On July 29, 2005, Floyd Norris of the *New York Times* reminded his readers of Cox's letter, yet the Senate Committee unanimously confirmed Cox later the same day. It was time to short CDOs, since the value added by the SEC's Cox seemed likely to shrivel.

When I read prospectuses for CDO deals and CDO-squared deals, I felt as if I had opened a box of candies and found only one or two good pieces. The rest were either missing altogether, or had a bite taken out of them with someone else's teeth marks. *These were definitely not See's Candies, a Berkshire Hathaway company.* Some CDO-squared deals were so bad it left me thinking: *Where is the candy?!*

To use an extreme example, if you only use subprime-backed fraud-ridden mortgage loans as collateral for residential mortgage-backed security deals, and the RMBSs lose 60 percent of portfolio value, if you use investment grade tranches but with ratings lower than the top AAA of these RMBSs as collateral for a CDO, *all of the collateral of your CDO will vaporize.* If you use tranches of this defective CDO in yet another CDO called a *CDO-squared,* you are starting out with nearly worthless collateral, so the entire CDO-squared is nearly worthless on the day the deal is brought to market. It seems to me that some investment banks knowingly participated in predatory securitizations.

One does not need to read hundreds of pages of prospectuses or perform complicated modeling to know that. Warren looks at every investment as if it is a business, and the only "business" these investments have are the loans backing them. *If the loans do not do well, the CDOs backed by them soon follow them down the tubes.*

It will be too obvious if all of the collateral you use is this bad, so you might mix it in with some Alt-A or even some prime collateral in an RMBS. That way, if you use this collateral for a CDO, it won't look so bad, and it will be devilishly difficult to analyze. For example, if you use BBB rated tranches of RMBS deals backed by a variety of types of loans, you can mix in 30 percent risky subprime loans. It sounds pretty safe, but losses will probably still eat through the BBB rated tranches.

Now you take those doomed BBB rated tranches and combine them with A and AA rated tranches to create a CDO. All of the BBB rated tranches will disappear and probably some or all of the single A. If you buy the AAA tranche of this CDO, and it has around 25 percent subordination, your principal may or may not be in jeopardy, but most of the tranches below it are in trouble. Now if you use those lower tranches to make a CDO-squared, most of those tranches will probably lose principal. In some deals, all of the tranches below the senior-most triple A will lose the entire principal amount, and the senior-most triple A will lose substantial principal.

Credit derivatives enable a further level of gamesmanship and opacity. The documentation of many CDOs is dense with all sorts of cash flow tricks, and the contracts for the credit derivatives embedded in the CDOs are not included with the prospectuses. *The ratings are completely meaningless.*

In January 2007, I noticed that U.S. institutional investors curtailed their buying of CDOs. But investment banks had created new types of structured investment vehicles called *SIV-lites,* or structured investment vehicles with less protection (or lite protection). These vehicles invested in the overrated AAA tranches of CDOs backed by subprime debt, and the rating agencies rated the vehicles AAA. These vehicles, in turn, issued faux AAA asset-backed commercial paper.

These new entities seemed like corporations, but the only "business" they have is investing in assets and those assets have to provide "earnings." Benjamin Graham's disciples look for better quality of earnings and for earnings growth.

As the collateral in the structured investment vehicles inevitably took massive downgrades, the vehicles had to liquidate their wasting collateral, and investors lost a significant amount of their principal. Mutual funds, bank portfolios, insurance companies, local government funds, private investment groups, and more lost billions. Canadians heavily invested, and our North American neighbors lost billions. Since these assets carried high ratings, European and Asian investors also took losses.

Despite their "efforts," investment banks were still stuck with tens of billions of unsold CDOs. They reduced exposures by buying bond insurance, buying credit protection from hedge funds, and doing a variety of leveraged sales. Some of that risk boomeranged back onto bank balance sheets.

The madness did not stop with mortgage loans. Collateralized debt obligations can be backed by any combination of debt: credit derivatives, asset-backed securities, mortgage-backed securities, other collateralized debt obligations, hedge fund loans, credit card loans, auto loans, bonds, leveraged corporate loans, sovereign debt, or any kind of combination of actual or notional debt man can imagine and create.

Stephen Partridge-Hicks, co-head of Gordian Knot, probably the best run structured investment vehicles in the world, felt the effects of a nervous market reluctant to invest in the debt of *any* investment vehicle. Risky overrated AAA commercial paper issued by risky structured investment vehicles caused investors to shun sound investments. He told me he bought *zero* subprime-backed investments and rejected a lot of other misrated AAA deals. Yet shortly after Lehman's bankruptcy, Sigma, one of his two funds, collapsed.

🖈 🖈 🖈

If I had a large bonus in my sights and mischief on my mind, how would I unload toxic CDO tranches? This is all hypothetical, mind you, but here's just one of a number of different gimmicks.

If you work at an investment bank and you stuff the toxic tranches of *only* your own CDOs into another CDO, it will be too obvious. You need help from your friends who work for other investment banks, hedge funds, and CDO managers. Since you all have toxic CDOs and still want to earn high fees, you can all play investment banking *hawala* similar to the complex, but highly effective, money brokering system used in the Middle East. *Hawala* makes it virtually impossible to trace cross-border money flows. It will be hard for anyone, except the SEC or someone with subpoena power to examine your trade tickets, to figure out what you are doing. Since the SEC seems to have lost its will to exist, you are good to go.

There is just one more thing. As Warren told me at lunch, many people seem to have a perverse desire to make things overly complicated. Yet, the fundamentals of finance do not change. Most value investors will not be fooled, and they actually read your documents. If you really think you can confuse unwary investors about the basics by hiding behind a label such as "synthetic CDO-squared," you are good to go.

Mix your toxic junk with your friends' toxic junk into a CDO-squared. Now you have deniability. After all, why would you buy someone else's CDOs if they were toxic? Now get the compliant rating agencies to rate a huge chunk of this risky hairball triple A. If you are lucky, you may find an investor to buy it. Failing that, you may find a bond insurer to insure it. Failing that, you may find an investment vehicle or hedge fund willing to do a credit derivative or other leveraged transaction. These diversions should get you through bonus season. After all else fails, your investment banks can beg the Federal Reserve Bank to take overrated AAA paper in exchange for treasuries.

There is one small problem with this. *If you know or should know* that you are not correctly pricing your balance sheet or if you knowingly sell overrated securities, you must disclose that, and you must be specific about it. If you know something is rated super-safe AAA; but it deserves a near-default rating of CCC, you cannot keep silent about it when you sell it.

When I pointed out to an investment banker that this is a classic situation for fraud, he told me: "Our internal OGC [Office of General Counsel] disclaims virtually all liability for [our investment bank] and its bankers in small print fully disclosing the risks in the prospectuses." I knew what he meant, but he sounded like a smart 10-year-old parroting an adult.

"I did not attend law school," I responded, "but I am pretty damn sure that just because you disclosed serious conflicts of interest, it does not protect you if you fail in your duty of care to investors. Your lawyers can't give you a license to kill."

The moral hazard swamped any risk the rating agencies' models could capture. One investment banker crowed to me that the rating agencies are eager for fees and the investment bank's structurers seeking ratings for their CDOs are "shrewd bullies."

One synthetic CDO deal with a notional amount of more than $2 billion went into liquidation, and *less than 3 percent* of investors' money was recovered. Even the investor in the top-most "AAA," the super senior tranche, lost principal. Perhaps everyone involved with this deal, including the CDO manager, was just very unlucky. But do you want to do business with unlucky people?[7]

CDO managers are supposed to be selling securities backed by *actual* assets—not *imaginary* assets.

In November 2006, I told *Asset Securitization* that CDO managers are unregulated, and only a handful of managers provide good value for the fees charged. Most do not have the expertise or resources to perform CDO management or surveillance. Many cannot build a CDO model. Many managers rely on the bank arranger both for structuring expertise and to take a lead role with the rating agencies to secure the initial ratings. Rating agencies rarely ask for background checks on CDO managers.

Chris Ricciardi, CEO of Cohen & Company, read my commentary and wrote me: "I LOVED it." He had been thinking about how to be "the best CDO manager in the business," had independently come to the same conclusions, and found my "insight very compelling." Yet in April 2008, Cohen & Company's CDO management arm, Strategos Capital Management, led managers with CDOs in default. The total original amount of the CDOs it managed that had events of default (with as yet undetermined recoveries) was $14.2 billion.[8]

On December 7, 2007, I wrote Warren that many asset-backed securitization CDO prospectuses are finance comic books. For example, Adams Square Funding I closed December 15, 2006. It was an "asset-backed" deal, a collateralized deal. It was rated by Moody's and S&P. Yet, before 2008 ended, the CDO unwound, meaning all of the underlying assets were sold in an attempt to pay investors back. Unfortunately, there was not enough cash after selling the loans to go around. According to S&P, investors in Adams Square Funding I got less than 25 percent of par value—more than a 75 percent loss—on average. Investors were wiped out, except for the investor in the seniormost AAA tranche.[9] Since the prospectus shows that the seniormost tranche made up 29 percent of the deal, it appears those investors may have lost some money, too. It is reminiscent of the opening scenes of the movie *Cliffhanger,* in which a climber's supports snap one-by-one ending in a spectacular steep fall. That last plastic buckle was AAA rated. Adams Square Funding I is not an isolated example, just a handy one, because it unwound. It is not even close to being the funkiest deal I have seen.

Warren's ability to say "no" when the risk is not priced correctly is a tremendous advantage to any investors.

The prospectus for Adams Square Funding I disclosed the conflicts of interest between the investors, Credit Suisse Alternative Capital (CSAC), and other Credit Suisse affiliated entities, including the Leveraged Investment Group (LIG) of Credit Suisse Securities (CSS).[10] I always recommend that investors eliminate this kind of moral hazard by insisting on changes to the deal. Conflicts of interest do not mean that there is anyone doing anything wrong, but when the moral hazard is enormous, things never seem to end well for investors. Rating agency models do not capture these huge risks, yet, the rating agencies never seem to refuse to rate these deals. I have written books and articles on this problem for years; the ratings on deals with this kind of risk are totally meaningless. Yet the rating agencies continue to defend their indefensible methods.

Among many classes of bad deals, the problems of CDOs named after constellations were well publicized. Approximately $35 billion of these CDOs had been underwritten by Citigroup, UBS, Merrill Lynch, Calyon, Lehman, and others. They are mostly fallen stars. I told the *Wall Street Journal* that Norma, a Merrill-underwritten CDO comprised mostly of credit derivatives linked to BBB rated tranches of other securitizations, "is a tangled hairball of risk."[11] It had come to market in March 2007, and by December 2007, it was worth a fraction of its original value. The rating agencies slashed its ratings to junk. I added "[A]ny savvy investor would have thrown this…in the trash bin."[12]

Constellation deals were not the only class of dicey deals, and it seems that CDOs bought in the last half of 2006 and during 2007 were particularly awful. Investment banks found they had a huge credibility problem with investors. Merrill Lynch was not alone in having credibility problems, but I happened to review all of their 2007 CDOs that I could track. I looked at 30 CDOs and CDO-squared deals with a notional amount of $32 billion that Merrill Lynch underwrote in 2007. As of June 10, 2008, *all of the deals I captured were in trouble at the AAA level.* One or more of the originally AAA rated tranches had been downgraded to junk (below investment grade) by one or more rating agencies. Merrill Lynch was not alone in having a poor track record, but this sort of unprecedented performance was hard to beat. CDO managers had nothing to be proud of, either, and many saw their streams of fee income dwindle. The securitization market was in a dead calm.[13] I made my concerns public.[14,15] As far as I was concerned, the Hall of Shame looked overcrowded. Losing trust was not the only problem. Financial institutions lost hundreds of billions of dollars.

Bloomberg keeps daily tabulations of subprime related losses world-wide. I told Yalman Onaran that although some mark-to-market losses may be reversed as markets recover, most of the losses are permanent impairments caused by surging defaults: "[O]f course we can't tell how much ... may actually be good stuff that will pay back at maturity."[16]

By June 18, 2008, Bloomberg estimated that global bank balance sheet losses due to write-downs and charge-offs at $396 billion. That figure may have been tainted with denial. By October 16, 2008, it nudged past $660 billion. Citigroup had written down $55.1 billion, Merrill Lynch $58.1 billion, and UBS $44.2 billion. Wachovia topped the list with losses of $96.7 billion; Washington Mutual's losses were $45.6 billion. The list was long and sobering.[17,18] Risky loans made to both risky borrowers and prime (high credit score) borrowers were only part of the problem. Predatory securitizations amplified losses. As a result, the entire landscape of global investment banking changed.

The damage to the global markets was much worse, however. Losses reported by the banks do not include losses to hedge funds, private equity investors, mutual funds, municipalities, insurance companies, pension funds, and more. The International Monetary Fund (IMF) estimates losses related to the U.S. subprime meltdown and its fallout could reach about *$1 trillion.*[19]

I blurted out to Warren that I was disgusted with the "*douche bags who got* [the nation] *into this mess*"; then I gasped at the realization of what I had just said. For his part, Warren says that the documentation uses arcane language and that it is impossible to read that many prospectuses just to analyze one deal. One had to read "hundreds of thousands of pages."[20] Warren once noted: "There seems to be some perverse human characteristic that likes to make easy things difficult."[21] The simple solution boils down to the principles that Warren has espoused for decades: *Don't lend money to people who cannot pay you back. If you do not understand something, do not invest.*

Chapter 7

Financial Astrology— AAA Falling Stars

I can't recall we've ever asked for management changes in companies we've invested in. If they did the wrong thing, they should go.
—Warren Buffett,
Wall Street Journal, May 23, 2008

At the end of 2007, Berkshire Hathaway owned 48 million shares of Moody's Corporation, one of the top three rating agencies (the same shares Berkshire owned when I first met Warren Buffett in 2005), representing just over 19 percent of the capital stock. The cost basis of the shares is $499 million. At the end of 2002, the value was just under $1 billion. By the end of 2006, the value was around $3.3 billion, but it dropped to $1.7 billion at the end of 2007.[1] The sharp increase in revenues is due chiefly to revenues generated from rating structured financial products, and the sharp decrease was due to the disillusionment of the market with the integrity of the ratings.

The collateralized debt obligation market grew from around $275 billion in 2000, to about $2 trillion in 2007; then the market stalled. By June 11, 2008, *Total Securitization* reported that CDOs in default exceeded $200 billion.[2] Investors included insurance companies, bank investment portfolios, mutual funds, pension funds, hedge funds, money mangers, and more. Every sector of society is affected as misrated products cause actual principal losses combined with loss in value due to declining market prices and illiquidity. More than that, liquidity—coming up with needed cash—is now a global problem, since investors are wary of lending money (by investing) against potentially misrated assets.

When I met Warren for the first time, I gave him a copy of another book that I had written, *Collateralized Debt Obligations & Structured Finance* (2003). It is a study of structured financial products in which I criticized holes so big in the rating agencies' methodology that you can drive a semi through them. In particular, I highlighted serious problems with inflated AAA ratings in securitizations that have inherent structural flaws, problems with supposedly investment grade rated collateral, and conflicts of interest that hold investors' capital hostage to the self-interest of "managers" and investment banks. Those conflicts of interest often result in substantial principal losses to investors, and the risk is not captured in the ratings. Cash flows held hostage to managers' conflicts of interest result in investment casualties.

Investors should act like the Israeli Defense Force when rescuing hostages taken in an airplane hijacking to Entebbe—move fast, minimize hostage casualties, and never let it happen again. Unfortunately, instead of taking measures to correct these flaws, the rating agencies seemed to brush aside my concerns and ramped up their flawed structured products ratings business.

As Warren points out, everyone makes mistakes. I have found that most people will forgive you anything if there was no evil intent. You acknowledge the error and apologize, correct the error, if possible, and make a commitment to change. Forgiveness comes easier if you did not—inadvertently or otherwise—cause them to lose a pile of money, or harm their children by, say, losing a pile of money intended for their benefit. This works as well in finance as it does in daily life.

The rating agencies seem not to care about the market's forgiveness since not only have they not apologized—a necessary, but not a sufficient condition—they seem to feel the *market* should change. Specifically, the market should change its point of view about what it expects from the rating agencies. Yet it seems that the market has the right to expect rating agencies to follow basic principles of statistics.

This tactic has mainly been successful because the rating agencies act as a cartel, leveraging their joint power to have fees magically converge and have ratings so similar that they have each participated in overrating AAA structured products backed by dodgy loans in 2007 that took substantial principal losses. Meanwhile, many market professionals, including me, pointed out in print that the AAA ratings were meaningless. The rating agencies presented a fairly united front in defending their methods (except for Fitch, which also participated in overrated CDOs and later seemed more responsive in downgrading structured products).

Furthermore, many investors have charters that require them to only buy products that have been rated by one or more of the top three rating agencies: Moody's Corporation (Warren's Berkshire Hathaway is a large minority investor); Standard & Poor's (S&P), part of McGraw-Hill Cos., Inc.; and Fitch, owned by France-based Fimalac SA. "Ma and Pa" retail investors found that AAA product ended up in their pension funds and mutual funds because their money managers gave too much credence to an AAA rating.

Of the three rating agencies, Fitch has the smallest market share, but it has unique style. Fimalac's chairman, Marc Ladreit de Lacharriere, and Veronique Morali, the chief operating officer, obeyed French disclosure requirements when she was paid a bonus of 8.7 million euros (around $9.94 million at the time) without board or compensation committee approval. According to the *Financial Times*, when the bonus was discovered in June 2003, the couple lived together, Fimalac's finances were tight, and Mr. de Lacharriere had pledged 40 percent of his Fimalac shares as collateral to banks. Upon learning the news, a Fimalac director was more than a little concerned: "I said to myself, 'Oh no, not this.' . . . In the U.S. or UK, this would be very serious indeed."[3] "From a legal point of view," said Ladreit de Lacharriere, "we have been meticulously correct."[4] In contrast, Warren Buffett suggested to his All-Stars that they should "start with what is legal, but always go on to what we would feel comfortable about being printed on the front page of our local paper."[5] *I have to admit, though, French perfume on the "odor of impropriety"[6] makes for entertaining reading.*

Most of the market is dominated by Moody's and Standard & Poor's, especially the U.S. market, where these two U.S.-based rating agencies have been entrenched and have most of the historical data.

Moody's awards a rating based on its estimate of *expected loss*, a single piece of information, and assigns a rating based on the safest (least expected loss) to the riskiest (highest expected loss): Aaa, Aa1, Aa2, Aa3, A1, A2, A3, Baa1, Baa2, Baa3, Ba1, Ba2, Ba3, B1, B2, B3, Caa1, Caa2, Caa3, Ca, C. Anything above Baa3 is considered investment grade, and anything below that is considered speculative grade. Standard & Poor's awards ratings based on *default probabilities* and label products AAA, AA+, AA, AA−, and so on. Fitch uses the same labels. As with Moody's, anything above BBB− is considered investment grade and anything below is considered speculative grade. I'll use AAA to denote the highest rating, but will specifically name Moody's (which uses the Aaa notation) when I am making a point specific to them.

Since many money managers cannot buy bonds that are not rated investment grade, and since some are required to sell bonds that fall below investment grade, ratings have a huge impact. This is why when Moody's admitted that impairment rates show no difference in performance between CDO tranches with a junk rating of BB− and an investment grade rating of BBB, it should have been headline financial news. It was not.[7] Moody's, Standard and Poor's, and Fitch have an NRSRO designation, meaning they are "Nationally Recognized Statistical Rating Organizations." Yet, when they rate many securitizations, particularly mortgage-loan-backed securitizations, they fail to follow basic statistical principles.

Statistics is the mathematical study of the probability and likelihood of events. Known information can be taken into account, and likelihoods and probabilities are inferred by taking a statistical sampling. The designation sounds impressive, but the rating agencies do not live up to it.

The rating agencies problems run deep. In late 2003, the *Financial Times* took rating agencies to task for misrating debt issued by scandal-ridden Parmalat, Enron, and WorldCom. Fitch protested that "credit ratings bring greater transparency."[8] Standard & Poor's retorted that "rating agencies are not auditors or investigators and are not empowered or able to unearth fraud."[9]

I responded that investors would be foolish to believe rating agencies provide greater transparency for structured financial products. In fact, the opposite is true. Investors relying on ratings to indicate structured products' performance are consistently disappointed in a variety of securitizations. S&P downgraded Hollywood Funding's deals backed by movie receipts from AAA, the highest credit rating possible, to BB, a noninvestment grade rating. Bond insurers raised fraud as a defense against payment, and S&P had thought payment was unconditional.[10]

Warren does not rely on the rating agencies since his fundamental analysis of a business's value is superior to anything the rating agencies are doing. If you understand the value of a business, you do not need to rely on a rating agency.

If everyone followed this guideline, the global credit meltdown could have been avoided. In fact, the rating agencies had warning of the need for change through a series of similar mishaps in the past. In 1998, they downgraded around $2 billion in securitizations backed by charged-off credit card receivables managed by Commercial Financial Services. Ratings went from investment grade to junk overnight. Rating agency failures cropped up again in subsequent years with respect to securitizations by Parmalat, manufactured housing loans, metals receivables, furniture receivables, subprime, and more.

When rating agencies make mistakes in securitizations backed by debt, the losses tend to be permanent and unfixable. The sole source of income is the portfolio of assets. *If you fail to understand the risk of the assets, you have blown the entire job.*

Unlike Warren, the rating agencies failed to drill down and examine whether the assets could generate the cash to pay back investors.

Rating agencies correctly point out that deal sponsors and investment bank underwriters are responsible for due diligence. Although the rating agencies do not perform due diligence for investors, they can demand evidence that proper due diligence has been performed before attempting to apply their respective ratings methodologies. In fact, it is not possible to perform a sound statistical analysis without it.

In the mortgage loan securitization market, a statistical sampling of the underlying mortgage loans should verify: integrity of the documentation, the identity of the borrower, the appraisal of the property, the borrower's ability to repay the loan, and so on. Rating agencies should take reasonable steps to understand the character of the risk they are modeling. Yet, they seemingly rated risky deals without demanding evidence of thorough due diligence.

When rating agencies use old data for obviously new risks, it is financial astrology. When rating agencies guess at AAA ratings (without the data to back it up), it is financial alchemy. When rating agencies evaluate no-name CDO managers without asking for thorough background checks, it is financial phrenology. In other words, the rating agencies practice *junk science*. The result is that junk sometimes gets a AAA rating.

Since the rating agencies are effectively a cartel, investors do not have an alternative to this flawed system other than to do their own fundamental credit analysis. *Like Warren Buffett, they should understand the investment.*

The rating agencies are swift to point out that they do not perform due diligence on the data they use and take no responsibility for unearthing fraud; they merely provide an opinion. In past legal battles, rating agencies successfully claimed journalist-like privileges, refused to turn over notes of their analyses, and continued to issue opinions. Independent organizations exist, however, that perform rigorous due diligence for a fee. Underwriters can hire them, and rating agencies can demand to see the results. Yet it seems the rating agencies failed to do so for many structured finance transactions. The rating agencies protest they are misunderstood rather than miscalculating when it comes to rating structured products. They claim the market misapplies ratings by expecting ratings to indicate market price and liquidity, but the former are merely symptoms of the real problem. They take data at face value, slap a rating on a dodgy securitization, and pocket a fat fee.

The Bank for International Settlements (BIS) and the Federal Reserve (Fed) may have embraced the rating agencies because these institutions are chiefly made up of economists. The Securities and Exchange Commission is loaded with lawyers. I do not expect lawyers to be rigorous in their analysis, but I expect more of the BIS and the Fed. While there is such a thing as "junk economics," economics itself is not considered a science. Even so, just because lack of rigor permeates economics, economists should not be allowed to let this seep into other fields, particularly when there is a scientific methodology that can be used as a basis. When they adopted the rating agencies labels as benchmarks, the BIS, Fed, and SEC enabled junk science.

Although they shouldn't, many investors rely on the rating and the coupon when buying structured financial products. Whereas Warren views an investment like a business, many investors view their jobs as getting an investment meeting consensus. That is similar to allowing the manic-depressive Mr. Market to tell you the right price. If you do not understand the value, neither Mr. Market's prices nor (sadly) the rating agencies will help you understand the value of a structured product any better. Many money managers feel buying a AAA investment is prudent; but if they do not understand these complex deals, they can quickly lose a chunk of principal.

Problems are not limited to mortgage loan securitizations. Ratings on leveraged synthetic credit products are often misleading, too. For example, when the products first appeared, I pointed out the triple A rating should never have been awarded to *constant proportion debt obligations* (CPDOs). These products are largely leveraged bets on the credit quality and market spreads of indexes based on U.S. and European investment-grade companies.

The high leverage of the products related to market risk puts investors' principal at risk. Investors essentially take the risk of the first losses on leveraged exposure to the indexes, *and that is the exact opposite strategy to Warren's margin of safety.* "Once again," I told the *Financial Times* in November 2006, "the rating agencies have proved that when it comes to some structured credit products, a rating is meaningless. All AAAs are not created equal, and this is a prime example."[11]

After rating an early CPDO transaction triple A, Moody's was criticized by industry professionals, including me. Moody's then changed its rating methodology, applying a different standard for subsequent transactions.[12] Investors were attracted by the AAA rating and the high coupons. The investment banks selling them were attracted to upfront fees of 1 percent plus annual servicing fees of up to 0.1 percent.

I thought the rating agencies may have been turning over staff too quickly and using incompetent rookies—who could be pushed around by aggressive highly paid investment bankers—to rate these deals. In May 2007, the *Financial Times* put Moody's actions in the harsh glare of a newly angled spotlight. It said Moody's original AAA ratings for CPDO were the result of a computer "bug," and the ratings should have been (according to Moody's) *four* notches lower. Fur flew. A friend joked: *Don't they mean forty?*

Moody's documents showed that after it corrected the "bug," it changed its methodology, resulting in the ratings staying AAA until January 2008, when the market fell apart and the original ratings seemed ludicrous. The CPDOs were downgraded several notches.

The part about Moody's changing its methodology was not news to me. I had included that information in a letter to the SEC on proposed regulations in February 2007, and I specifically objected to the AAA rating on this product. I do not even recall who told me about the change. If it was a secret, it was an open secret. All three rating agencies' models have more patches than Microsoft software.

The news is that the AAA rating seemed to be due to something more than a serious disagreement with my opinion. Moody's internal memo said that the bug's impact had been reduced after "improvements in the model."[13] This suggests that there may be a cause and effect—the inconvenient lower ratings may have been masked by the methodology change. Chairman of the House Financial Services Committee, Barney Frank, said: "Moody's alleged conduct in this matter raises questions not only about its competence, but more importantly its integrity."[14]

By January 2008, just under a year after my written comments to the SEC, Moody's analysts wrote that two of the originally AAA rated CPDOs would "unwind at an approximate 90 percent loss to investors."[15] The CPDOs were projected to have a *90 percent loss* from the rating agency that claims its AAA rating is based on *expected loss*.

Standard & Poor's had also rated CPDOs AAA. In fact, it was the first to do so, and Moody's followed suit. S&P vigorously defended their ratings methodology, even after it downgraded CPDOs. In the wake of the negative news, it put Moody's commercial paper on credit watch. S&P later disclosed that it too found an error in its computer models, but said: "This error did not result in a ratings change and was caught and remedied by our ratings process."[16] *Now we all feel better.*

In February 2007, Bear Stearns research analyst Gyan Sinha wrote a report encouraging investors to take a long position in the ABX.HE.06-2 BBB− index (an index based on the value of BBB− rated residential mortgage-backed securities backed by subprime home equity loans).[17] Simultaneously, I wrote a letter to the SEC recommending it revoke the NRSRO designation for the credit rating agencies with respect to structured financial products, asserting *"ratings are based on smoke and mirrors."*[18]

On February 20, 2007, Gyan Sinha appeared on CNBC with Susan Bies, a Fed governor who had recently tendered her resignation. Bies thought it could take a year or two for housing inventory to be worked out, and housing had further to fall. She was concerned that hidden inventory was high, houses built for investors were vacant, and the numbers did not reflect the problem. She was surprised that subprime mortgages originated in 2006 had gone bad so quickly. It usually took a couple of years for loan delinquencies and defaults to peak, but 2006 vintage loans were delinquent in just a few months. It seemed to her that loans were made that never should have been made. She echoed Warren Buffett's 2002 complaint about mortgage lenders in the manufactured housing market.

Gyan Sinha agreed with Susan Bies's assertion that subprime delinquencies could reach 20 percent or a bit higher. He too was concerned about the early delinquency trends, but said that based on his research, at 6 to 7 percent cumulative losses, only 1 of the 20 residential mortgage-backed securities in the ABX index would experience a write-down. Furthermore, he stressed that 75 percent of the capital structure of a CDO is AAA rated.[19]

It seemed to me Sinha only had part of the story. He did not mention that ersatz AAA rated tranches did not deserve that rating, or that prices of AAA rated tranches in the secondary market were trading at discounts among savvy investors. I projected a 21 percent cumulative loss rate for *first-lien mortgage loans*, and the ABX included home equity lines of credit and *second liens*, so losses would hit the loans backing the ABX much harder than that. Based on my projections, the ABX index would plummet.

In January 2007, I had lunch with Bethany McLean, coauthor of *The Smartest Guys in the Room*, a bestselling book about the Enron debacle. She was intrigued about my assertion that AAA and AA rated products were overrated. That meant that bond insurers such as Ambac, MBIA, FGIC that also insured municipal bonds would have substantial losses. It also meant pension funds, bank investment portfolios, mutual funds, and more were buying investments with a high-rated label, but in reality they had the risk of losing substantial principal. I told her: "No one believes the ratings have any value."[20]

Some AAA rated tranches traded around 95 cents on the dollar in the secondary market. Losses were already being absorbed by lower-rated, but still investment-grade, tranches, and first loss investors of conventionally structured deals were wiped out. Her article appeared on March 19, 2007, St. Joseph's Day, the patron saint of the homeless. The rating agencies denied there was a problem: "All of the rating agencies say they have scrubbed the numbers, and slices of debt that are rated investment grade will mostly stay that way, even if the collateral consists of subprime mortgages."[21]

Investment banks kept up the front. None of them took the massive write-downs I expected in the first quarter of 2007. Instead, they cranked up the CDO machines. They offered toxic product to unwary investors.

On March 22, 2007, I wrote Warren that John Calamos Sr., chairman and CEO of Calamos Investments, does not rely on the rating agencies, either:

> He mortgaged his house to start his fund, and he did not seek outside money. . . . Initially they tried using Moody's and S&P ratings as benchmarks, and they got smoked a couple of quarters. They set up their own credit models and use those to the exclusion of ratings.

The following year, on Tuesday, March 11, 2008, *Bloomberg News* reported that AAA subprime residential home equity loan backed bonds were not being downgraded despite having delinquencies exceeding 40 percent. As Bear Stearns gasped its last breaths, I appeared on *Bloomberg TV* that morning to discuss the structured finance ratings folly. The rating agencies were *still* in denial. Incapable of accurately measuring the present, the rating agencies provided no useful information for predicting future performance. The ABX indexes referenced 80 faux AAA bonds, and according to *Bloomberg*'s analysis, *none* of them merited that rating. According to its interpretation of S&P's data, *Bloomberg* asserted that only six of the 80 AAA rated bonds in the ABX index would merit a rating above BBB–, the lowest possible investment grade rating.[22] In other words, 90 percent of the bonds in the AAA index were not even investment grade.

Contrary to the assertions of Nassim Taleb and the Talebites, the mortgage meltdown is not a black swan event (an unlikely occurrence—unless one lives in Australia or New Zealand). It is not even Benoit Mandelbrot's *gray swan*, a flawed model that does not foresee disaster.[23] Those labels would have described the 1987 portfolio insurance catastrophe affecting around $60 billion in equity assets, when sophisticated mathematical models originated in academia failed to take into account what happens when a large crowd tries to sell at the same time.

Portfolio insurance is a form of "dynamic" hedging that mimics a series of put options—as the stock price falls, the program automatically sells a given amount of stock and invests in cash. If the price falls further, the program sells more stock. In the week before the "Black October" crash of 1987, the Dow fell 250 points, and a large backlog of sell orders accumulated. The following Monday, portfolio insurance kicked in, and portfolio stock and index futures were sold. The market fell more. The market dropped around 500 points, the equivalent of around 2,500 points today. This was a classic liquidity crunch, brought on by model-driven selling, followed by the panic of general investors. The price at which managers were able to sell was much lower than the model's price because they could not get out in time. To add insult to financial injury, the stock market as a whole was up 2 percent per year. If investors had simply held onto their positions during the "crash," they would have been much better off. Instead, the models sold at lows, and then repurchased as prices rose. Portfolio insurance is a form of dynamic hedging, which I call *death by one thousand cuts.*

Benjamin Graham was not a fan of market formulas or program trading: "Never buy a stock immediately after a substantial rise or sell one immediately after a substantial drop."[24] At least not for the sake of it. As more people rely on formulas, they become less reliable. For one thing, *conditions change.* Secondly, when a formula becomes very popular, it may cause the stock market herd to "stampede."[25] At the time, Warren also derided the models. If the *price falls* far enough, the model *sells* everything and the manager is 100 percent in cash; when prices *rise*, the model tells you to *buy.* Warren loves to buy more when the price of a good value stock falls and seeks to sell, if ever, at a profit.

Instead, the mortgage meltdown was caused by *Black Barts.* Black Bart is said to have robbed California stagecoaches without ever firing a shot, and the mortgage meltdown involved some bloodless robbery. The risk was fully knowable, fully discoverable in the course of competent work. The mortgage meltdown had a direct cause and effect, and the result was predictable in advance. At the outset, symptoms of financial disease were as obvious as an advanced outbreak of mad cow. If one examined the loans they looked like downer cows, stumbling and sickly. Financial professionals including Warren Buffett, Charlie Munger, John Paulson, James "Jim" B. Rogers, William "Bill" Ackman, William "Bill" Gross, Whitney Tilson, Jim Melcher, David Einhorn (head of Greenlight Capital), myself, and others had been specific in sounding the alarm both verbally and in print for many years.

♟ ♟ ♟

Money market funds and pension funds often rely on ratings. The SEC is proposing that mutual funds should not rely on ratings, but the SEC is missing a piece. The SEC should not allow an investment below a previously required rating. For example, if an investor relied on an AAA rating before and it did not work out, that should not mean the investor should ignore the requirement and invest in something with a lower rating, either. Rather, the investor should still be required to have an AAA rating *and* should be required to understand that the value of the investment lives up to the rating.

There is often a difference between an investor with a lot of money to manage and a sophisticated investor. For example, municipal funds usually lack the sophistication of Goldman Sachs Asset management. That is why many compliance departments at investment banks ask that brokers and institutional salespeople "know the customer." The idea is to sell complex products to investors that have the ability to understand and analyze the risk.

Or better yet, do as Warren does. Don't make your investments unnecessarily complex and thoroughly understand the risk. That way, if you make a mistake, it is very unlikely it will be a big one.

In spite of this wisdom, funds in Europe and the United States—including local government-run funds—often find they do not understand the risks of complex structured financial products they own, because they rely on AAA ratings for guidance. These Main Street government investors have no choice but to cut costs, aggressively go after back taxes, and—if the problem is bad enough—*raise taxes.* Main Street's list of investors that feel burned is long and growing.

For example, the Springfield (Massachusetts) Finance Control Board alleged that Merrill Lynch & Co. sold it AAA rated CDO products backed by subprime debt without fully disclosing the risk. State law limits Springfield's investments to government securities and short-term liquid investments. Regarding Springfield, I told the *Wall Street Journal:* "Merrill has to know its customers and sell them what's suitable and appropriate. These CDOs are not."[26]

Springfield was fortunate that its troubles received publicity. It seemed to own the chlorine trifluoride of CDOs. The AAA rated tranches were unstable and lethally toxic to portfolio value. The three CDOs Springfield originally purchased for $13.9 million in the summer of 2007 were valued by Merrill at around $1.2 million by January 2008. Merrill repurchased the CDOs for the full amount of $13.9 million.

Vickie Tillman, executive vice-president at Standard & Poor's defends its AAA ratings: "of the 26,000 structured securities originally rated AAA by S&P between 1978 and 2007, fewer than 0.1 per cent [sic] subsequently defaulted."[27]

That may be true. It may even be true that AAA ratings on securities that were imploding did not have ratings withdrawn to remove them from the data set. But that is not the point. When it counted, when the U.S. housing markets and municipal bond markets depended on the integrity of the ratings, the rating agencies failed. *There were a lot of teeth marks in those "boxes" of CDOs backed by mortgage loans.* Smart investors avoided CDOs and ate some See's Candies.

In August 2008, a draft version of an SEC 38-page report on the rating agencies revealed that an S&P analyst emailed a colleague that they should not be rating a particular structured finance deal. The colleague responded that they rate every deal: "it could be structured by cows and we would rate it."[28]

Deal after CDO-squared deal brought to market in 2007 had AAA rated tranches downgraded below investment grade within months after the deals came to market. *This is unprecedented.* Deals brought in 2006 are similarly troubled as are deals brought in the last half of 2005. Dollar values involved are in the hundreds of billions. It is a travesty. Investors in AAA structured finance products are losing substantial principal. Some nominally, AAA bond insurers were downgraded from AAA to junk. The AAA ratings of others Slid lower. Municipal bond markets and student loan markets are in confusion. Investment banks sold auction-rate securities with long maturities as if they were money market instruments. They told customers that the coupons reset at regular auctions at short-term intervals, and if the auctions failed to find buyers, the investment banks would step in and buy back the securities. Investors could not get their money. Investors from large corporations to condominium boards investing members' assessments held frozen assets. Yet they had been told the bonds are exactly like cash. By the fall of 2008, banks and investment banks were compelled to buy back auction rate securities from retail investors to settle claims with U.S. regulators that they improperly sold these bonds to uninformed customers.[29, 30] Larger investors are forced to settle their own disputes.[31]

In the face of its contribution to enabling a cycle of shoddy home loans resulting in massive foreclosures, declining housing prices, deteriorating ratings of bond insurers, and lack of liquidity due to shaken confidence in the markets, Standard & Poor's demonstrates a curious combination of arrogance and truthiness.

The markets have nothing to replace the rating agencies other than individual initiative. Rating agencies are currently protected by government regulation, barriers to entry, institutionalized investor reliance, and the profit margin of approximately 40 percent that they make on their traditional business of rating corporate credits. As maddening as the recent actions of the rating agencies might seem, they are like a fellow who knowingly sells a horse to an investment banker named Black Bart. Without investors' money funneled through investment banks to predatory mortgage lenders, the problems would have died an early death. It is very convenient for investment banks that Congress and the SEC are focused on the rating agencies, because investment banks—not the rating agencies—are the securities dealers obliged to perform due diligence appropriate to the circumstances.

The rating agency business will probably pull in steady business in the future because the market has nothing to replace them. That does not mean, however, that the market is satisfied with the cartel's performance. Warren Buffett avoids interfering with the management of the companies with which he invests but he made an unprecedented statement during his European excursion to find new investments. In May 2008, he said if Moody's management did something wrong, "they should go."[32] Weeks earlier, Warren told me he is "not proud" of Moody's. One could say the same for Standard & Poor's and Fitch. Misleading ratings contributed to the global market meltdown, because many financial institutions used "high" ratings as a sign of "safety" to justify their use of excessive leverage.

Chapter 8

Bear Market (I'd Like a Review of the Bidding)

It's easy to put on leverage, but not as easy to take it off.

—Warren Buffett

(*Wall Street Journal,* April 30, 2007)

In 2007, both Warren and I thought many hedge funds were over-leveraged. If the book value of Berkshire Hathaway stock falls 5 percent, investors have "lost" 5 percent for the moment, but Berkshire Hathaway's strong earning power (from subsidiaries and investments) will likely cause the price to rise satisfactorily again in the future. Berkshire Hathaway has value and its value is growing. A leveraged hedge fund that invests in *collateralized debt obligations* (CDOs) can only rely on those CDOs for "earnings." If the CDOs deteriorate due to, say, defaults on the loans backing them, there is *permanent value destruction*. There is no bouncing back from that. Furthermore, leverage magnifies the losses for investors. Bear Stearns Asset Management managed two hedge funds that provided classic examples.

On January 30, 2007, Jim Melcher of Balestra Capital (a $100 million hedge fund) and I appeared on CNBC to discuss hidden price deterioration in subprime CDOs. Diana Olick, CNBC's Washington-based real estate correspondent taped the segment. Olick may be the best reporter on any channel on this topic; she closely followed developments before the mortgage meltdown was big news. She reported that housing prices were softening and had risen only 1 percent the previous year for existing homes against the double-digit increases of the prior few years. Subprime mortgage loans had reached around $1.3 trillion in outstanding loans of the total $11 trillion (at the time) U.S. mortgage market. The foreclosure rate was already 13 percent (in the years before the 2005 risky loan explosion delinquency rates were in the low to mid-single digits) and climbing fast and steeply for more recent (2006) vintages.

Based on my projections, foreclosure rates for subprime loans made in 2006 could reach 30 percent and recovery rates would probably be only around 30 cents on the dollar. This was based on my experience during other times of severe mortgage loan stress combined with poor underwriting standards. This meant that recent subprime loan securitizations were in trouble. Most investment-grade-rated residential mortgage-backed securities were in serious trouble at the lower levels, and the AAA tranches did not have enough protection to merit that rating. CDOs compounded the problem and CDO-squared products amplified it further. For those deals, even the AAA tranches had significant risk of substantial losses.

I told Olick that investors who bought non-Fannie Mae and non-Freddie Mac securitizations should be very worried. Deals were overrated and overpriced, and prices would plummet. Jim Melcher was short the ABX index, the ABX HE 2 06 BBB– series, to profit on overrated and overpriced subprime-backed CDOs. He had tripled his money the prior two months and was one of the few hedge fund managers willing to publicly discuss the trade. He hung on anticipating further profits. I explained to CNBC that one didn't even need to own the securitizations, you could have a gain "if the price in *someone else's* portfolio takes a hit."[1]

Ralph Cioffi, a senior managing director of Bear Stearns Asset Management and a former colleague, had seen the segment and gave me unsolicited feedback. "You sounded good," he said, "and you looked mahvelous as Billy Crystal used to say." When his leveraged hedge funds failed a few months later, I wondered if he had listened to the content.

In early February 2007, the shares of aggressive subprime mortgage lender, New Century Financial Corp., then the second largest subprime in the United States, plummeted after it alerted that it was short of cash. London-based HSBC Holdings Plc, the largest bank by market value in Europe, unexpectedly reported that it had $1.8 billion of losses due to subprime lending.[2]

Bear Stearns' fixed income research gave the horrific news a positive spin indicating that the worst might be over and recommended customers go *long*—the opposite of Jim Melcher's *short* money-making position.[3] ResMae Mortgage Corporation went bankrupt on February 13, 2007, the day after Bear Stearns Fixed Income Research issued its report. ResMae was selling assets for mere pennies on the dollar.[4]

By the end of February 2007, New Century was trading at around $15 per share, after its share price fell around 50 percent during the prior three weeks. Rumors circulated that the lender was in its death throes. Perhaps Bear Stearns didn't get the memo, even though it had a "longstanding"[5] relationship financing New Century's mortgage operation. On March 1, 2007, Scott R. Coren, a Bear Stearns stock analyst, *upgraded* New Century, saying that $10 per share would be the downside risk, if New Century needed rescuing. About a week later, New Century announced it had probably been unprofitable during the last six months of 2006 and needed to restate its earnings. Lenders yanked their credit lines. In April 2007, New Century filed for bankruptcy, joining more than 100 failed mortgage lenders. Countrywide, the nation's largest mortgage lender, also showed signs of strain.

Hidden leverage threatened the global markets. Many hedge funds used CDOs' artificially high ratings as an excuse to leverage their "safe highly rated" investments. It is an extremely risky proposition. *Debt purchased near full price has little or no price upside, but there is a lot of room for*

the price to go down when things go wrong. Combine that with leverage, and you have a very risky strategy.

What if prices drop because everyone finds out that the assets are overrated? What if prices drop because of defaults by overextended homeowners, defaults due to a collapse in housing prices, or permanent value destruction due to fraud? There is no other income to give you upside potential, and a leveraged position has no hope of springing back. If a fund does not have gobs of liquidity in reserve, investor capital is quickly wiped out. Investors take a stomach-churning toboggan ride straight down risk's icy slope. Creditors that lent the fund money to buy assets are lucky if they do not lose money, too.

Most of us use high degrees of leverage when we buy a home. A homeowner might buy a $1 million dollar home and mortgage $900,000 of the purchase. If the price drops to $950,000, the "homeowner" loses $50,000 of his initial equity of $50,000, or 50 percent of his equity. If the price drops to $900,000, the "homeowner" loses all of his initial investment. If a bank forecloses on the $900,000 mortgage, it does not even break even after fees. If the price drops below $900,000, the bank's cushion of the first loss taken by the "homeowner's" $100,000 is gone, and the bank, the creditor, will not get the full amount of the loan paid back. Some of the mortgage loans made in 2006 and 2007 had zero money down, were made against aggressively appraised homes, and defaulted almost immediately. The investors in the hedge funds are like the homeowners that make a down payment (the investor had equity in the hedge fund), and investment banks (that give the lines of credit to hedge funds) are like the bank that gives out the mortgage. If asset prices drop and wipe out investors' equity, the investment bank is next in line to take losses on its credit lines.

Many hedge funds use *total return swaps,* a type of credit derivative, in order to borrow money and leverage up their investments. Warren saw the negative consequences of this strategy first-hand with Long-Term Capital Management. Total return swaps easily thwart the intent of margin requirements, they create much more leverage, and it is virtually invisible. At the end of April 2007, Warren told Susan Pulliam at the *Wall Street Journal* that the global financial system is so leveraged that it makes the leverage used before the Crash of 1929 "look like a Sunday-school picnic."[6] I told her that if cash-strapped funds are forced to sell assets in a market downturn it "could lead to a vicious cycle of selling that would feed on itself."[7]

The collateral the hedge funds put up to back their borrowings is often illiquid and difficult to trade, and prime brokers such as Credit Suisse and JPMorgan do not disclose the amount of total-return swaps that they have made to hedge funds on their books. The strategy is very risky since the assets a hedge fund "buys" may come back on the balance sheet of the bank (the lender) if the fund implodes. For example, if a hedge fund uses 15 times leverage, and asset prices irreversibly drop just a tiny amount, investors lose some principal. If prices irreversibly drop just seven percent or more, investor capital is wiped out, and creditors have no choice but to seize the assets, some of which were sold by the investment banks in the first place.

Regulators fed the folly. Within days of Warren's warning, the New York Fed claimed that despite market similarities to the risk levels at the time just before LTCM blew up, there were different causes then, so the existing market environment now was less alarming.[8] England's Financial Services Authority (FSA) piled on pablum. The FSA released results from a partial survey of hedge funds and thought that "average" leverage had declined.[9]

Dr. Sam Savage coined the term "flaw of averages." He asserts that using an average number to forecast an outcome can lead to huge errors. For example, if a swimming pool's average depth is four feet, but the deep end of the pool is eight feet, a nonswimmer is presented with lethal risk. A drowning man learns the hard way that the "average depth" mischaracterizes the peril. The average leverage number might suggest that hedge funds on balance are safer, but if an individual hedge fund employs a high degree of leverage, the average for all hedge funds is meaningless. Furthermore, hedge funds had massive hidden risks—inherently risky over-rated assets. On May 7, 2007, I wrote the *Financial Times* that the regulators were dead wrong. The current situation was not less alarming that that presented by LTCM, it was *more* alarming. Hidden leverage does not show up by polling prime brokers. Hedge funds, structured investment vehicles, and other investors use structured products combined with derivatives and leverage, "illiquid structured products will experience a classic collateral crash when hedge funds try to liquidate these assets to meet margin calls."[10]

A few weeks later, Bear Stearns Asset Management proved my point.

In May 2007, Ralph Cioffi was the senior managing director of Bear Stearns Asset Management (BSAM), a subsidiary of Bear Stearns, and cochief executive officer of Everquest Financial Ltd., a private financial services company. He reported to Richard Marin, the chairman and chief executive officer of BSAM. Warren Spector, cochief operating officer of Bear Stearns and a former trader of exotic mortgage products, was the key sponsor of Bear Stearns' foray into hedge funds. Bear Stearns Asset Management managed several CDOs and it also managed several hedge funds. Before the summer of 2007 ended, my former colleagues Ralph Cioffi and Warren Spector (along with Richard Marin) lost their positions due to CDO investments combined with leverage in hedge funds managed by BSAM.

I had worked at Bear Stearns in the late 1980s and remembered amiable newcomer Ralph Cioffi to be Bear Stearns' most talented and successful salesman of mortgage-backed securities. He was usually even tempered, always hard working, and thoughtful. I headed marketing for the quantitative group run by both Stanley Diller, one of the original Wall Street "quants," and Ed Rappa (now CEO of R.W. Pressprich & Co, Inc.), a managing partner. Ralph was a popular salesman with my colleagues and a heavy user of our quantitative research. In gratitude for analytical work that helped him make sales, Ralph presented our group with an $800 portable bond calculator purchased out of his own pocket. When I was lured away from Bear Stearns by Goldman Sachs, Ralph Cioffi tried to persuade me to stay, matching the offer. Around 20 years had passed and since then we occasionally stayed in touch, but we were not close friends.

I knew Warren Spector, too. He had been a talented trader of exotic mortgage products, which at the time meant collateralized mortgage obligations including the volatile interest-only and principal-only slices of those deals. He had come a long way from the somewhat awkward young man who spilled red wine all over a white linen tablecloth at one of our client dinners. Before CDOs undid his career, he was a Bear Stearns favored son with a good shot at taking over Jimmy Cayne's position as CEO.

We did not correspond. However, a couple of years previously I shared my concerns with Spector about a call I received from a fund representative. He claimed that Bear Stearns had agreed to underwrite his firm's securitization backed by life insurance policies. The macabre idea was that when policyholders died, investors got the money from the life insurance policies net of expenses and fees—very heavy fees. Documents posted on the SEC's Web site showed that if the holders of the life insurance policies did not die before additional money was needed to pay ongoing policy premiums, investors would be asked for more money. Investors could lose more than their initial investment if policyholders inconvenienced them by living a long life. I had done a quick background check on the fund representative. The SEC was conducting an investigation and alleged that the fund representative's former employer was a Ponzi scheme. My concerns were bad news to Warren Spector as well. He checked into it and I missed his return call, so he left me a voice message: "There are lots of people peddling this idea and it's extremely unlikely that we will do anything with any of them, so I appreciate knowing who's dropping our name."

The last time I spoke to Warren Spector, we discussed the hedging of synthetic CDOs that were constructed using credit derivatives. Bear Stearns' proprietary trading desk had large derivatives positions with a number of investment banks. After JPMorgan Chase purchased Bear Stearns, the New York Fed estimated that Bear had around 750,000 derivatives contracts outstanding.[11] Based on what I knew, I thought Bear Stearns had scary volume in tricky credit derivatives. Keeping track of the true risk and long-term profit is a complex task. As I discussed with Warren Spector, any manager would have difficulty determining whether traders were actually making money (or losing money) relative to a risk-neutral fully hedged position. One could temporarily create huge revenues, but enormous risk could soon turn revenues into losses. In contrast, Warren Buffett worked hard to *reduce* the number and complexity of derivatives contracts owned by Berkshire Hathaway. Warren Buffett told me that after years of whittling down Gen Re's derivatives positions, he knows (and understands) every derivative contract owned by Berkshire Hathaway.

Buffett and Spector are very different Warrens. Warren Buffett used derivatives to turn junk into gold. Warren Spector oversaw at least one Bear Stearns affiliate (BSAM) that turned "high grade" into junk.

Among other hedge funds, Bear Stearns Asset Management (BSAM) managed the Bear Stearns High Grade Structured Credit Strategies fund. By August 2006, the fund had a couple of years of double-digit returns. BSAM launched the Bear Stearns High Grade Structured Credit Strategies Enhanced Leverage fund taking advantage of the first fund's "success." *There must be more money!*

Both funds managed by BSAM included CDO and CDO-squared tranches backed in part by subprime loans and other securitizations (collateralized loan obligations) backed by corporate loans and leveraged corporate loans. In August 2006 when BSAM was setting up the Enhanced Leverage fund, other hedge fund managers (like John Paulson), *shorted* subprime-backed investments.

Investors in the two funds managed by BSAM had been getting double-digit annualized returns on high-grade debt at a time when treasuries were yielding less than 5 percent. In fixed income investments, that usually means investors are taking risk.

Ralph seemed to have similar views to mine on CPDOs, the leveraged product that I had said did not deserve a AAA rating. Ralph told me he thought the AAA rating could "lull the unsophisticated investor to sleep," and that for the purposes of his hedge funds, if he liked an investment-grade-rated trade he could have the same trade without paying fees and "easily lever up . . . fifteen times." *To paraphrase Warren Buffett, if the price of your investments drops, leverage will compound your misery.*

♟ ♟ ♟

On May 9, 2007, Matt Goldstein called and asked me if I had a chance to look at the registration statement for a new initial public stock offering (IPO) called Everquest Financial, Ltd (Everquest). Everquest is a private company formed in September 2006, and the registration statement was a required filing in preparation for its going public. The shares were held by private equity investors, but the IPO would make shares available to the general public.[12]

Everquest was jointly managed by Bear Stearns Asset Management Inc, and Stone Tower Debt Advisors LLC, an affiliate of Stone Tower Capital LLC. I was curious, but I was swamped. I told him no, I was very busy and had not even had a chance to glance at it. He called again asking if I had seen it, and again I said no, "Go away." Then Jody Shenn of *Bloomberg* left a voice message about Everquest, but I was still busy. The next morning I ignored Matt's voice mails, but finally took his call the afternoon of Thursday, May 10, telling him that I still had not looked at the registration statement and had no plans to do so that day. My first call on the morning of Friday, May 11, 2007, was again from Matt Goldstein. He thought the IPO might be important.

I went to the SEC's Web site, and as I scanned the document I thought to myself: *Has Bear Stearns Asset Management completely lost its mind?* There is a difference between being clever and being intelligent. As I printed out the document to read it more thoroughly, I put aside the rest of my work and said: "Matt, you are right; this is important." I was surprised to read that funds managed by BSAM invested in the unrated first loss risk (equity) of CDOs. In my view, the underlying assets were neither suitable nor appropriate investments for the retail market. I did not have time for a thorough review, so I picked a CDO investment underwritten by Citigroup in March 2007[13] bearing in mind that if the Everquest IPO came to market, some of the proceeds would pay down Citigroup's $200 million credit line. Everquest held the "first loss" risk, usually the riskiest of all of the CDO tranches (unless you do a "constellation" type deal with CDO *hawala*), and it was obvious to me that even the investors in the supposedly safe AAA tranches were in trouble. Time proved my concerns warranted, since the CDO triggered an event of default in February 2008, at which time Standard & Poor's downgraded even the original safest AAA tranche to junk.

The equity is the investment with the most leverage, the highest nominal return, and is the most difficult to accurately price. The CDO equity investments were from CDOs underwritten by UBS, Citigroup, Merrill, and other investment banks.[14]

Based on what I read, Everquest's original assets had significant exposure to subprime mortgage loans, and the document disclosed it, "a substantial majority of the [asset-backed] CDOs in which we hold equity have invested primarily in [residential mortgage-backed securities] backed by collateral pools of subprime residential mortgages."[15] Based on my rough estimates, it was as high as 40 percent to 50 percent.

If that was not bad enough, there was huge moral hazard. Bear Stearns Asset Management provided the assumptions for valuing the CDOs. Small changes in the assumptions could create huge differences in prices. Greg Parseghian, formerly of Freddie Mac, was listed as one of the outside directors of Everquest.[16] Among the many criticisms levied against Freddie Mac (due to events at the time Parseghian worked there) was its failure to use *third-party assumptions* instead of concocting its own, thus exposing itself up to moral hazard. Parseghian's bosses left under a cloud, and he was promoted to CEO of Freddie Mac. Parseghian himself stepped down after a couple of months. OFHEO—the Office of Federal Housing Enterprise Oversight—then Freddie Mac's regulator, said that before Parseghian's promotion to CEO, he "failed to provide the Board with adequate information . . . to make an informed decision" in regard to some transactions. In this respect Parseghian's actions illustrated Freddie Mac's "culture of minimal disclosure."[17]

BSAM earned management fees for the hedge funds, management fees on some of the CDOs, and fees for managing Everquest. If Everquest's Board replaced the managers, it had to pay a "break-up" fee of one to three years worth of the management fees—*breaking up's so very hard to do.*[18] The registration statement stated that one of the risks is "the inability of our financial models to forecast adequately the actual performance results."[19] *Yet, fees partially depended on performance.*

I explained my concerns to Matt in a general way. Among other concerns: (1) money from the IPO would pay down Everquest's $200 million line of credit to Citigroup; (2) the loan helped Everquest buy some of its assets including CDOs and a CDO-squared from two hedge funds managed by BSAM, namely the Bear Stearns High-Grade Structured Credit Strategies Fund that had been founded in 2003 and the Bear Stearns High-Grade Structured Credit Strategies Enhanced Leverage Fund ("Enhanced Leverage Fund") launched in August 2006; and (3) the assets appeared to include substantial subprime exposure.

Matt Goldstein posted his story on *Business Week's* site later that day. Initially it was called: *The Everquest IPO: Buyer Beware,* but after protests from Bear Stearns Asset Management, *BusinessWeek* changed the title to *Bear Stearns' Subprime IPO.*[20] I hardly think that pleased Bear Stearns more.

Bloomberg's Jody Shenn also wrote an article on Everquest that day. I expressed to him that "the moral hazard . . . is just mind-boggling." He noted that Lehman thought that CDO assets had lost $18 billion to $25 billion in value industrywide as mortgage delinquencies rose. I thought industrywide losses were already much larger, they just were not being reported.[21]

Ralph Cioffi contacted me about the *BusinessWeek* article. He said that dozens of IPOs like Everquest had been done—mostly offshore so as not to deal with the SEC. According to Ralph, BSAM's hedge funds and Stone Tower's private equity funds would own about 70 percent of Everquest stock shares (equity), and they had no plans to sell "a single share at the IPO date." They planned to use the IPO proceeds to pay down the Citigroup credit line and possibly buy out unaffiliated private equity investors.

I responded that verbal assurances that there are no plans to sell a share at the IPO date are meaningless. Publicly traded shares can be sold anytime. But even if the funds kept their controlling shares, it was not good news. Retail investors would have only a minority interest, which would be a disadvantage if they had a dispute with the managers.

Ralph claimed that subprime was "actually a very small percent of Everquest's assets." He reasoned that on a *market value* basis the exposure to subprime was actually *negative* because Everquest hedged its risk. Technically, Ralph might have been correct—but the registration statement for the Everquest IPO itself suggested otherwise: "The hedges will not cover all of our exposure to [securitizations] backed primarily by subprime mortgage loans."[22]

It is fine to talk about *net* exposure (left over after you protect yourself with a hedge), but one usually also discusses the *gross exposure* (of the assets you originally bought). Hedges cost money, so they can reduce returns.

Ralph Cioffi said CDO equity is "freely traded and easily managed." I countered that CDO equity may be easy for Ralph to value, but investment banks and forensic departments of accounting firms told me they have trouble doing it. I told him that if this were a CDO private placement, it would have to be sold to sophisticated investors and meet suitability requirements, but since it is in a corporation, it can be issued as an *initial public offering* (IPO) to the general public. It seemed to be a way around SEC regulations for fixed income securities, and it was not suitable for retail investors in my view.

Ralph said he would talk to his lawyers about changing the IPO's registration statement to add a line about third-party valuations. We seemed to be talking at cross purposes, since the registration statement already said that third-party valuation would occur at the time of underwriting. The problem with that was that the *assumptions* for pricing would be provided by a conflicted manager, and assumptions are critical in determining value. Moreover, on an ongoing basis, one had to rely on a conflicted management's assumptions for pricing.

Ralph did not seem to want to end the discussion, so I asked him if there was something he wanted me to do. He said it would be great if I issued a comment saying I was quoted "out of context," that my being quoted in *Business Week* lent credibility to the article and was not helping me, and that I would be "better served" writing my own commentary. I ignored what I perceived to be a thinly veiled threat. I told him that if he wanted me to write a commentary, I would do a thorough job of raising all of the objections I had just raised with him. Ralph seemed unhappy, but my thinking he was a hedge fund manager from *Night of the Living Dead* was the least of his problems.

♟ ♟ ♟

At the end of January 2007, the Enhanced Leverage Fund had $669 million in investor capital and $12 billion in investments for a leverage ratio estimated at around 17 to 1. Some estimates said that leverage increased to more than 20 to 1 the following month as assets increased and capital decreased slightly. The less-leveraged fund was estimated to have been levered over 10 to 1, a high degree of leverage for risky assets. On May 15, just days after the *Business Week* article appeared, Bear Stearns asset management told investors in the Enhanced Leverage fund that April losses were 6.75 percent. Questions about both the Bear Stearns High-Grade Structured Credit Strategies and the Enhanced Leveraged fund flooded the marketplace. The funds' credit line providers were alarmed.[23,24,25]

♟ ♟ ♟

Bear Stearns faced other challenges. In April 2007, Bear Stearns asked the International Swaps and Derivatives Association, Inc. (ISDA) to modify credit default swap documents to make it clear that it had the right to modify mortgage loan agreements. On the surface, trying to maximize recovery by allowing homeowners to stay in their homes while continuing to make payments is a good idea. Foreclosure costs are expensive, and one should try to minimize losses in any way possible. But Bear Stearns's timing could not have been more unfortunate; it provoked its own public relations disaster.

A few weeks later, more than 25 hedge funds led by John Paulson, the heavy shorter of the ABX index, all but accused Bear Stearns of seeking to manipulate the market. The seller of credit protection (perhaps Bear Stearns) on mortgage-backed securities, the other side of Mr. Paulson's trade, could use its investment in residual or servicing rights on a mortgage-backed security to buy out and revive defaulted loans. The protection seller could buy a loan at par, instead of its deeply discounted price, and it would artificially prop up the prices of the trust investments and the underlying securities that made up the ABX and other indexes. Since a protection seller in a lower-rated index has a leveraged position, for a relatively small investment it would gain (or protect) tens of times what it paid out. John Paulson maintained that Bear Stearns was trying to avoid making billions of dollars in payments on credit default swaps. "We were shocked," said Michael Waldorf, a vice president at Paulson's firm: He said Bear Stearns introduced language that "would try to give cover to market manipulation."[26] In March 2008, less than one year later, many market participants remembered Paulson's concerns when *Bloomberg* revealed that assets backing the ABX indexes appeared wildly overrated and credit default protection sellers (perhaps Bear Stearns?) would possibly have to come up with more collateral to back these trades.

Bear Stearns withdrew its request to ISDA for additional clarification, claiming it now realized that market participants understood its right to modify loans, but the damage was done. With voices stentorian, the hedge funds had given ISDA and the entire subprime market a vote of no confidence in the motivations of Bear Stearns Companies, Inc.

Warren Buffett had admonished his managers not to do anything they wouldn't want to read about in the newspapers. Bear Stearns and its affiliates were seeing themselves in the press constantly—and not in a good way.

On June 6, 2007, Bear Stearns Asset Management froze redemptions on the approximately $600 million Enhanced Leveraged fund that had been founded the previous August, whereas up until then, investors were accustomed to withdrawing funds with 30-days notice. Its value had fallen 23 percent from the start of the year, and by June 7, BSAM restated its May 15 statement of April 2007 losses from a 6.75 percent loss to a loss of 18.97 percent. BSAM had little choice. Bear Stearns's lenders: Citigroup Inc., J.P. Morgan Chase & Co., Merrill Lynch & Co., Morgan Stanley, Goldman Sachs Group, Inc., Barclays PLC, Dresdner Kleinwort, Deutsche Bank, and others had begun marking down the value of the funds' assets and demanded more collateral; the banks made margin calls. The Enhanced Leverage fund faced $145 million of margin calls as of June 8, and the less-leveraged fund faced $63 million of its own margin calls.[27]

Bear Stearns asked for forbearance. When that didn't work, BSAM met with the funds' lenders, and asked for a moratorium on margin calls and a return of derivative collateral back to the fund. In effect it was asking for more leverage and an extended loan.

The meeting was punctuated with a breathtakingly arrogant flourish when BSAM distributed handouts ending with what it needed from the funds' counterparties. The creditors were not rookies. They had expected BSAM to announce some sort of solution worked out in concert with its parent, Bear Stearns. Of all of the hedge fund managers in the world, the last thing they expected was that Bear Stearns Asset Management would ask them to bend over and think of Ben Bernanke.

BSAM and Bear Stearns Companies, Inc. seemed unaware they had just made an enormous tactical error. They must have been walking around in a dissociative fugue. *Bear Stearns Asset Management wanted new conditions from lenders? BSAM was worried about the prices its creditors might put on the assets it managed?* The mood of at least one of the funds' creditors had just shifted from "let's see what they've come up with" to "#★?! those guys."

In 1994, Bear Stearns had been very quick—some said much too quick—off the mark to seize and liquidate exotic CMO collateral (the kind of assets Warren Spector traded early in his career) of three commingled funds managed by Askin Capital Management. Bear Stearns seemed to have made a fast profit—and a greater profit than the other creditors involved—after reselling seized assets.

Despite David Askin's belief that he could consistently produce returns as high as 15 percent in both up and down markets, he ran into pricing and liquidity problems.[28] At the end of February 1994, Askin did not use the mark-to-market prices supplied by Wall Street firms that had lent him money—including Bear Stearns—but a court-appointed trustee could not find Askin's models, either. Askin's disclosure to his investors the following month about not using dealer pricing was one of the triggers that sparked the market sell-off that led to that fund's bankruptcy.[29]

Questions were also raised about the prices used by the investment banks that eventually liquidated the assets they seized from the funds. The investment banks did not seem to be using a defensible model based on observable assumptions. Prices seemed to be arranged over the phone between dealers and designed to show a "print" for the records, since customer business had dried up. The prices became a market joke: *I'm just Askin'* . . . *What's the price of this CMO?*

The final bankruptcy report for the Askin funds noted that Bear Stearns had a 12-hour head start and seemed to make much more profit than the other firms when it resold the assets it seized from Askin. The hasty liquidation may have made any attempt for a bailout moot. The report said Bear Stearns's seizure and sale of collateral was "at prices below its own contemporaneous assessments of value."[30] To be fair to Bear Stearns, we will never know how it came up with new prices over the phone on that day, since—despite a court order—Bear Stearns said it "inadvertently"[31] recorded over its trading floor telephone tapes several months after it was required to produce them. *What happened to the evidence? We're just Askin'.*

Bear Stearns was consistent in its take-no-hedge-fund-prisoners philosophy. In 1998, after Long-Term Capital Management turned down Warren Buffett's bid, the New York Federal Reserve Bank helped arrange a bailout for LTCM with 16 banks and investment banks. James "Jimmy" E. Cayne, Bear Stearns's CEO, famously refused to help. The rest of Wall Street never forgot it.

The head of risk management for J.P. Morgan wasn't askin' anything when he pointed out to Ralph Cioffi and his boss Richard Marin that they might have to seek help from Bear Stearns, their parent company, to figure out a way to meet margin calls. He thought they were "underestimating the severity of the situation." *When you are playing for keeps in finance, you dispense with insults such* as "you're a lying scumbag," *and replace it with something along the lines of* "you are gravely mistaken"—*meaning take it back, or there will be war.*

On June 23, 2007, Richard Marin later wrote on his blog, *Whim of Iron* (whimofiron.blogspot.com), that he had spent the previous two weeks defending "Sparta against the Persians [sic] hordes of Wall Street." One of my business contacts joked that Marin meant me, since my last name is a Persian name, an artifact of my ex-husband. But Marin seemed to be referring to the popular film, *300,* about the battle at Thermopylae, in which a small army of Greeks perished after battling and delaying tens of thousands of Persians. Their sacrifice bought time for the Greek armies, who ultimately drove back their enemy. Marin thought he had prevailed, but like the doomed soldiers in the *300,* he lost his battle to maintain his top position at BSAM. On June 29, 2007, Marin moved aside and became an advisor to Jeffrey Lane, BSAM's new chairman and CEO, an import from Lehman Brothers.[32]

Initially, Alan Schwartz and Warren Spector, Bear Stearns's cochief operating officers, emphasized that they were not bailing out the funds. Ralph Cioffi tried to save the funds and announced to his creditors that he had hired a consultant, Blackstone's Timothy Coleman, to help him restructure the funds. Blackstone owned a large private equity share of FGIC, a bond guarantor that insured risky subprime-backed CDOs (among other things). FGIC thought the tranches it insured were "safe," but a fundamental analysis would have shown otherwise. In June 2007, FGIC was still rated AAA, but ironically, it was downgraded to junk in March 2007, just a few days before Bear Stearns failed.[33]

There was talk of Bear Stearns coming to the rescue with a $2.5 billion loan. "People close to the situation"[34] claimed that losses would have little impact on Bear Stearns. They were wrong.

On June 15, Merrill Lynch seized collateral and others began testing the market. The news was dismal. Even though most of the assets on bid lists were nominally rated AAA, only some of assets fetched prices close to asking prices. Others were less than 50 cents on the dollar, and some of the harder to sell assets were not even shown around. Many people were angry that BSAM had not managed the funds better. Now that the bid lists were hitting the market, it would be harder than ever to avoid marking down the investment banks' enormous exposures to CDOs. Bid lists from JPMorgan Securities and Morgan Stanley found their way to *Reuters.* It counted $1.44 billion in CDOs. Managers included Tricadia, headed by Michael Barnes, an alumnus of the Bear Stearns's mortgage department and later UBS, Cohen Brothers' Strategos—later to distinguish itself with highest notional amount of defaulted CDOs, and BSAM.[35, 36]

Among the funds' assets were collateralized loan obligations partially backed by leveraged loans. The SEC had several pricing investigations underway into these types of securitizations. The leveraged loan market had not been getting as much attention as the mortgage market, but collateral quality was mixed. Some loans had assets backing them, and some did not. Investment banks looked at the bid lists and saw that they did not have time to drill down into the loans to figure out how to bid.[37]

By late June, Bear Stearns said it would invest $1.6 billion to bailout the Enhanced Leverage fund. BSAM had already begun reducing leverage. Bear Stearns also stated that the less-leveraged Bear Stearns High-Grade Structured Credit Strategies fund would not need to be rescued.[38]

By not stepping up immediately, Bear Stearns let BSAM circulate asset lists that aired Wall Street's dirty laundry. At the end of June 2007 I told the *Wall Street Journal's* Serena Ng that the poor bids raised the question of why investment banks were not reporting losses, and no one wanted to ask the question. "That would open the floodgates. Everyone is trying to stop the problem, but they should face up to it. The assets may all be mispriced."[39]

It wasn't as if the coming market mess could have been avoided. Bear Stearns simply had the misfortune of an arrogant past, and now it was the first to show everyone's losing cards. By the end of June, Bear Stearns's share price closed just under $139 per share, down 15 percent for the year. The worst was yet to come. *As Warren Buffett joked to me during lunch, you cannot multiply your investments when you multiply by zero.*

Bear Stearns had only bailed out creditors, not fund investors. By mid-July, Bear Stearns told investors in the Enhanced Leverage fund that they would probably get back *nothing.* Investors in the less-leveraged fund were told they would probably get only 10 cents on the dollar.[40] In the eyes of some investors, Bear Stearns Asset Management went from hero to zero.

Iain Hamilton, a portfolio manager for Infiniti Capital, a fund of funds in Zurich that had invested a 3.25 percent allocation in BSAM managed hedge funds, felt misled. At a conference in Sydney, Hamilton exclaimed that BSAM represented the subprime exposure was "6 percent, but it had 40 percent hidden elsewhere."[41] He could take losses. He had losses in another fund, but hadn't felt misled. According to him, it was misrepresentation. Whether this was a misunderstanding of net versus gross exposures, or something else, will have to be decided by the courts.

🌱 🌱 🌱

Ralph Cioffi left Bear Stearns by mutual agreement on November 28, 2007, at the age of 51. His compensation reportedly soared to eight figures during his BSAM days. The less-leveraged fund had positive returns for several years, and colleagues invested money with him after noting he was returning around 1 percent per month—more than 12 percent per year—in an interest rate environment in which 10-year Treasuries were yielding less than 5 percent. It was an old story: If it sounds too good to be true, it is.

Warren Spector did not last as long as Cioffi. Like Warren Buffett, Warren Spector and Jimmy Cayne are avid bridge players. On August 5, 2007, Spector became the highest ranking bridge player—one of the world's top 300 contract bridge players—to lose his job over the mortgage lending crisis. *Bridge is a great comfort in your old age. If it distracts you from business, it can help you get there faster.* Spector had been the lead promoter for Bear Stearns to get into the hedge fund business, and Cayne held him responsible. Cayne's ire may also have been sparked by the fact that while the funds faltered in July, Spector was at a bridge tournament playing perfect hands of bridge and racking up 100 master points. Cayne played less well at the same bridge tournament, and apparently he thought Spector should have been closer to the hedge fund problem, even if Cayne himself did not feel compelled to fly back to New York.

Unlike Cayne, Spector had sold millions of shares of his Bear Stearns stock in 2004. *Bloomberg* reported that Spector, 51, earned $228 million in cash from 1992 to 2006, and got another $372 million when he cashed in most of his Bear Stearns shares.[42] Jimmy Cayne, 74, resigned in January of 2008, after serving 15 years as CEO. His Bear Stearns stock had been worth more than $975 million in January 2007 and was worth around half of that when he resigned in January 2008. Cayne did not liquidate until after JPMorgan's March 2008 takeover. The stock was worth only $61 million.

Cayne may feel lucky in comparison to Ralph Cioffi and Matthew Tannin, Ralph's cohead at BSAM. On June 18, 2008, they were indicted on allegations of securities fraud, among other charges.[43, 44]

Prosecutors focused on electronic exchanges between Tannin and Cioffi. The partners may have stumbled over the truth, picked themselves up, and hurried on. In late April, they saw a negative report prompting Tannin to write to Cioffi: "If the report was [sic] true, the entire subprime market was toast."[45] Yet they did not seem to share those concerns with investors. Perhaps the partners gave themselves unwarranted reassurance.

It reminded me of a bridge joke I sent Warren Buffett after our lunch. *It was a partnership misunderstanding. My partner thought I knew what I was doing.*

Chapter 9

Dead Man's Curve

I evaluate the probable loss myself. I don't use a model.

—Warren Buffett
to Janet Tavakoli, September 2005

Benjamin Graham was not a fan of market timing, in which investors try to forecast stock market prices (or oil spreads, interest rate spreads, or prices of CDOs). He was sure those who followed forecasting would "end up as a speculator with a speculator's financial results."[1] Instead, Graham advocated buying a stock if it was trading below its fair value and selling when it was above its fair value after doing a fundamental analysis. He knew that his views were "not commonly accepted on Wall Street."[2] Even after Warren Buffett achieved a successful track record following (and then modifying) Graham's principles, many on Wall Street still did not accept these views.

A recent example is the demise of Bear Stearns, which was preceded and partly triggered by the deaths of Peloton, a European-based hedge fund cofounded by Ron Beller, and one of the funds of the Carlyle Group, a Washington-connected private equity firm. At the time of its demise, Peloton held long positions of the type that Bear Stearns's research group touted in February 2008.

Ron Beller first made big headlines in 2004 when Joyti De-Laurey, personal assistant at Goldman Sachs to his wife, Jennifer Moses, went on trial and was convicted of forging the Bellers' and Moses' signatures to filch funds from their personal accounts. Beller and his wife asked De-Laurey to work for them personally when they both left Goldman Sachs, but De-Laurey stayed to become the personal assistant of another Goldman Sachs partner, Scott Mead. She was also convicted of filching funds from him. De-Laurey reportedly took £4.4 million (around $8.75 million in 2008 dollars) from the collective accounts of Scott Mead, Jennifer Moses (Beller's wife) and Ron Beller. Neither of the Bellers noticed that De-Laurey had taken millions from their personal accounts for several months. Is it any wonder that during the trial De-Laurey referred to Mr. Beller as "an absolute diamond"?[3] Yet, when Beller co-founded London-based Peloton in 2005, investors seemed eager to let him manage their money.

Ron Beller and Geoff Grant, another former Goldman Sachs partner, ran Peloton Partners, named after the vee-like bird formation adopted by endurance bicycle riders that lead the pack by taking advantage of drafting to reduce wind friction. In January 2008, Peloton Partners LLP was riding high. It had two funds, the $1.6 billion Peloton Multi-strategy fund, and the $2 billion Peloton ABS fund.[4] The latter fund won *Eurohedge*'s best new fixed-income fund of the year award, after reporting a stunning *net* return of 87.6 percent for 2007. When the fund's returns were announced, some of the attendees at the awards ceremony "gasped."[5] *Shock and awe.* Beller and Grant were lauded as "hedgie heroes."[6] Within two months of receiving these accolades, Peloton's $2 billion ABS fund collapsed, and Peloton put its offices up for sale.

Beller told potential investors that his strategy was to make bets on a variety of assets to make money from global economic trends. He made *leveraged* bets on these trends, and for that to work, he had to be on the right side of the trend.

Initially, the ABS Peloton fund took short positions in subprime mortgage backed securities making huge bets against the U.S. housing market as John Paulson had done very successfully. Since the prices of those securities plummeted in 2007, the short position had huge gains. But what would Peloton do for an encore? There had to be another big trade. If only Peloton Partners could pedal to where there was luck—*there must be more money!* After all, spread relationships for AAA and AA rated products looked out of line with historical relationships. The spread curve *should* revert back to historical levels, according to the market timer's nursery rhyme. So the fund also bet that the "highly rated" mortgage securities trading at more than 90 cents on the dollar would be protected by subordinated investors eventually paying back all of the principal, and he went long these assets. Like market timers before them, Peloton Partners ended up with speculator's results. A fundamental analysis of the type Graham had advocated suggested that those "highly rated" products were *overpriced* and *overrated*. The prices were not going to revert back to "historical" levels; the prices would drop to reflect a lower fair value based on imperfect (but highly negative) loan performance data combined with the illiquidity that uncertainty about one's imperfect data brings. This is a market timer's worst-case scenario. Peloton Partners lost $17 billion in "a matter of days."[7]

The Peloton ABS fund used credit derivatives (it sold protection) to go long $6 billion of exposure to two ABX indexes (the 2006 AAA and 2006 AA rated ABX indexes). In all, it was long $15 billion on various mortgage-backed assets and only partially hedged with short positions. Peloton was said to have leveraged up four or five times, "normal for a credit fund."[8] Leverage "averages" are misleading when the assets themselves are inherently very risky (mispriced in the opposite direction to your trade). When the price of the "highly rated" 2006 ABX indexes continued to drop, Peloton's 14 lenders, including UBS, Goldman and Lehman, asked the fund to come up with more money to top up its cash cushion. Peloton's ABX positions headed around Dead Man's Curve and the fund skidded off the edge of the cliff.

Since Peloton liked bicycle analogies, this simplified one may help explain its problem with leverage. Suppose Peloton's assets consist of a fleet of uninsured bikes originally worth $1 million purchased with $200,000 of its investors' money and $800,000 of money borrowed from an investment bank. The investment bank says that at all times, Peloton must keep a balance of pledged assets—any assets—against the $800 million loan of $1 million in value. The extra $200,000 is margin collateral for the loan, a cushion for the investment bank making it unlikely that the investment bank will lose money. Initially, Peloton pledges the entire $1 million fleet of bikes as collateral for the $800,000 loan with the investment bank. If Peloton damaged 5 percent of its bikes due to rough riding, the assets would only be worth $950,000, and the bank would ask Peloton for another $50,000 in collateral to maintain the cushion. This is known as a *margin call*. If Peloton has enough cash on hand there is no problem. But if Peloton does not have enough cash (or *liquidity*) to meet the investment bank's demand, it will have to liquidate the assets—sell the bicycles and *unwind* the position—to pay back the bank. Since the bikes are worth $950,000, the bank is paid its $800,000 in full, but the original investment of $200,000 is now only worth $150,000 for a 25 percent loss on the investors' original capital. That's the downside of leverage on fixed assets.

Now suppose that 25 percent of Peloton's bikes round Dead Man's Curve and skid off a steep cliff. One quarter, or $250,000, of the value of the fleet disappears. Peloton loses the investors' entire original $200,000. More than that, if the bank repossesses the fleet and sells it— known as *unwinding the position*—it will not get back the full amount of the $800,000 since the $200,000 cash cushion the investors provided has been used up. The bank loses $50,000 and only gets back $750,000 of its original $800,000 loan. The investors lose 100 percent of their initial equity; *the investors are wiped out.* But the investment bank, the creditor, loses 6.25 percent of the original principal on its loan.

Bear Stearns's shareholders and creditors had Peloton's demise fresh in their minds when, a couple of weeks later, a confluence of events raised questions about Bear Stearns's solvency. If Peloton were an investment bank, *shareholders would be wiped out,* and only the bond-holders and other creditors would recover some (or all) of the origi-nal amount of the debt. That is the power of leverage. When things are going your way, everyone is euphoric and gasping with delight. When things do not go your way, shareholders can be wiped out. The results can be dramatic and swift, and instead of gasping with delight, shareholders are gasping for air.

Funds that leverage risky debt assets without sufficient liquidity are doomed to collapse. Yet, time and again, bankers extended credit lines to funds using fully priced tranches of collateralized debt obligations, turning a blind eye to the unwind potential.

When we first met, Warren explained that he evaluates the underlying collateral: its probability of default and its probable recovery value. He avoids leverage and looks for a risk premium payment to cover potential losses and more. Peloton was about as far away from Warren Buffett's philosophy as one can get.

Peloton's problem with making leveraged bets on fixed-income securities was that they had little or no upside, and the securities underlying the ABX index were overpriced when Peloton put on the trade even though they had already dropped from par to prices ranging from 90 to 95. The downward price swing was due to irreversible damage in the underlying collateral, and unlike a manufacturing company, there is no source of future earnings to make up for the lost cash.[9]

In January 2008, when Beller accepted his award, Peloton thought it had solid credit lines and thought its $750 million in cash was more than enough liquidity to meet margin calls. It was wrong. On February 25, 2008, the ABX index prices dropped and when Peloton tried to sell assets to meet margin calls, brokers wouldn't bid. At one point Beller, like the rocking horse winner, "collapsed on a couch in distress."[10] On February 28, lenders seized the assets of the Peloton ABS fund.

Beller, Grant, and a third partner had around $117 million[11] of their own money plus the previous year's fees invested in the ABS fund; Beller's individual loss is said to be $60 million. Beller may not have learned his lesson. He reportedly believes that the Peloton ABS fund failed because the prices were only *temporarily* depressed when his bankers made margin calls and pulled their credit lines. The reality is that the delinquencies of the loans backing the poorly structured assets in the home equity indexes ensure prices will not recover to the lofty levels at which Beller put on his trades. Peloton's long positions were partially hedged with short positions in lower quality mortgages.[12] It seemed to me the damage to "higher rated" tranches had yet to be acknowledged by a market that was still in denial. Investors seemed to avoid fundamental analysis at the time Peloton put on its original trades. BlackRock Inc. and Man Group PLC among others also lost money on their investment in the fund.

The $1.6 billion Peloton Multi-strategy fund had contributed $500 million in investor money to launch the Peloton ABS fund. Investors' assets were frozen and Peloton Partners wound down the fund. It is estimated that within the month of February 2008, investors in the Multi-strategy fund lost half of their capital. Beller and Grant wrote a letter to investors during the last week of February 2008 bemoaning the fact that their creditors had "severely" tightened their terms "without regard to the creditworthiness or track record."[13] In early March, a week after the Peloton ABS fund collapsed, Peloton Partners put its offices in London's Soho district on the market.

As Benjamin Graham observed, the market is not there to instruct you. The market isn't trying to teach you something when prices rise or fall (or when spreads widen or narrow) relative to where they were historically. You can stuff all of that information into a model (or your head) if you want to, but manipulating market numbers—if that is all you are doing—will not tell you anything about value. It is up to you to analyze the fundamental value and compare it with the market. Peloton Partners was not alone in skimping on fundamental analysis, but Peloton was not as well connected as the Carlyle Group, which had a fund of its own rounding Dead Man's Curve.

Washington-based Carlyle Group is the world's second largest private equity firm, and the most well-connected. As of March 13, 2008, it managed $81 billion in 60 venture capital funds.[14] Louis V. Gerstner Jr., former CEO of IBM, chairs the group founded by Dan D'Aniello,

William E. Conway, also chairman of United Defense Industries; and David Rubenstein, former policy advisor to former President Jimmy Carter. The Carlyle Group's employees past and present include former President George H. W. Bush; his former Secretary of State James Baker (also President Ronald Reagan's Chief of Staff and later his Secretary of the Treasury); former Carlyle head (until 2003) Frank Carlucci, President Reagan's CIA director and defense secretary; former British Prime Minister John Major, Ken Kresa; former CEO of defense contractor Northrup Grumann; and Louis Giuliano, former CEO to military and oil electronics supplier ITT Industries. One of Carlyle's investors is Shafig bin Laden, one of Osama's many brothers. Shafig was one of the honored guests at a Washington-held Carlyle conference on September 11, 2001, the day his brother's Al Qaeda terrorists hijacked U.S. passenger airliners and piloted them into the Pentagon and the World Trade Center.[15, 16]

Carlyle Capital Corporation Ltd. (Carlyle Capital), one of the funds managed by the Carlyle Group, was troubled since July 2007, the day it launched its initial public offering. The fund was registered in the island of Guernsey in the United Kingdom, run out of New York, and its IPO listed and traded on the Amsterdam Stock Exchange. The IPO was scaled down and delayed due to a nervous market. It ultimately raised $345.5 million, $54.5 million under its initial target of $400 million. Carlyle Capital Corporation ominously chose CCC as its stock ticker.[17] Within two months the market would ask whether CCC stood for its stock ticker or a near-default credit rating.

Like the doomed hedge funds managed by BSAM, Carlyle Capital financed its asset purchases with repurchase agreements. It had around $940 million in investor capital backing $22.7 billion in leveraged borrowings. CCC was around 24 times leveraged, meaning that if the price of its assets dropped 4 percent, the initial investment of its investors would be wiped out if it were forced to liquidate assets.[18] If the price dropped more than that, its creditors, including a number of U.S. investment banks, would also lose money. Given that there were questions about the quality of the mortgage loans backing AAA rated securities, and given the low prices revealed when the BSAM's bid lists circulated, a price drop of more than 4 percent was very likely.

By August 2007, the month the Fed indirectly bailed out Countrywide's asset-backed commercial paper, the Carlyle Group provided CCC with a

$100 million unsecured revolving credit facility to help meet margin calls. The value of CCC's investments in AAA U.S. government agency residential mortgage-backed securities, declined in value. At the end of February 2008, the Carlyle Group increased its credit line from $100 million to $150 million.[19] Carlyle Capital reported a net profit for 2007 of $16.8 million while downward price pressure on its assets persisted. In early March 2008, CCC received a notice of default for failing to meet a margin call, and it announced that since August it had sold around $1 billion in assets in an attempt to decrease leverage and increase liquidity. On March 7, 2008, after CCC could not meet additional margin calls, trading in CCC shares was suspended.[20]

JPMorgan Chase vice chairman James Lee Jr., warned a Carlyle Group founder, David Rubenstein, that unless it could line up a huge capital injection, the funds' collateral would be seized to satisfy its debts. The problem was that the only likely source of capital for the fund was the Carlyle Group itself. JPMorgan Chase was asking the Carlyle Group to bail out its hedge fund the way Bear Stearns had bailed out BSAM's doomed funds. If the Carlyle Group bailed out its fund the way Bear Stearns had bailed out the funds managed by BSAM, it could lose some of its own principal, and losses would probably eclipse its $16.7 million in profits reported for 2007. On the other hand, investment banks seizing collateral would use up much needed liquidity. If investment banks were forced to immediately liquidate Carlyle's billions in assets, they would take losses and drive market prices down even further. As of March 10, 2008, Carlyle Capital stared down the barrel of around $400 million in margin calls it couldn't meet, and it asked its lenders for a standstill agreement.[21]

Bear Stearns had its own liquidity problems that week as the market speculated on its exposures. Even the breaking Governor Spitzer pay-to-play sex scandal could not upstage the March 10 Moody's Investors Service's downgrade of tranches of mortgage-backed debt issued by Bear Stearns Alt-A Trust. *Bear Stearns was one of Carlyle Capital's creditors and now this.* Throughout the day of March 10, rumors circulated that Bear Stearns was sinking fast from lack of liquidity and possibly even insolvency. Bear Stearns officially denied it, saying there was "no truth to the rumors of liquidity problems."[22]

In reaction to the market's reaction, Moody's clarified that its ratings actions did not affect Bear Stearns' corporate ratings, which it viewed as stable. The rumors persisted. At the end of the day, Bear Stearns issued a press release quoting Alan Schwartz, then its president and CEO. "Bear Stearns' balance sheet, liquidity and capital," he said, "remain strong."[23]

On March 11, 2008, *Bloomberg News* issued its article suggesting the rating agencies propped up AAA rated subprime residential home equity loan-backed bonds backing the ABX index. According to its analysis of S&P data, *none* of the assets backing the index merited an AAA rating and it took only a short step for readers to realize that 90 percent of the bonds in the AAA index were not even investment grade.[24] "Peloton," I told an investment banker, "was leveraged and *long* an ABX index, so the news suggests the depressed prices may not rebound and investment banks will take losses on those positions. Carlyle's CCC is *long* AAA agency assets, and it cannot meet its margin calls. No wonder they want the Carlyle Group to put up more collateral (margin)."

The Carlyle Group was not alone. *Anyone* who was long would have to put up more collateral. Was John Paulson correct the previous summer when he hypothesized that, when Bear Stearns appealed to ISDA, it was trying to avoid making billions of dollars in payments on credit default swaps?[25] If so, the *Bloomberg* article was devastating news. At a minimum, Bear Stearns would have to come up with more collateral to back those trades and it might eventually have to make payments to cover defaults.

The Federal Reserve Bank took unprecedented action that had the effect of being an indirect bailout for the Carlyle Group. It created a new Term Securities Lending Facility (TSLF). Instead of lending overnight it extended the term to 28 days to primary dealers and would accept "federal agency debt, federal agency residential mortgage-backed securities, and nonagency AAA and Aaa rated private label residential MBS." The program would start through weekly auctions beginning March 27, 2008, and the Fed would lend up to $200 billion of Treasury securities in exchange for the collateral.[26] *How soon can you stuff overrated AAA assets to the Fed so you don't have to show a loss on your balance sheet?*

Traditionally, the Fed freely provides liquidity to the U.S. banking system's securities arms including: Banc of America Securities LLC, HSBC Securities (USA) Inc., and J. P. Morgan Securities Inc. But the Fed had never before opened securities lending to all primary dealers including some foreign banks, U.S. brokers and investment banks: BNP Paribas Securities Corp, Barclays Capital Inc. Bear, Stearns & Co., Inc.,

Cantor Fitzgerald & Co., Countrywide Securities Corporation, Credit Suisse Securities (USA) LLC, Daiwa Securities America Inc., Deutsche Bank Securities Inc. Dresdner Kleinwort Wasserstein Securities LLC., Goldman, Sachs & Co., Greenwich Capital Markets, Inc., Lehman Brothers Inc., Merrill Lynch Government Securities Inc., Mizuho Securities USA Inc., Morgan Stanley & Co. Incorporated, and UBS Securities LLC. Although the program would not begin until March 27 for primary dealers, banks should now be more willing to provide back-door financing for them in the meantime.

The Fed was supposed to protect *banks* not *nonbank investment banks and nonbank primary dealers.* Primary dealers included the worst actors in the subprime lending crisis. The Fed not only failed to speak out against the bad guys before or during the crisis, it had just announced it was bailing out some bad guys after-the-fact.

Similar to the terms of its August 2007 bailout of Countrywide's borrowing problems, the Fed would lend up to 28 days. The primary dealers had to pledge securities to secure the loans. The Fed announced it would accept mortgage-related assets having AAA ratings as well as other assets with any kind of nominal investment grade rating. The Fed proposed to "haircut," or discount those securities by 5 percent, but that would not be nearly enough to cover potential losses. The only condition was that the assets could not be on negative credit watch. Given how poorly the ratings agencies had "watched" up until then, it seems that the Fed will take in assets worth much less than a nominal price of 95 cents on the dollar. The prices on overrated mortgage-backed assets had proven to be wildly inflated. Did the Fed think no one would notice? In the coming weeks, the Bank of England would launch a bailout of its own and demand *five to six times the discount* asked for by the Fed.

I was against the Fed's actions. It was like watching a trailer for the Fed's version of a financial horror movie: *28 Days Later—four weeks after the Fed debases the dollar by exchanging treasuries for trash, the raging virus of inflation infects the planet.*

The Carlyle Group was off the hook; only investors in Carlyle Capital's fund would lose money. On March 13, 2008, Carlyle Capital announced the fund's collapse. It had failed to find financing and it had failed to negotiate the standstill agreement it sought. On March 13, 2008, Carlyle Capital announced it defaulted on about *$16.6 billion* in loans.[27] The Fed had conveniently provided Carlyle's creditors with a source of liquidity. Now Carlyle Capital's assets need never come under public scrutiny. Carlyle Capital said its assets were mostly agency AAA mortgage-backed paper, but the agencies had owned up to having AAA rated subprime-backed RMBS tranches, so what exactly backed Carlyle's investments? Carlyle Capital's $940 million fund went under and its creditors took approximately $22.7 billion in assets back on their balance sheets. Now they had to fund them (with a little help from the Fed).[28, 29, 30, 31] Some said the Carlyle Group took a hit to its reputation, but others disagree. One banker told me: "This shows how much clout the Carlyle Group really has."

As for the investors that lost money in the Carlyle Capital fund, David Rubenstein made a cryptic remark: "We will try to make this experience ultimately feel better than it does today."[32] I do not recall ever before hearing a fund manager say anything like that to investors that lost money in a fund. *Don't worry, we'll make it up to you; we're connected, so you're connected.*

Carlyle's creditors included Bear Stearns, Merrill Lynch & Co., Deutsche Bank AG, and Citigroup, Inc.[33] Bear Stearns could not yet access the Fed's largesse, since the proposed borrowing plan for primary dealers was not yet in effect. One might be tempted to blame market rumors for Bear Stearns's demise, but there were plenty of troublesome facts to infer that anyone with exposure to Bear Stearns should consider reducing that exposure.

Benjamin Graham had warned of new conditions causing a nervous market to stampede, and creditors could infer they had reason to be nervous.

Neither Moody's affirmation that Bear Stearns' rating was stable, nor the press release issued by Bear Stearns convinced the market that Bear Stearns had enough liquidity. The morning of March 11, Bear Stearns' CFO Sam Molinaro appeared on CNBC to flatly deny that Bear was having liquidity problems. Bear had used up its good will, an important source of Wall Street liquidity in a crisis. Carlyle had not yet announced its March 13 collapse but market watchers wondered: *How much exposure did Bear Stearns have to Carlyle Capital? What about the money-losing credit derivatives (long exposure to subprime CDOs) trades that Paulson mentioned the previous year? What about the assets Bear Stearns took back on balance sheet from the two hedge funds in the summer of 2007—how were they doing?* One could infer from publicly available information that these were reasonable questions, but Bear Stearns again created its own PR disaster by failing to anticipate these concerns.

Rumors circulated that highly leveraged Lehman Brothers was also having liquidity problems. Lehman informally denied it, and unlike Bear, Lehman still had many market supporters (Lehman would not declare bankruptcy until six months later).

On March 11, SEC Chairman Cox said he was comfortable that Bear Stearns, Lehman Brothers, Merrill Lynch, Goldman Sachs, and Morgan Stanley had enough capital. *Based on what, exactly?* "We are reviewing the adequacy of capital at the holding company level on a constant basis, daily in some cases."[34] This statement gave me no comfort. The SEC's failure to shut down investment banks' financial meth labs (Byzantine CDOs) made it as credible as a rating agency in my eyes. Given that investment banks priced tens of billions of dollars of assets using only managements' assumptions, and given their excessive leverage, *no one* should have been comfortable.

Earlier in the day, rumors spread that Goldman Sachs[35] or CSFB[36] or both had sent an e-mail letter bomb to hedge fund clients saying that it would no longer take fees for intermediating Bear Stearns' derivatives transactions. Up until then, investment banks pocketed cash to stand in the middle of the hedge funds' derivative trades with Bear Stearns. In credit derivatives speak, sending an e-mail like that was as good as saying you expected Bear Stearns to lose its investment grade rating and possibly go bankrupt. Goldman later told *Fortune* the e-mail did not say it would categorically refuse to sell credit protection on Bear Stearns.[37] By the end of the day, on Tuesday, March 11, 2008, it seemed the entire credit derivatives market was reluctant to sell credit default protection on Bear Stearns.

That afternoon, I spoke with Jonathan Wald, CNBC's senior vice president of business news, saying there was a lot of turmoil. I mentioned that it looked as if there would be a large fund failure. I was referring to Carlyle Capital Corporation Ltd., but did not name it (it collapsed two days later). Wald said we might get together for coffee the following day, unless Eliot Spitzer resigned since the sex scandal would cram his schedule. I responded, "In that case, we should schedule it another time." Spitzer was out of options.

On the morning of Wednesday, March 12, 2008, Alan Schwartz, then CEO of Bear Stearns for less than one fiscal quarter, was in Palm Beach, Florida. He gave an early morning interview to CNBC. Schwartz claimed he saw no liquidity pressure on Bear Stearns. He said the holding company had a liquidity cushion of $17 billion in cash, plus there were billions of dollars in cash and unpledged collateral at the subsidiaries. He smiled and I thought he looked relaxed. CNBC was not trying to be funny when, partway through Schwartz's interview, a female commentator broke in to announce that Eliot Spitzer would resign that day.[38]

Was Schwartz bluffing? It appeared to me he was. He said the previous week had been a "difficult time" in the mortgage market with rumors about problems at the government-sponsored entities (Fannie Mae and Freddie Mac), funds (he did not mention Carlyle Capital Corporation by name) invested in "very high quality" mortgage instruments with high leverage that were having problems, and that people might "speculate" that Bear Stearns also had problems since it was a "significant" player in the mortgage market.[39] The only part of Schwartz's spin that the market bought was his observation that in tough markets, there is a tendency to "Sell first and ask questions later."[40]

While $17 billion sounds like a large number, if market prices moved down 5 percent—$17 billion and more could disappear faster than a car in *Gone in 60 Seconds.* For securitized lending, the market now asked for 3 percent more collateral for mortgage-backed bonds issued by Fannie Mae and Freddie Mac (Carlyle Capital–type assets); and was now asking for 30 percent collateral on Alt-A backed bonds. Jeffrey Rosenberg, head of credit strategy research for Bank of America, said this funding dried up and "that appears to have been Bear's problem."[41]

In fact, the Fed's new lending program may have contributed to Bear Stearns's downfall. Banks took Carlyle Capital's assets knowing the Fed would soon provide liquidity for them, but the program was not yet in place, and Bear Stearns had fewer funding options than other banks.[42] As one CEO of a boutique investment bank told me: "Bear Stearns had no friends." The Fed indirectly bailed out Carlyle's creditors—and saved the Carlyle Group from pressure to come up with bailout money—but now *Bear Stearns* had a problem.

Kevin O'Leary, the managing director of Boston's Tibbar Capital, was in St Bart's with other hedge fund managers. The hedge fund managers did not mess around. O'Leary said they felt Bear Stearns might be forced into bankruptcy, and it was not worth the risk of losing a part of their cash by leaving it tied up in margin accounts at Bear Stearns. They simply pushed the button and *boom*, billions moved out of their trading accounts and into custodian accounts, so Bear Stearns was no longer able to borrow against these assets.[43] That made quite a dent in Schwartz's cash and unpledged collateral at the subsidiaries.[44]

The CEO of a small New York investment bank said he was concerned about his clearing account, given that Bear Stearns' sources of liquidity were turning their backs. He explored other alternatives. He was relieved after Jamie Dimon announced his bid for Bear Stearns a few days later and told me: "It doesn't get better than a guarantee from JPMorgan Chase *and* the Fed."

On Friday March 14, 2008, there was still hope for Bear Stearns; it was not yet dead. The Fed announced a stop-gap loan (Bear Stearns later found out it was only good for a day), but since its lending program was not yet operational, it agreed to accept collateral via JPMorgan Chase. It was odd. If JPMorgan Chase had confidence in Bear Stearns's collateral, it could have accepted the collateral itself (on a recourse basis) and made the loan to Bear Stearns. JPMorgan Chase has access to the Fed and could meet its own liquidity needs there. The announcement made it seem as if JPMorgan Chase did not trust the value of the assets. *The market will price the assets, but you may not like the price.*

That day, I discussed this move both Bloomberg Television and Canada's business news network, BNN. The market still questioned the survival of Bear Stearns, but Lehman Brothers was able to get financing. There seemed to be a view that "a firm is only as solvent as people think it is." I pointed out that is not true. *If you are liquid, solvent, have a positive cash flow and you have no leverage—you do not have to borrow money—and it does not matter what the market thinks about you.*

If you are *solvent* but not liquid (you need cash but the value of your assets make you more than good for it) and if you can *prove* you are solvent, you tend to get the *liquidity,* since people will lend you money. But if you are highly leveraged, it only takes a small negative change in the perception of the value of your collateral for you to be in trouble.

The investment banks were playing a very dangerous game, and they were losing that game. They could not prove they were solvent (if they were). No one trusted their own pricing, and there was no transparency.

If no one can figure out if an investment bank is solvent, short-term financing disappears. *In fact, the investment bank itself may not know whether or not it is solvent.*

If you lend a brother-in-law $100,000 for the down payment on a $1 million home, and the price of the home goes to $1.1 million, you might be willing to give him a short-term loan of $1,000 knowing he's temporarily short of cash, but he's good for it. If you know, however, that the price of all of the homes in his neighborhood are down to $900,000, you know he will be lucky to pay you any of the money you originally lent him. You might say no to an additional short-term loan of $1,000.

Warren Buffett and Charlie Munger avoid leverage so that they are not at the mercy of the manic depressive Mr. Market. By supplying investment banks with liquidity, the Fed introduced huge moral hazard. The Fed rewarded those who brought down the housing market.

I told *Bloomberg*: The $200 billion lending program "is really bad for the dollar; the Fed is now practicing junk economics." The Fed agreed to accept ersatz AAA rated paper in exchange for treasuries, and the rating agencies now had further incentive not to downgrade these securities. The problem is lack of trust in the underlying collateral. The problem goes right back to the mortgage market and leveraged corporate loans on investment banks' balance sheets. The Fed swept the problem under the rug by taking the collateral. "This is a bailout of the rich . . . You are worried about recession? *You should be terrified about inflation.* Inflation is the great destroyer" The Fed is *counterfeiting* dollars, but we call it debasing the currency because the Fed is behind it instead of gangsters.[45]

Bruce Foerster, president of South Beach Capital Markets, told Bloomberg Television that the publicly traded large investment banks and commercial banks are a "national asset."[46] A commodity trader in Chicago heard Foerster's comments "Bear Stearns," he said, ". . . a 'national asset' *Gag!*"

I observed that large investment banks had failed before; for example, Drexel Burnham Lambert went bankrupt in the 1980s. In the 1990s GE made a quick sale of its troubled Kidder Peabody holdings to Paine Webber. Let it happen. Jim Rogers, head of Rogers Holdings, asserts that a bear market cleans out the system, and it is good for capitalism and the markets. Bear Stearns was the fifth largest investment bank in the United States. If you believe the Fed's excuse that the whole system is so fragile that will fall apart if Bear Stearns goes under, what happens when one of the *larger* investment banks goes under? The Federal Reserve is using up its balance sheet. It will have no weapons in its arsenal for the next time.[47]

By the weekend, Bear Stearns was looking for a rescuer. Warren Buffett turned down a request to lead the rescue. He could not evaluate Bear Stearns in one weekend, and he didn't have enough capital.[48] Alan Schwartz later told Jamie Dimon that Bear Stearns directors wanted a double-digit bid because there was a "psychological limit."[49] Warren studied under Graham, who would probably advise that emotional directors should not set a stock price any more than the emotional Mr. Market should set the price at which an investor buys or sells. A low price does not mean a company is trading at fair value, and *not even Warren Buffett can come up with a value on these hard-to-price assets in that period of time.*

JPMorgan Chase bought Bear Stearns with some assistance from the Federal Reserve. Now JPMorgan Chase has to decode Bear Stearns's $400 billionish balance sheet including mortgage backed securities valued at $56 billion.[50] No matter how one spins this, JPMorgan Chase bought a pig in a poke, and it is not in the interest of the health of the financial system for banks to be forced to operate that way.

Since Bear Stearns was so highly leveraged, the stock was probably worth zero, and it was unclear if all of the creditors of Bear Stearns would be paid in full. Those who later talked about the "value" of the Bear Stearn's headquarters building may not have realized that in bankruptcy, sales of all of Bear Stearns's assets—including the building—might not have covered its debts. Creditors would probably have had to write off bad debts, and there would be nothing leftover for shareholders.

Even if every Bear Stearns investment banker hocked their jewelry and watches, it probably wouldn't be enough. That is the nature of leverage.

It would have looked bad if Jamie Dimon bid, say *a penny* or a dollar for Bear Stearns's stock, so JPMorgan Chase bid $2. This was still probably $2 too high, but if it wanted to take control, Dimon had to possess the shares. Jamie Dimon told Congress: "We could not and would not have assumed the substantial risks of acquiring Bear Stearns without the $30 billion facility provided by the Fed. . . . We are acquiring some $360 billion of Bear Stearns assets and liabilities. The notion that Bear Stearns' riskiest assets have been placed in the $30 billion Fed facility is simply not true. And if there is ever a loss on the assets pledged to the Fed, the first $1 billion of that loss will be borne by JPMorgan alone."[51] As part of the deal, the Federal Reserve agreed to take $30 billion of Bear Stearns's securities, and JPMorgan Chase put up only $1 billion as security (at 3.3 percent, this is less than the margin the Fed proposed for its lending program). However, if the price of the assets declined, JPMorgan Chase could walk away. Were the assets already overvalued? Who knows? As Dimon himself said: "Buying a house is not the same thing as buying a house on fire."[52, 53] The Fed did not provide the necessary transparency for anyone on the outside to offer an independent opinion. JPMorgan Chase may have paid $1 billion for the right to put potentially overvalued and deteriorating assets to the Fed. Within three months the Fed admitted that if it used market prices, JPMorgan Chase's $1 billion would be history and the Fed itself had a loss.[54]

The deal temporarily went sideways after JPMorgan Chase discovered it had inadvertently given away a valuable option for free. Buried in the 74-page agreement brokered and partially financed by the Fed was a clause putting JPMorgan on the hook to finance Bear Stearns's trades for a year, whether or not shareholders accepted the deal. In the end, JPMorgan Chase increased its bid from $2 per share to $10 per share (or $2.2 billion—not counting the $1 billion at risk that JPMorgan put up as collateral to the Fed) and the shareholders approved the deal. By the end of May 2008, Bear Stearns was no more.[55, 56]

Was the bailout necessary? It is convenient that supporters cannot prove their case, and I cannot prove mine, either. But I can hypothesize. If Bear Stearns failed, the banking system could have bid on Bear Stearns's derivatives books just as it did when Drexel went under. The system may have purchased cheaper assets if Bear Stearns had gone bankrupt. While temporarily painful, once the system trusted each other's prices, easier trading might have resumed. I am much more worried about the inflationary consequences of the balooning bailouts.

Was the purchase of Bear Stearns a good idea for JPMorgan Chase? The rushed weekend purchase of a highly leveraged company led to a costly mistake and is the same thing as buying a bag of mystery meat. JPMorgan Chase looked in the bag, and it is still trying to figure out what it is. It seems to me that JPMorgan Chase overpaid, and Jamie Dimon seemed a bit testy afterwards. When Vikram Pandit, Citigroup's CEO, asked a question about long-term guarantees during a conference call, Jamie said: "Stop being such a jerk."[57] *This is when I first realized that Jamie and I graduated from the same charm school.*

When Dimon testified before Congress, he might have used more balanced candor about Bear Stearns. Specifically, it might have been *better* for the financial system to let Bear Stearns fail. Within two months JPMorgan revised its estimates of merger-related costs 50 percent upward to $9 billion. Richard "Dick" Bove of Laden Burg Thalmann & Co. said that Bear Stearns would not add to JPMorgan's profits and Bear "should have gone bankrupt," noting it has a nice office building in Manhattan—"big deal."[58]

On June 16, 2008, JPMorgan stated that Bear Stearns is worth more than the $10 per share it paid.[59] But financial firms can trade at single digits during recessions. Salomon Brothers had a saying: "Our assets ride down the elevator at night," meaning the people that generate the fees, make the trades, and attract the *customers.* Bear Stearns lost customers (in addition to employees). Given the opacity of investment banking products, there is no reason to accept JPMorgan's claim at face value. Suppose it were true that Bear Stearns was worth more than $10 per share (and I can fly). That is all the more reason the Fed should not bail out an investment bank. In bankruptcy, everyone has a chance to bid on the assets and the net result may net shareholders more.

If, however, Bear Stearns' stock was worth zero, it still doesn't make sense to bail it out. Bear Stearns would go into bankruptcy and JPMorgan Chase could have cherry picked the assets and paid less. If Dimon were after Bear Stearns' employees, they would have been ripe for hire.

I find my theories more plausible than the *Apocalypse Now* story the Fed told to Congress, but now we will never know.

Was Warren Buffett even tempted by Bear Stearns? I do not know for certain, but I have a point of view. On September 27, 2007, *BusinessWeek's* Matt Goldstein asked me if I had seen a *New York Times* article suggesting that Warren Buffett was considering the purchase of a stake in Bear Stearns. The original article stated that "Mr. Buffett did not return telephone calls seeking a comment."[60] It did not surprise me; *it is hard to talk and laugh at the same time.* Goldstein was not suggesting I had a particular reason to know, it was just that everyone was talking about it. Many news outlets picked up the viral rumor and CNBC aired at least five segments that day on the rumor that Buffett was a potential buyer.[61]

I told Goldstein that I had no way of knowing for sure, but *heck no.*

Chapter 10

Bazooka Hank and Dread Reckoning (AIG, Fannie, Freddie, Lehman, Merrill, and Other Fluid Situations)

If they sell five percent of it, they'll get the market price.
—Warren Buffett
to Janet Tavakoli, August 10, 2007

B efore the fall of 2007, few besides Warren Buffett, John Paulson (Paulson & Co.), Bill Ackman (Pershing Square), David Einhorn (Greenlight Capital), Jim Rogers (Rogers Holdings), and I specifically challenged investment banks' prices of complex structured products. On August 9, 2007, I told CNBC that "when you get truthiness in lending you get truthiness in pricing." Even with corporate leveraged loans, there is "too much foam and too little beer."[1] Many AAA rated money market investments were losing money because they were backed by CDOs backed by subprime loans. Becky Quick of CNBC asked who is vulnerable, and I responded just about every investor: hedge funds, REITs, insurance company investment portfolios, mutual funds, and money market funds might lose money.

The next day, I challenged American International Group Inc.'s (AIG) accounting, after it told analysts it did not need to show a loss (reflecting a change in market prices) on its credit derivatives portfolio for its second quarter ending June 30, 2007. Yet, accounting practices required AIG to mark to market its portfolio using market prices or a close approximation to market prices. The rule did not say *only if you feel like it*. AIG seemed to take the position that (1) nothing like this is currently trading, so there is no market price; and (2) AIG would never have to make any cash payments because its portfolio was so "safe." Accounting gives one a lot of room to make reasonable assumptions, but how could AIG say nothing had changed?

For example, AIG wrote credit default protection on a whopping *$19.2 billion* "safe" investment that had exposure to subprime loans (a super-senior tranche of a CDO backed by BBB rated tranches—the lowest rating that is still investment grade—of residential mortgage-backed securities, and these were backed by a significant amount of subprime loans. By August 2007, the prices of the collateral backing the super senior had tanked.)[2] Anyone who buys insurance knows that even if you are "safe," if you are in a high-risk category, your cost of insurance goes up. If AIG were to pay someone to take over its insurance-like obligation, AIG would have to pay more than it had received, and AIG should have shown this as a loss.

AIG's stance seemed bizarre given that five insurance executives from AIG and Berkshire Hathaway's Gen Re Corp (even Warren Buffett cannot control every action of every employee) were under investigation (and eventually found guilty) of conspiracy to inflate AIG's reserves and mislead investors about AIG's earnings.[3]

I told Dave Reilly at the *Wall Street Journal*: "There's no way these aren't showing a loss."[4] That is simply a market reality. *This is Wall Street speak for:* In my humble opinion, you are a big fat liar. AIG responded: "We disagree."[5] *That is Wall Street speak for:* No, YOU are a big fat liar!

Before Dave Reilly wrote his article, he talked to experts, including me, for background. Then he called AIG to ask them for their thinking. AIG stood firm. Then Reilly called me again. He didn't want the *Wall Street Journal* to look stupid, but told me, "they pay me to go out on a limb." He said he needed me to go on the record. It would make the article more forceful. I did not think that AIG would tell Reilly: *You know, you have a point, maybe we should recheck our homework,* but I did not anticipate arguing with AIG in the *Wall Street Journal's* "Heard on the Street" column. I hesitated. AIG, a large global conglomerate, has the resources to crush me like a bug. On the other hand, *I am not fat.* I finally agreed to go on the record.

By June 2008, AIG recorded two back-to-back quarters of its largest losses ever. AIG took more than $20 billion in write-downs on its derivative positions through the first quarter of 2008; net losses for the fourth quarter of 2007 were $5.3 billion, and in the first quarter of 2008, AIG reported losses of $7.8 billion. In February 2008, its auditor said it found "material weakness"[6] in AIG's accounting. Eli Broad, a billionaire real estate baron, Shelby Davis of Davis Selected Advisers LP, and Bill Miller of Legg Mason Inc., were AIG shareholders controlling 4 percent of the company (more than 100 million shares). These already accomplished men may have a hidden talent. Apparently, they can read my mind. These shareholders wanted changes in senior management and a *new* CEO, and they wrote AIG's board: "The facts presented . . . preclude any individual who was in a position of significant responsibility and oversight during the last three years from having the credibility to lead this company on a permanent basis."[7] *That is shareholder speak for:* We are not calling those responsible for oversight big fat liars, we are just saying they have no credibility.

By the summer of 2008, more than nine months after the August 2007 *Wall Street Journal* story, the Slumbering Esquire's Club (also known as the SEC) and the Department of Justice were investigating whether AIG had overstated the value of its credit derivatives exposure to subprime mortgages.[8] In the summer of 2007, the SEC might have questioned *everyone's* accounting. Well, not everyone's—just several large investment banks and various other entities that the SEC regulates.

Likewise, OFHEO, then regulator of Freddie Mac could have questioned Freddie's accounting. In 2004, David A. Andrukonis, then chief risk officer for Freddie Mac, was concerned about Freddie's purchases of bad mortgage loans. He told then CEO Richard Syron that the loans would probably "pose an enormous financial and reputational risk to the company and the country."[9] While taking on more risk was bad enough, the Department of Treasury reviewed Freddie's books in preparation for a bailout and concluded in September 2008 that its capital cushion had been overstated by Freddie Mac's accounting methods.[10]

On July 15, 2008, ex-Goldman Sachs banker and then Treasury Secretary Henry ("Hank") Paulson asked Congress for the authority to buy stakes in Fannie Mae and Freddie Mac. Paulson asserted: "If you have a bazooka in your pocket, and people know you have a bazooka, you may never have to take it out."[11] In my experience, boasting about a big bazooka just tempts the curious to see how you measure up in exciting circumstances, and the person to do that might be named Mr. Gross. Bill Gross manages the Pimco Total Return Fund, the world's largest bond fund with large exposures to Fannie Mae and Freddie Mac (and AIG along with a number of investment banks as of September 2008). Gross is a fan of Fed intervention, and his investments reflected it. His fund reportedly gained $1.7 billion after the U.S. government took over Fannie Mae and Freddie Mac on Sept 7, 2008.[12] Fannie Mae and Freddie Mac were placed in conservatorship to be run by their new regulator, the Federal Housing Finance Agency (FHFA) headed by James Lockhart, the same gentleman that headed up their former regulator, OFHEO. What was the thinking on choosing Mr. Lockhart—*let's give him another chance, because he cannot possibly do a worse job than he did before?* The Treasury may purchase up to $200 billion of stock, dividends were suspended (long overdue in my opinion), and the CEOs were replaced. Both Fannie Mae and Freddie Mac were removed from the S&P 500 on September 9.[13] Herb Allison, a former CEO of TIAA-CREF, will head Fannie Mae. David Moffett, retired vice chairman and chief financial officer of U.S. Bancorp, became the CEO of Freddie Mac. Mr. Moffett was most recently a senior advisor to the Carlyle Group.[14, 15] *Business as usual in Washington.*

In September 2008, AIG's problems grew worse. One of the reasons AIG may have initially resisted showing losses on its credit derivatives positions is that price declines triggered a need for more cash to meet collateral calls from AIG's trading counterparties. Warren was right. Credit derivatives are weapons of mass *liquidity* destruction. By the end of July 31, 2008, the company that refuted my August 2007 assertion that it had risk from credit derivatives, had already put up $16.5 billion in collateral. To paraphrase Warren, *AIG sucked its thumb in 2007.* AIG was in the midst of a strategic review and had set its deadline at September 25, 2008.[16] The Fed took over AIG on September 15.

Moody's rated AIG Aa2 at the beginning of May 2008, and downgraded it to Aa3, the lowest double-A rating, on May 22, 2008. In early September 2008, AIG's rating neared single-A territory. AIG had lived in denial for more than a year. It had failed to sell assets to raise the cash it needed to face additional margin calls (triggered by the downgrade) of $14.5 billion. AIG has valuable assets, but the assets are illiquid and AIG was short of cash. On September 15, 2008, AIG was downgraded to single-A. AIG asked the Fed for a loan. When the Fed resisted, it sought a $75 billion loan from Goldman Sachs and JPMorgan Chase.[17] No dice.

Goldman Sachs said its exposure to AIG is not material.[18] Of course, it wouldn't be if Goldman's trades have collateral triggers (or if it bought credit default swap protection on AIG). A better question is, what is the combined trading, insurance and reinsurance exposure of Bazooka Hank's old firm if AIG did not have to pony up so much of its cash and if Goldman had no default protection on AIG? *Is it material?* JPMorgan is one of the largest credit derivatives traders in the world, and with its acquisition of Bear Stearns, it was probably the largest. AIG sold credit default protection on $441 billion of assets to a number of European and U.S. counterparties. If AIG could not make good on its promises, it would affect the entire financial community.[19] The technical term for this is *systemic risk.* In this case it is the result of *global financial institutions doing foolish things at the same time.*

The Fed changed its mind and decided to give AIG the loan after all. Although the Fed never regulated AIG, it agreed to provide AIG with a $85 billion credit line for two years (similar to a credit card with an $85 billion limit – *wouldn't you just love one of those?*) in exchange for interest payments and stock warrants (the right to buy, under certain conditions, up to 79.9 percent of AIG). The Fed will end up controlling a private insurer *with the help of U.S. taxpayer dollars.*[20] What gave the Fed the right to do that? It invoked an obscure rule under section 13(3) of the Federal Reserve Act with the full support of Bazooka Hank's Treasury Department, just as it did when it helped JPMorgan Chase purchase Bear Stearns.[21] The new Wall Street speak for institutions like AIG that have illiquidity problems requiring intervention is that the "situation is fluid." It remains to be seen how successful the Fed will be in stabilizing and making a profit (or loss) from AIG.

Bill Gross's Pimco Total Return Fund had sold $760 million of default guarantees (as credit default swaps) on AIG, and it would have cost him if AIG went under.[22] Mr. Gross might have thought he had a good idea of how the Fed would behave. Pimco had hired Alan Greenspan as a consultant.[23] I was not surprised when Bill Gross said the Fed intervention was a "necessary step."[24]

AIG seemed to have lost the plot on its cash needs, especially those linked to CDOs. In April of 2008, Warren told a group of University of Pennsylvania students that when it comes to CDOs, "Nobody knows what the hell they're doing. It's ridiculous."[25]

Accountants do not seem to know what they are doing, either.

*   *   *

Accountants allow corporations to put assets into three "levels." The "level" indicates how easy it is for someone to check your work, with Level 1 being the easiest. Level 2 requires you to accept assumptions that you can supposedly recreate with enough hard work and data. *Do you have several hundred thousand dollars and an army of geeks?* Level 3 requires you to trust management assumptions that you cannot see and they do not disclose—it is reminiscent of teenage boys at their first prom: *trust me, I will love you in the morning.*

Level 1 is mark-to-market-based on observable market prices. For example, if you own stocks, you can find the prices very easily online.

It is easy to calculate the value of your stocks every day. This is what accountants mean by mark-to-market. Since it is easy to do and anyone can check your work, it is *transparent*.

Level 2 is mark to model. Prices are based on models using observable assumptions. Accounting gives you some room to make assumptions. You cannot easily find prices in the market on many CDOs. You can debate mark-to-model prices. For instance, the creditors of BSAM challenged the April 2007 prices of the two hedge funds. Since management can control the assumptions, even with "observable" inputs, Level 2 can be "mark to myth."

Level 3 accounting allows management to come up with prices based on models using *unobservable* inputs. In the absence of any other disclosure, I consider Level 3 purely mark to myth. It is a black box. *You have no evidence that management is leveling with you.*

Benjamin Graham put it another way. The formulas may be precise, but the assumptions may be self-serving and can be used "to justify practically any value .. however high."[26]

FASB board member Donald Young says that mark-to-market accounting is "most valuable"[27] when markets are tough. If prices decline, it signals investors that assets are under stress. If managers make up their own estimates instead of marking-to-market, it can be "mark-to-management"[28] or as Warren Buffett says again, it can be "mark to myth."[29] If companies think prices will recover in the future, they can explain it in their regular reports (the regulatory filings with the SEC).

In August 2007, Warren told me that if financial institutions sell 5 percent of their position, they will get the market price, and it will still be a higher price than they would get if they tried to sell 100 percent of a large illiquid position. He laughed as he added: "No one wants to do that." In September 2007, *Fortune* reported that some financial institutions might appear healthy, but leveraged institutions might actually be insolvent if they marked-to-market instead of marked to model. "Many institutions," Warren said, "that publicly report precise market values for their holdings or [sic] CDOs are in truth reporting fiction," adding "I'd give a lot to mark my weight to 'model' rather than to 'market.'"[30] Warren explained that selling 5 percent of their positions would reflect reality. I wrote Warren that I call this *Warren Buffett's Five Percent Solution*. He wrote back: "In the print edition of *Fortune* they changed

"of" to "or" in the first sentence, though I got it corrected online."
I responded: "I am usually fast and accurate, but rarely impeccable and
precise." *He sets a high bar.*

The SEC seemed to have another idea. The last weekend in
March 2008 (a couple of weeks after the Fed said it would exchange
AAA assets for Treasuries), the SEC's Division of Corporate Finance
issued a letter that could have been called *Retroactive Amnesty for Potential
Alleged Accounting Fraud.* The letter concerned public companies and
disclosure issues they "may wish to consider"[31] when preparing their
regulatory filings. It said that under current (tough) market conditions,
public companies might be required to use models with "significant
unobservable inputs"[32] So, as of January 1, 2008, the companies could
put those assets in a black box (Level 3).

The SEC appeared to override the accounting board. Since when
does the SEC interpret accounting rules that contradict public pro-
nouncements by FASB? Yet the SEC seemed to encourage investment
banks to classify more assets as "Level 3." Classify they did. For example, in
early May 2008, Goldman Sachs Group Inc. announced that for its fiscal
quarter ending in February, it increased its Level 3 assets by 39 percent or
by more than $27 billion. It had $96.4 billion in assets sitting in its Level
3 accounting bucket. Morgan Stanley had $78.2 billion in assets sitting in
its Level 3 accounting bucket. Merrill Lynch announced that its mark-
to-myth assets increased from $48.6 billion at the end of 2007 to $82.4
billion for the first quarter ending March 31, 2008 (Merrill is on a different fiscal calendar), an increase of 70 percent.[33] The list goes on. Merrill
Lynch's new CEO, John Thain, brought in 51-year-old Tom Montag from
his old Goldman Sachs stomping grounds to head up global trading for
around $40 million.[34] Wouldn't you think that for that kind of money,
Merrill could disclose their assumptions?

How could one value Merrill Lynch, Lehman, or any of the other
investment banks? How could anyone trust their numbers?

Lehman announced a probable loss for second quarter 2008 of $2.8
billion, the first loss since going public in 1994. It came as no surprise
when Lehman said it might boost its Level 3 assets. It raised $12 billion
in new capital between February and the end of May, and said it would
raise $6 billion in new equity diluting shareholder equity by 30 percent.
Through sales, it reduced leverage from 31.7 times to 25 times. It sold

$130 billion in assets (*but it did not specify how it sold all of those assets so quickly or to whom*).[35]

Richard "Dick" Fuld, the 62-year-old then CEO, was a Lehman lifer. In December 1983, when Fuld was chief of trading operations, he made a presentation to Lehman's board as it met over lunch to assess capital needs. Richard Bingham asked Fuld how he had made money in his trading operations the previous five years and how he would make it the next five. Fund responded: "I don't know how I made it over the last five years."[36] Fuld added he had hired people "to study how we're going to do it over the next several years."[37] An appalled Bingham asked how long that would take. Fuld responded: "Two years."[38] *I wonder if Fuld completed the study.*

The SEC quickly moved to give the appearance it was on top of things. After all, we wouldn't want another debacle like Bear Stearns, would we? The SEC said it would require Wall Street to report its liquidity levels and its capital starting later in 2008. The SEC wants disclosures "in terms that the market can readily understand . . ."[39] *Oh, really? About that letter the SEC sent in March. . . .* That ship has sailed. After financial institutions stuff tens of billions of dollars worth of assets into a black box (Level 3 accounting buckets), how is the market supposed to readily understand? The Federal Reserve Bank, the new liquidity provider for Wall Street, seemed to have no idea of what was going on, either. The American taxpayer should ask for a refund for the money allocated to keep the SEC in operation. It makes one wonder just what it would take to get Christopher Cox booted out and have a thorough housecleaning at the SEC.

I do not as a rule weigh in on quarterly earnings statements, but I will occasionally volunteer my views just to keep making the point. I had publicly challenged AIG's writedowns in August 2007, Merrill's in early October 2007, and challenged Citigroup's reported numbers in January 2008. I told the *Wall Street Journal* that Citigroup might need $3.3 billion more in write-downs on its "super safe super senior" positions to reflect market prices. That would have increased Citigroup's overall write-down due to subprime from $18 billion to $24 billion. Citigroup raised new capital that diluted shareholder equity by 10 percent. In the new world of financial topseyturveydom, *diluting shareholder equity was touted as a good thing.*[40, 41] Warren aims to *preserve* shareholder value.

Oppenheimer's bank analyst Meredith Whitney wrote a report on October 31, 2007, saying that Citigroup's dividend exceeded its profits, saying, "it was the easiest call I ever made."[42] Since that Halloween day in 2007, Wall Street has been paying closer attention to Meredith Whitney's reports. It seemed to take more than a month before other Wall Street analysts woke up to the problem. Bear Stearns' bank analyst David Hilder thought her concerns were overstated. He was wrong, of course. *Where did Bear Stearns find these guys?*

Citigroup's losses continued to mount. As of October 2008, Citigroup's subprime-related write-downs are $60.8 billion.[43] Vikram Pandit had been CEO of Citigroup just over a month when the numbers I challenged were reported. Pandit cofounded Old Lane Partners in 2006 and sold it to Citigroup in July 2007 for $800 million. His personal take for his share was $165 million, but he plowed $100.3 million of it back into the fund. By June of 2008, Citigroup shut it down. The *Wall Street Journal* reported the fund "has been dogged by mediocre returns and the loss of its top managers." Old Lane had raised $4 billion from investors and borrowed $5 billion more. Citigroup agreed to take $9 billion of assets onto its balance sheet after writing down $202 million. Whatever you may think of Pandit's qualifications to lead Citigroup, it seems he knows how to time a sale.[44]

Lehman was not so lucky with its sales; it could not raise cash when it needed it. Many questioned Lehman's accounting. David Einhorn of Greenlight Capital had publicly questioned Lehman's first quarter accounting numbers. Lehman reported a $489 million "profit" and only took a $200 million gross write-down on $6.5 billion on its holdings of asset backed securities. Einhorn complained that (among other things) Lehman did not disclose its significant CDO exposure until more than 3 weeks later when Lehman filed its 10Q (a required financial report).[45] In October 2008, Lehman and Tishman Speyer engineered a $22.2 billion leveraged buyout of Archstone, an apartment developer. *Fortune* said Dick Fuld declined to talk to it for months and it seemed to *Fortune* that the Archstone deal had losses almost from the start.[46]

Richard Fuld tried to sell a stake in his separate asset management unit to stay afloat. He was unsuccessful. Lehman Brothers worked during the weekend of September 13 and 14 with a group of potential buyers. Bankers wanted the Fed to participate, but the Fed refused. Bankers fretted about how they would unwind (sell out) their derivatives trades with Lehman. On Monday, September 15, 2008, Lehman Brothers Holdings Inc., a 158 year-old firm, filed for bankruptcy. It is still alive in the minds of its creditors, since they will not know what they have left until Lehman's assets are finally liquidated.[47, 48] Hedge funds that used Lehman Brothers as their prime broker found "their" assets temporarily frozen. Like many other prime brokers, Lehman had provided financing for hedge funds to purchase assets, and now it was not clear whether Lehman or a hedge fund owned a particular asset. Like creditors, Lehman's hedge fund customers will have to wait until the mess is sorted out. Warren had been correct in warning that the leverage unwind would be painful, and it seemed hedge funds and investment banks failed to imagine all the ways it could cause pain.

John Thain as CEO of Merrill Lynch recognized that a Lehman bankruptcy could have negative implications for Merrill. He and Ken Lewis, Bank of America's CEO, hammered out an agreement, and on September 14, a Sunday night, Bank of America Corp. agreed to purchase Merrill Lynch & Co. in an all-stock deal for $29 per share (at the time of the announcement worth about $50 billion), a premium to its closing price the previous Friday. The combined firm will be a behemoth if the deal closes as planned in early 2009. Bank of America will get a broader global reach; Merrill's huge wealth management business; a huge trading operation; a prime brokerage business; and around half of Blackrock, an investment manager with $1.4 trillion under management.[49] The Fed said it did not participate in a bailout, but it expanded its lending facility just after Lehman declared bankruptcy. It would take a wider variety of securities including *equities.*

In August 2008, Warren told me he read every page of Lehman's financial report. In March of 2008, Warren told me he had been approached about helping Bear Stearns, but he could not come up with a value in a weekend (and did not have $60 billion in capital). He expanded on that to the students from the University of Pennsylvania when he said that bailing out Bear Stearns "took some guts that I didn't want to match."[50] The balance sheets of the investment banks are so difficult to figure out that one cannot tell whether one is getting a good deal.

Pimco's Bill Gross found there is a limit to the Fed's largesse, and his Lehman investment lost money. In March, Bear Stearns, the *fifth* largest investment bank, was deemed too big to fail, but the Fed refused to help Lehman, the *fourth* largest investment bank. As Jim Rogers predicted, larger investment banks than Bear Stearns had problems, and the Fed had other problems besides investment banks—Fannie, Freddie, and AIG. Pimco's investments were only partially protected by the Fed. The Total Return Fund's return slumped, and it will be interesting to see if Gross ends up a net winner or a net loser as the market struggles for balance.

Jamie Dimon, JPMorgan Chase's CEO, bought Bear Stearns, and Ken Lewis, Bank of America's CEO, bought Merrill Lynch. Did either of them get a good deal? Did both of them get good deals? Who got the better deal? Ken Lewis certainly passed up Jamie Dimon in size, but only time will tell how this plays out. For my part, it seems that Ken Lewis is the more underestimated of the two.

In May 2003, I heard both CEOs give luncheon speeches at the Federal Reserve's Conference on Bank Structure and Supervision. Jamie spoke the day before Ken Lewis. Jamie dressed in a light suit and spoke rapidly, sounding as if he had just drunk a pot of coffee. He seemed to suggest he had solved all of the problems at Bank One in the vein of a public relations speech (this predated its merger with JPMorgan Chase). He seemed uncomfortable with silence. In between questions the microphone was passed around for a few seconds. Jamie added to his already complete answers, and it seemed an attempt to fill dead air. The next day Ken Lewis spoke. He wore a conservative dark blue suit with a flag pin in his lapel. His grooming was impeccable. His speech flowed. Unlike Jamie, he spoke about corporate governance, the topic at hand. He gave clear and balanced reasons why (contrary to popular wisdom) it made sense in Bank of America's case for him to occupy the position of both chairman and CEO. Ken Lewis left me with the impression that he is a very ambitious man who comes prepared. He did not underestimate his audience.

Perhaps these CEOs have a better crystal ball than Warren Buffett and I. The list of accounting distortions seems endless,[51, 52, 53] but the key is to understand business fundamentals first, and then consider what the accounting statements imply.

By October 2008, J.P. Morgan acquired Bear Stearns and Washington Mutual; BofA acquired Merrill; and Wells Fargo acquired Wachovia. Morgan Stanley and Goldman Sachs became bank holding companies. The Treasury invested tens of billions of dollars in each. AIG got a bail-out. Lehman was bankrupt. The situation is fluid. Meanwhile, Berkshire Hathaway has limited debt (leverage) and a lot of cash.

* * *

Starting around 1980, Berkshire Hathaway's *nonreported (undistributed) earnings* from the ownership of equities exceeded *reporting earnings* generated by the business it owns. That means there is a lot of hidden value that does not show up on accounting statements. Earnings and return on equity are important measures, but the *intrinsic value* of the company is the key.

Today, investors can purchase low-fee index funds, so a reasonable benchmark is the S&P 500. Each year, Berkshire Hathaway compares its performance with the S&P 500. Warren Buffett and Charlie Munger strive to increase intrinsic value, the true value including value that is obscured by accounting statements. They say that if they cannot beat the S&P that way, then they are not doing anything an investor cannot do on his or her own.

So far long-term Berkshire Hathaway investors, including me, have been delighted. No one can predict future performance, but long-term investors continue to hold their stock. Not only does Berkshire Hathaway invest in stocks and pieces of companies, many of the companies owned by Berkshire Hathaway also invest. If Berkshire Hathaway owns less than 20 percent (accounting rules are subject to change, so this percentage is just an example) of a company, it does not have to include (consolidate) the company's earnings on Berkshire Hathaway's balance sheet, even when this represents a huge wealth increase.

In 1990, Berkshire Hathaway owned 17 percent of Capital Cities/ABC, Inc. (Capital Cities). Berkshire Hathaway's share of Capital Cities earnings was $83 million, but Capital Cities retained more than $82 million (of Berkshire Hathaway's earnings) for future growth. Berkshire Hathaway only got about $530,000 net after-tax dividends. According to *generally accepted accounting principle* (GAAP), Berkshire Hathaway only had to record the dividends as earnings, so it recorded $530,000 (not $83 million). If Capital Cities/ABC, Inc. sounds unfamiliar to you that may be because Disney bought it in 1995[54] Berkshire Hathaway sold its holdings in Disney a few years after the takeover. *Warren's favorite holding period may be forever, but that does not mean he will hold something he no longer favors forever.*

Berkshire Hathaway prefers to purchase companies that generate earnings that do not have to be reported. If Berkshire Hathaway buys an entire business, Berkshire Hathaway must report the earnings. Sometimes, however, Berkshire Hathaway can acquire a minority interest in a company more cheaply (on a pro rata basis) than it would have paid for the entire company. Furthermore, Berkshire Hathaway does not have to report the earnings for the minority interest. The price is a relative bargain, and the unreported earnings should eventually become capital gains. In turn, the capital gains will increase Berkshire Hathaway's intrinsic value.

When Berkshire Hathaway acquires a company or part of a company, it looks for good managers. If the stock price falls below the value of the business the managers should buy back the stock. If the price is above the business value, however, managers will either (1) retain earnings if they can increase market value by a dollar for every dollar of earnings they retain; or (2) if they cannot do that, they should pay dividends. Good managers know these finance basics and follow them.

Accounting also misleads when it comes to the stock price that is recorded on the books (the carrying price). Berkshire Hathaway's subsidiaries may carry value at one price, while Berkshire Hathaway itself carries the same stock on its book at another price. Again, that is legal and proper accounting.

Highly leveraged investment banks stuff tens of billions of dollars worth of assets into black boxes (Level 3 accounting) and use other methods to avoid showing market prices for assets (hold-to-maturity portfolios). The investment banks may have hidden problems. *Investment banks may be worth less than their accounting reports suggest.* In contrast, Berkshire Hathaway has *hidden value.* Berkshire Hathaway does not report retained earnings or capital gains on long-term investments unless the investments are sold.

Berkshire Hathaway reports fluctuations in market prices of its derivatives, however. Berkshire Hathaway took a loss on derivatives in 2007 and in first quarter 2008. Berkshire Hathaway's invested $4.88 billion in premiums (up from $4.5 billion at the end of 2007) for puts it wrote on equity indexes, and the first payment—in the unlikely event one ever comes due—is 2019. Berkshire Hathaway took a mark-to-market loss it can afford, a write-down of $1.7 billion in the first quarter of 2008. Magen Marcus, a medical doctor who has been a Berkshire Hathaway shareholder for five years, called them "unrealized losses."[55] *He is an informed shareholder.* In his 2007 shareholder letter, Warren told us that he and Charlie Munger are not concerned about the price fluctuations: "even though they could easily amount to $1 billion or more in a quarter—and we hope you won't be either."[56] They are willing to cope with reported earnings volatility "in the short run for greater gains in net worth in the long run."[57]

Berkshire Hathaway does not chase revenues for the sake of revenues; the price must be right. When rating agencies suggested that Berkshire Hathaway should increase insurance revenues to maintain its AAA rating, Warren told me he rejected their premise. Berkshire Hathaway is happy to do nothing when the risk is not priced correctly, but many insurance companies did not feel the same way. This critical difference led to an opportunity for Warren Buffett he never sought. An insurance regulator knocked on Berkshire Hathaway's door when it needed help.

Chapter 11

Bond Insurance Burns Main Street

You have been writing some terrific stuff. I send it along to Ajit and he's now a big fan.

—Warren Buffett
to Janet Tavakoli, January 3, 2008

When he was in his twenties, Warren Buffett put three-quarters of his money (around $10,000) into property and casualty insurer GEICO, and reaped a healthy profit. Since then, he has been keenly interested in insurance opportunities. The credit crisis dropped an opportunity in Berkshire Hathaway's lap.

As Bear Stearns and the Carlyle fund struggled for their survival on March 12, 2008, news about bond insurance was not a highlight, but it should have been. In what would become an ugly pattern, one of the bond insurers that had been AAA at the start of 2008 was downgraded several grades (by Fitch), and it filed a lawsuit in an attempt to nullify a nearly $2 billion guaranty.[1]

Bond insurers traditionally provided credit enhancement for municipal bonds needed to fund roads, schools, water treatment plants, and many other necessary public works. Now bond insurers are an integral part of the credit bubble problem. Most of the bond insurers (or *monolines*[2]) have exposure to subprime home equity loans or troubled loans bundled in risky securitizations. Most bond insurers have done dicey deals dirt cheap. Most of them need more money. It is as if they offered hurricane insurance on homes and insured everyone in Florida without enough money to cover potential obligations. Instead of insuring homes, the insurers were insuring bonds without enough money to cover the potential obligations or to keep their AAA ratings. Their folly affects the average American taxpayer and many retail accounts.

Bond insurers provide guarantees for municipal bonds, which often have very long maturities. The interest rate is set at periodic auctions, and these auction-rate securities (ARS) were sold as if they have been like a cash instrument or a money market instrument. The same day in March 2007 when the bond insurer filed its lawsuit, I was in New York. I met with the CEO of a large foreign manufacturing company. He told me he was suing the investment bank that sold his cash manager more than $10 million in auction-rate municipal bonds guaranteed by a bond insurer. "[The investment bank] told him it is the same as cash." By February 2008, around 70 percent of the $330 billion auction-rate securities market for municipalities, student loans, and colleges failed when investment banks and banks stopped bidding for the "insured" bonds that investors wanted to sell (or did not want to buy).

Usually auction-rate bonds are bought and sold at a prespecified short period such as every 7 or 28 days. The interest rate is determined by buyers. If the auction fails, the interest rate goes up, usually to a rate specified in the documents. In some cases, the rate for unsold bonds rises as high as 20 percent (rates vary by bond), and the investor is left holding the old bonds. Auctions have rarely failed, so the market was in a panic. Some ARS were a bargain, but that meant municipalities were paying higher interest costs solely due to the confusion. For municipalities, that means taxpayers may pay higher taxes. Municipalities struggle to find a way to refinance into reasonable fixed rate debt in the dicey market, and as of June 2008, only 25 percent have refinanced. Local tax rates may increase to cover their problems.

Banks and investment banks are hurting from lack of ready cash (liquidity) and would not buy back bonds since everyone's confidence is so shaken that it is hard for the banks to trade them. Many investors were told by their bankers that the bank would always buy the bonds if an auction failed. Many investors were told these bonds were as safe as T-bills. Investors felt scammed. Some investors did not even see a prospectus until the auctions failed. Cash management accounts across the globe ranging from large corporate clients such as Google to small condominium associations could not sell their ARS. That may not be a crisis for Google, but customers like some condominium associations could not pay their bills and have to ask condo owners for more money.

Even pension funds invested in these "AAA money market" securities. These assets are "guaranteed," but many bond insurers are in trouble, so their "guarantee" is not worth anything. In some cases the underlying assets seem sound (so the "guarantee" does not matter), but in other cases there is a genuine risk of principal loss *and the guarantee people depended on is worthless because "sophisticated" bond insurers guaranteed bad products manufactured by investment banks.* Some but not all of the top underwriters (sellers) of municipal auction-rate securities included players in the subprime market: Citigroup, UBS, Morgan Stanley, Goldman Sachs, Bear Stearns, Merrill Lynch, Wachovia, Bank of America, JPMorgan Chase, Royal Bank of Canada, and Lehman Brothers, but few of the underwriters have clean hands when it comes to this new problem. Class action suits abounded. Banks and investment banks had undisclosed conflicts of interest with their retail customers, and seemed to pass on their liquidity problems to their customers.[3, 4, 5] Many banks paid fines to settle claims with U.S. regulators and agreed to buy back ARS at full price (par) from retail clients and small businesses.[6, 7] The buy-back was unprecedented, but it did not include all customers. Larger customers are deemed to be sophisticated enough to know what they are doing, whether or not that is actually true. Those customers are usually left to work out their disputes themselves.[8]

Many of the small accounts are handled by the "retail" side of banks and investment banks. Small investors thought their banks had a fiduciary responsibility to them. Yet, it now seems as if finance has become a game of "every man for himself." In *The Spanish Prisoner,* Steve Martin plays a confidence man who advises: "Always do business as if the other person is trying to screw you because most likely they are, and if they are not, you can be pleasantly surprised." In the current financial environment, it has come to that, because regulators failed to do their jobs.

A certain and stable AAA rating is extremely valuable to any bond insurer. Investors pay for the guarantee believing it means uninterrupted cash flows and that belief means market liquidity. Even if interest rates in general rise and prices drop somewhat, the fact that one can count on cash flows makes reliable AAA bonds easier to price and trade. But if ratings are in doubt, the market freezes.

In December 2007, seven bond insurers were rated AAA. Standard & Poor's said underwriting quality for several of the bond insurers was high, but that was not true. The underwriting standards were actually naïve and bond insurers overly relied on faulty models. It was as if the rating agencies were daring the market to contradict them.[9,10] *So we did.*

William ("Bill") Ackman, head of Pershing Square Capital Management, warned the market for years that bond insurers underestimated the risk of structured finance business. Whitney Tilson, a value investor, made presentations at conferences with Bill Ackman supporting his view. David Einhorn, founder of Greenlight Capital, also made public his concerns about the overrated bond insurers. Ackman sold short the holding companies of the two largest publicly traded bond insurers, MBIA and Ambac. In 2007 he announced that he would donate his personal gains to the Pershing Square Foundation, a charity.[11] Pershing

Square's hedge funds stand to reap billions, which benefits Ackman in the long run.

Ackman took the extraordinary step of using Internet-based Open Source to post the subprime related holdings of Ambac and MBIA. He, in turn, obtained the positions from an investment bank he declined to name. Usually, outing positions is not the done thing, but in this case I heartily approve. Ackman took flack because he put out high loss numbers for the bond insurers. He tried to make his opinion transparent, but the spread sheet is a black hole of time-sucking minutiae.

Armed with Ackman's publicly available information, I simplified the analysis. According to Ackman's spreadsheet, many of the CDO positions held by Ambac and MBIA are horrifying. Most bond insurers had CDO-squared positions, with inner CDOs including constellation deals and other CDO-squareds.[12] On January 3, 2008, I wrote my clients that most of the bond insurers deserved much lower ratings, and *all* of the major bond insurers, including Ambac and MBIA—the largest insurers of municipal bonds—deserved to lose their AAA ratings.[13] This was bad news for the municipal bond market. Ambac and MBIA insure around $2 trillion in securities, and FGIC insures another $315 billion. Ambac and MBIA insure most of the public finance market including $1 trillion of U.S. "guaranteed" municipal bonds. What's more, investment banks that bought protection from bond insurers already had billions in mark-to-market losses. Investment banks would have to take losses of many billions more.

In early January 2008, I told CNBC that the bond insurers are in deep trouble: "They did the financial equivalent of insuring drunk drivers with bad driving records at the same prices as they would insure teetotalers with good driving records."[14] Management will have to go and there will have to be a restructuring. MBIA and Ambac need capital and there is a "crisis of confidence in that management."[15] CNBC's Becky Quick asked why people were surprised by something that I had been predicting for a long time. Jack Caouette, then vice chairman of MBIA, had written a blurb for my 2003 book on securitization saying *caveat emptor*—yet, the bond insurers had been careless.

CNBC contributor David Kotok, chief investment officer of Cumberland Advisors, an investor in municipal bonds (among other things), did not agree with me. He said there are "seven triple-A municipal bond insurers,"[16] and thought this was an opportunity. He said the municipal bond insurance would be fine. He seemed unaware of the ratings peril.

On January 10, 2008, MBIA paid 14 percent in interest to raise $1 billion in capital; the 10-year U.S. treasury yield was less than 4 percent.[17] The market no longer seemed to believe that MBIA was AAA rated. Warren laughed as he asked me: "Did you ever think you would see a triple-A raise money at 14 percent [with treasury rates so low]?"

In January of 2008, Eric Dinallo, the New York insurance regulator, called a meeting of investment banks to discuss the way forward for the monoline insurers. Based on market feedback, Dinallo knew the bond insurers needed capital, and cash-strapped investment banks did not want to cooperate. Dinallo, however, had more to say.

A key feature of credit derivatives is that fraud is not a defense against payment. That means that if a default occurs, both sides settle up, and if there is a problem, allegations of fraud can be litigated later. Bond insurers had done a particular type of credit derivative contract called pay-as-you-go. Dinallo pointed out it looks like an *insurance* contract, and he is an insurance regulator. According to one banker, Dinallo brought up the fact that there is an extraordinary amount of fraud associated with mortgage loans backing the deals guaranteed by the bond insurers. Dinallo suggested these were unusual circumstances.

The smarter investment banks were alarmed. If push came to shove, bond insurers might use fraud as an excuse to avoid payments, or the bond insurers might try to nullify contracts. That would mean billions of dollars of losses for the investment banks.

On January 25, 2008, I told CNBC's Joe Kernen that the underwriters (not the rating agencies) are responsible for doing due diligence, and Dinallo raised the issue of insurance and fraud. The investment banks might have to take the loans back on balance sheet, and they took Dinallo very seriously.

Charlie Gasparino asserted the rating agencies are the "culprit."[18] I responded that blaming rating agencies without mentioning the role of the underwriters is incorrect, since investment banks buy and sell the securities and are obliged to do due diligence.

Dinallo, Gasparino said, "is probably hiding under his desk," and that "what he did is completely irresponsible," referring to the bailout plan. He added that Dinallo "has a little explaining to do."[19] But Matt

Fabian of Municipal Market Advisors observed that investment banks and rating agency interests are aligned, and "the bailout plan is a pretty obvious one."[20] Fabian said the investment banks must have a problem coming up with the money.

The investment banks struggled to hold off a wave of write-downs and were dismayed by the prospect of coming up with money to help the bond insurers. The banks were worried that the bond insurers would figure out a way to get out of the contracts and all of that risk would come right back on the investment banks' balance sheets.

By the end of June 2008, MBIA and Ambac lost their AAA ratings and three other bond insurers had been downgraded from AAA to junk (below investment grade).[21] Some bond insurers sued, others investigated options to nullify contracts. But they left it too late. The bond insurers have been damaged and investment banks took more losses as they took risk back on their balance sheets. The fights will go on for years. *Eric Dinallo is not the one with a little explaining to do.*

Strong municipalities do not need guarantees from bond insurers. Besides, the guarantees are worse than worthless. In many cases, municipal bonds can get a strong investment grade rating on their own merits. During the summer of 2008, municipalities worthy of a single-A rating on their own merits—and many merited higher ratings—found their bonds would trade more easily without the guarantee. As of September 2008, the municipal bond market remained in a state of flux as Moody's announced that in about a month hence it would change the way it assigns ratings to tax-exempt borrowers. This would result in higher ratings for many municipalities, but of course, this is not an actual upgrade in quality; it is merely a relabeling.[22] By the time this book is published there may be more clarity and consistency in municipal bond ratings, but until there is, the confusion may make it more difficult for municipalities to predict their borrowing costs.

♟ ♟ ♟

When we first met, I told Warren that I am an avid Benjamin Franklin fan and have read his short autobiography several times. Warren looked at me as if I were pulling his leg. He handed me a copy of *Poor Charlie's*

Almanack—Vice-Chairman of Berkshire Hathaway and longtime friend Charlie Munger's self-styled finance homage to Franklin. Munger is also a great admirer of Benjamin Franklin, the statesman, philosopher, author, founder of the first North American library, publisher and inventor. Those are reasons enough for admiration, but Franklin was also the father of the North American insurance business, a lynchpin of Berkshire Hathaway's success.

Inspired to take action after a 1730 fire destroyed the shops on Fishbourn's wharf in Philadelphia, Benjamin Franklin wrote a guide on "different accidents and carelessnesses by which houses are set on fire . . . and means of avoiding them."[23] Shortly thereafter, Benjamin Franklin started Union Fire Company, the first volunteer fire department in North America. Even more important to the future success of the as-yet-unborn Warren Buffett and Charlie Munger, Franklin also started the Philadelphia Contributionship for the Insurance of Houses from Loss by Fire, the first successful (Charles Town's earlier effort was unsuccessful) fire insurance organization in North America. The first board meeting was held in 1752, the year the colonies switched from the Julian calendar to the Gregorian calendar, two years before the British colonies sent representatives to the Albany Congress, and 24 years before those colonies declared independence from Britain. Franklin noted that when it came to fires: "An ounce of prevention is worth a pound of cure,"[24] but for what one cannot prevent, insurance helps provide the pound of cure.

Run properly, underwriting risk is a money-making machine that makes a commercial bank look like a child's piggy bank in comparison. A successful insurance operation generates *float,* premiums received before losses are paid—sometimes years or decades before losses, if any, are paid. An insurance company does not technically own its float, called *reserves,* but it has the use of the reserves for investment purposes. *A rising tide lifts all boats, and an increasing stream of well-invested float lifts all returns.*

Americans love to buy insurance. My cyber-friend, Andrew Tobias, wrote a classic book on the insurance industry, *The Invisible Bankers,* more than a quarter of a century ago. Some regulations have changed, but the fundamental principles of making money in the insurance business have remained the same. Tobias cites a *Playboy* survey in which 91 percent of the men thought a car is a necessity—and it is difficult to use that necessity without car insurance. 88 percent of the men thought health insurance was a necessity. Even though only 60 percent of the men surveyed were married, 79 percent of the men responding thought that life insurance was a necessity, not a luxury. Only 16 percent of the men thought that dining out every week was a necessity.[25]

So the question isn't whether or not Americans will buy insurance, but rather, *how much will they buy and from whom?*

The competence of the insurer is crucial, because Mr. Market's manic depressive cousin prices insurance risk. The magic trick in the insurance business is to avoid volume just for the sake of volume.

Auditors do not seem competent to evaluate reported reserves, since anyone can create huge reserves by underwriting bad business. *How did that work out for MBIA and Ambac?* The rating agencies seem even worse than the auditors. When rating agencies told Berkshire Hathaway they liked to see an increasing revenue stream in AAA insurance companies, Warren told me he said he would never let revenues be his target. Anyone can increase revenues by underwriting risk at the wrong price. In a shareholder letter, he wrote:

> Where "earnings" can be created by the stroke of a pen, the dishonest will gather.[26]

Warren's insurance businesses only underwrite insurance risks when market prices are favorable. Insurance success depends on pricing premiums so that premiums exceed losses and expenses. When prices aren't favorable, Berkshire Hathaway ignores Mr. Market's cousin. But when it can underwrite risk at premium prices, Berkshire Hathaway's insurance businesses participate massively.

Simonides, a Greek poet and philosopher, was among a handful of survivors after an earthquake destroyed the great hall of a palace where he attended a party. The crushed victims' bodies were so badly disfigured that grieving relatives could not identify the corpses for burial. Simonides recalled each of the two hundred guests by name and

remembered each guest's exact location in the hall, allowing the mourn-
ers to separate and identify the bodies of their friends and relatives. He
hadn't anticipated the earthquake. His mental picture was formed *before*
the disaster.

Simonides is not around anymore, but fortunately for Berkshire
Hathaway, it has Ajit Jain to tend to Geico and General Reinsurance,
Berkshire Hathaway's large insurance company holdings. He joined Berkshire
Hathaway in 1986, and built its reinsurance business from scratch. The *reinsurance* business may be even better than primary insurance. Jain tries
to price premiums so that no matter who verifies the claims, the insurance business remains profitable.

For the right price, Berkshire Hathaway's reinsurance companies
underwrite the excess risk other insurance companies are eager to shed,
reducing their maximum possible loss. Insurance companies sometimes
need to expand capacity, exit an insurance business, or protect themselves against rare catastrophic losses, and they are often willing to pay
up to meet these needs. For nothing more than a promise, Berkshire
Hathaway receives large premium payments in advance. Losses and loss
payments are usually delayed far into the future. In the hands of skilled
investors like Buffett and Munger, those payments compound to levels
that can far exceed any potential future payments.

The *super catastrophe* or *super-cat* business may be even better than
the reinsurance business, but no one really knows. Berkshire Hathaway
is also in this business, and reaps very high upfront premiums. But in a
horrific year, the super-cat business will take a huge hit. When it comes,
the compounding of the cash has to be great enough to cover the losses.

In December 2007, Ajit Jain set up Berkshire Hathaway Assurance
to take advantage of opportunities in municipal bond insurance. In an
unprecedented move, New York insurance regulators proposed the idea
to Berkshire Hathaway and quickly cut through red tape. In late January
2008, Jonathan Stempel at *Reuters* asked me if Warren Buffett planned
to reinsure the monoline's structured finance positions. I stopped myself
from laughing, and suggested he check his facts directly with Berkshire
Hathaway.

Warren has repeatedly said he wants to do "premium business at
premium prices,"[27] and he insures risks he can understand. Stempel
could not reach Ajit Jain or Berkshire for comment, but I had already

told this much: "I would be surprised if he were to touch the financial guarantors' [bond insurers'] structured products, given that the underwriting standards seemed so poor."[28]

After the municipal bond market auction failed in the second week of February 2008,[29, 30] Warren Buffett's Berkshire Hathaway Assurance reinsured $50 million of bonds and was paid a 2 percent premium, double the original 1 percent premium for primary insurance from the bond insurers. Put another way, Berkshire Hathaway Assurance received *two times the original premium to back up the existing insurance,* in case the insurer cannot pay.[31] By the end of February Berkshire Hathaway Assurance did 206 transactions and was paid an average of 3.5 percent on business that the primary insurer originally underwrote at 1.5 percent.[32]

Warren is happy to do zero business when risk premiums make no sense. Berkshire Hathaway's triple-A rating is trusted as a genuine rating. Its stated intention of doing premium business at premium prices may leave the largest of the legacy bond insurers scrambling for scraps.

Chapter 12

Money, Money, Money (Warren and Washington)

That's the problem . . . you can't regulate it anymore. You can't get the genie back in the bottle.

—Warren Buffett
(in Reuters), May 24, 2008

In the spring of 2008, both Warren and I said the United States was already in a recession. In May 2008, Warren told CNBC that "it will be deeper and last longer than many think."[1] Yet many economists sound like the Merchants of Death (MOD squad) in *Thank You for Smoking*: "Although we are constantly exploring the slowdown, there is currently no economic evidence to suggest the economy is in a recession."

The classic definition of a recession calls for two consecutive quarters of negative growth, and as of the summer of 2008, the numbers did not yet show it. Election years bring out the best in the economy. In the long run, we need to improve productivity and spend less—I will get to that later. In the short run, Warren is right. The United States is in a recession combined with inflation and low growth, a condition called *stagflation*.

How did this happen? For most of this century, Washington has pumped money into the economy by keeping interest rates low. Easy money tempts crooks. Speculators and fraudsters had a party. Regulators became enablers. Cheap money fueled bad lending, including predatory lending, and cheap money expanded the housing bubble. There are genuine victims of predatory lending. The war on poverty became a war on the poor. Those victims face crushing debt, a weaker dollar, and rising prices. Now even the average American is the victim of bad policies combined with widespread financial crime. Most Americans feel the negative wealth effect of rising prices, falling home values, and tighter credit. Consumers cut back on spending while struggling with higher food and gas prices. Bailouts of poorly regulated investment banks and corrupt mortgage lenders mean Washington is printing more money, which weakens the dollar. Inflation adds to the misery. Americans feel poorer. The United States is in a recession combined with stagflation.

Washington is supposed to provide a strong national defense; but we were attacked from within our own borders—sometimes by those charged to protect us. Washington failed in one of its most important duties. Washington failed to protect our money.

What is money? *Money is a store of value.* It does not matter whether we talk about gold coins, silver, diamonds, bearer bonds, pieces of paper with pictures of dead presidents, salt, cacao, tulip bulbs, or a signed check. We accept these things as money, because we have a common agreement (or hallucination) of their value.

Our idea of value changes as circumstances change. If crops fail and I am starving, I'd prefer to stockpile wheat rather than gold. If you have no wheat, I would prefer to have gold than take your credit, since it will be easier for me to convert gold into food than to convert your credit into food. *We invented money to enhance our probability of survival.* The best money is an abundant store of value measured in a standard and reliable manner. When anyone—especially someone we elected to a position of authority—messes around with the value of money, we should all take it very seriously. *Homeland security requires a secure homeland currency.*

There are three basic kinds of money. The first is commodity money, something usable that humans value. Children quickly grasp the concept of commodity money the first time they swap toys. Commodity money is gold, silver, rice, wheat, oil, salt, or any number of usable goods. Beads went out of fashion as currency in the United States soon after Europeans used them to purchase Manhattan from Native Americans. Gold is still in fashion because the global community agrees it has value. The gold standard was dissolved in 1971, but before that, Europe relied on it both officially and unofficially for about 900 years. Central banks still stockpile physical gold. Gold is still considered a benchmark, even though it is no longer the standard.

Warren invests in businesses that make things that people use and that are unlikely to go out of fashion (for a long time). For example, people enjoy eating Dairy Queen's ice cream treats, and human taste buds are unlikely to evolve to new preferences in our lifetime.

Credit is the second kind of money. Most of us have checking accounts. People who accept our checks assume our credit is good enough that the check will clear. Our assets in the form of checking deposits back our check, and the currency in our checking account will keep its value long enough to have the same purchasing power when the check clears. If there is hyperinflation, merchants will not accept checks. Credit has been around since humans shared food with the expectation that they would benefit from a future meal—an asset—provided by their fellow tribesmen. Shipping merchants have used trade receivables for centuries using credit against a shipment of saleable goods. This only worked, because everyone expected your "ship to come in." International banking was born, because we wanted to trade goods between distant lands.

Warren and Charlie Munger avoid leverage, because it makes it much easier for people to trust that Berkshire Hathaway will always meet its obligations and keep its genuine AAA rating. Furthermore, since its businesses are throwing off so much cash, Berkshire Hathaway's ship is always coming in. Berkshire Hathaway's businesses throw off cash of around $100 million per week. It has no problem meeting obligations. Its problem is finding more good businesses in which to invest all of this money.

The third kind of money is *fiat* money (this is not money to buy a designer car, as many young Wall Street bankers seem to think), such as the pieces of paper your government prints and issues as its currency notes. Fiat money is not backed by a commodity. Fiat money is not backed by assets (unlike a check which is backed by checking deposits). The *faith and credit* of a government back fiat money. The world relied on commodities such as gold until we formed the nation-states. Until then, we did not trust each other's coins and printed papers. Until the beginning of the twenty-first century, *hard currencies,* defined as reliable currencies, included the U.S. dollar, Swiss franc, pound sterling, Deutsche mark (now replaced by the euro), and Japanese yen. The Deutsche mark (before the euro) and dollar held premier positions as reliable global currencies. By 2008, the dollar's reliability as a store of value lost credibility as the world looks askance at the United States' inconsistent policies and disastrous dollar diluting actions. China's currency, the renmimbi, is gaining credibility. Some consider it an emerging hard currency, but that remains to be seen. *When it comes to money, government matters.* If you live in a Third-World country and your government is run by corrupt thugs who loot the treasury and destroy the local economy, your country's fiat money will be nearly worthless to the international community. It is a lot harder to shake down a currency like the United States dollar. The United States is still a rich country, so a little corruption will not destroy the currency. But a lot of corruption combined with making promises for which we cannot pay (a $9 trillion national debt) and lower productivity are destroying faith in the U.S. dollar. Lately, the United States policymakers have demonstrated a twisted genius for causing the dollar to lose value.

In finance, credibility is extremely important. Warren Buffett and Charlie Munger educate Berkshire Hathaway's 40,000 odd shareholders so that they understand that Berkshire Hathaway's AAA rating is solid. The entire financial community trusts it. Washington should have worked hard to make sure the dollar kept its credibility in the global financial markets.

The dollar is weakening partly because of growing U.S. current account deficit. The United States used to produce more than it consumes, and the rest of the world owed us. We reached a turning point in 2006 and headed in the wrong direction. We started consuming more than we produce. We now shovel $2 billion per day out the door and into the pockets of the rest of the world. It is as if we have a large lot of land and are selling off the fringes of our gardens so we can buy more consumable goods for the house. We are transferring a part of the ownership of our country abroad. For the first time in about 100 years, we are relying on credit with the rest of the world and have become a net seller of our assets to subsidize our spending habits. The current generation is spending and building up a large debt. How will your children and grandchildren feel if after you die they have to spend part of their time working to pay off tens of thousands of dollars of credit card debt you left behind? While the debt we are taking on is not credit card debt, our children and grandchildren will have to pay it off if we do not come up with a better solution soon. The solution is to start producing more than we consume, and it will not be easy. America is aging, and the number of workers is declining.

Washington has created a $9 trillion gross national debt. The size of the debt is around 80 percent of the $11.5 trillion U.S. residential mortgage market, or about $38,000 for each citizen of the United States (counting children and those no longer working). The only way to reverse this course is to increase national productivity relative to spending, practice sound lending (*especially* for the housing market), stop bailing out those responsible for this mess, and force the bloated regulatory system to go on a diet and do its job. American ingenuity and innovation may create future productivity gains, but we cannot depend solely on that.

Since we are so wealthy and since our lifestyles will improve with the debt we are accumulating, it is easy to avoid thinking about the fact that we will eventually get to a point where the amount of debt is uncomfortable. Then things will slide. That will be decades away, and our children will suffer the effects of our foolishness. Our enormous debt is growing slowly, but it is *growing*. Meanwhile the dollar is weakening.

There is a high cost of doing nothing. Around 100 years ago, Britain was the world's greatest power, generating vast wealth from its sprawling empire. Britain is currently in no danger of becoming a Third-World country, but at times it seems like a very strong "Second-World" country. For all of the vast resources of the United States, in 50 to 100 years, we will become tomorrow's Britain. After I commented on these problems in an interview with Harlan Levy of Connecticut's *Journal Inquirer* in the fall of 2007, Warren wrote me: "Your answers in the interview . . . are 100 percent on the mark. Congratulations."

Warren's late mentor, Benjamin Graham, said it requires "considerable will power to keep from following the crowd."[2] In finance, following a bad crowd can lead to enormous financial gain (in the short term), so bankers can be tempted to take the easy road to riches instead of the high road. Sadly, regulators themselves sometimes succumb to temptation, and it is particularly vexing when it causes us to lose a strong advocate of investors' interests. Washington failed to regulate Wall Street, failed to regulate mortgage lenders, and regulators failed to regulate themselves.

On Valentine's Day 2008, the *Washington Post* printed New York Governor Eliot Spitzer's screed on the Bush administration's enabling role in the subprime lending crisis. The former New York attorney general's aggressive prosecution of malfeasance relating to the dot com and Enron scandals had earned him the nickname the "sheriff of Wall Street." His article castigated the Office of the Comptroller of the Currency, the national bank examiner, for its 2003 actions that protected national banks and predatory lenders from states' lending laws. Spitzer did not stop there. He labeled the Bush administration a "willing accomplice" of unfair lending. He wrote that the administration thwarted state attorneys general with "an aggressive and unprecedented campaign to prevent states from protecting their residents . . . " from predatory lenders.[3] Aggressive in his methods, arrogant in demeanor, ruthless when exercising "prosecutorial discretion," Eliot Spitzer's often excessive zeal was excused by the media because he directed most of his energy at financial malfeasance. Spitzer may have imagined himself the arbiter of moral high ground, but he was no Thomas Moore.

On March 10, 2008, the *New York Times* broke the Spitzer scandal. More than one financier protested to me that in Europe, Spitzer's escapades would not even be a crime. Unfortunately for Mr. Spitzer, the news did not break in Amsterdam, it broke in *New* Amsterdam. Spitzer neutered himself. In his previous role as attorney general of New York, he oversaw the organized crime task force that prosecuted prostitution rings. By Spitzer's own standards, he was done. On the day Spitzer's article appeared in the *Washington Post,* the then-governor of New York and alleged Client 9 of the Emperor's Club VIP, gave his many enemies the ammunition they sought. He allegedly met with call girl "Kristin" in room 871 of Washington's Mayflower Hotel and paid her $4,300. The post-911 Patriot Act, legislation allowed authorities to track Spitzer's legal money transfers and record cell phone conversations referring to the alleged illegal prostitution transaction. The Bush administration could not capture Osama Bin Laden, but it got "Sheriff" Spitzer.[4]

His downfall is a tragedy for those trying to balance the scales of justice in the financial markets and a cause for snide soaked relief among the many targets of his investigations. Yet, for Spitzer himself, there is little pity; he engineered his own political suicide by cop. Spitzer announced his resignation as governor of New York on March 12, effective at noon on March 17, 2008. News of his disgrace broke just in time for the Fed to announce its $200 billion liquidity bailout that for the first time extended directly to investment banks and indirectly to private equity funds and hedge funds. His resignation occurred the same day the JPMorgan Chase announced its Federal Reserve and Treasury orchestrated purchase of Bear Stearns.[5, 6]

Among other issues with the Fed actions, just as with its liquidity bailout of Countrywide in August 2007, there was no *quid pro quo.* The Fed does not regulate investment banks, insurance companies, private equity firms, hedge funds, or thrifts. If it is going to hand out our money, it should ask for concessions designed to make the U.S. financial system safer—to do otherwise ratchets up moral hazard.

Yet, just as with the August 2007 liquidity bailout of Countrywide, the Fed extracted no concessions when it aided JPMorgan's purchase of Bear Stearns and when it handed out massive liquidity to highly leveraged investment banks in the first quarter of 2008. It opened the national purse and let investment banks reach in.

In early April 2008, Fed Chairman Ben Bernanke testified before the U.S. Senate's Committee on Banking in a speech devoid of inflationary language. His reason for the Federal Reserve's agreement (in consultation with the Treasury Department) to provide funding to Bear Stearns through JPMorgan Chase was "to prevent a disorderly failure of Bear Stearns and the unpredictable but likely severe consequences for market functioning and the broader economy."[7]

What happened to the $30 billion in Bear Stearns' mortgage-backed products that the Federal Reserve bought through JPMorgan? From March to June 2008, it lost more than more than $1.1 billion in value; it has already eaten through JPMorgan's $1 billion "cushion" and is now eating into taxpayer dollars. It is a *sticky bomb,* as dangerous as the makeshift explosives stuck to tanks during World War II. In June 2008, the Fed admitted that it priced the assets as if we were in an "orderly market."[8] But we are not in an orderly market, so the price should be lower, meaning we do not know how much taxpayer money is at risk. Who is helping the Fed price these securities since it cannot price the sticky bomb itself? Blackrock. Blackrock lost money when it invested in the Peloton fund that bought overrated and overpriced mortgage backed securities. *They should know all about getting taken for a ride.* Jamie Dimon claimed he by no means saddled the Fed with Bear Stearns's riskiest assets. Given the performance of the assets the Fed took on board, JPMorgan's shareholders may not feel reassured by Jamie's testimony before the Senate Banking Committee.

Bernanke seems to think the Bear Stearns bailout did not create a moral hazard problem, because shareholders lost money. Bear Stearns' share price bubble burst, but the Federal Reserve Bank inflated moral hazard. Shareholders in leveraged companies should expect to take risk. Bernanke bailed out Bear Stearns' *creditors.* Investment bankers—not shareholders—are the key architects of the mortgage meltdown. Many investment bankers lost money on their own stock holdings, but others sold and diversified their holdings. Some earned high salaries and a significant portion of their bonuses in cash.

If the Fed feels investment bankers have learned anything from the Bear Stearns debacle, it might consider Jim Rogers's point of view.

"You don't see any 29-year-old cotton farmers driving around in Maseratis," he observed, "but you see a lot of 29-year-olds on Wall Street driving around in Maseratis. This is not the way the world is supposed to work."[9] Warren Buffett put it another way: "Wall Street is going to go where the money is and not worry about consequences. You've got a lot of leeway in running a bank to not tell the truth for quite a while."[10]

The securitization markets presented a high potential for fraud known as the *fraud triangle*: need, opportunity, and the ability to rationalize one's behavior. Many financial professionals have great needs: the need for a larger house in the Hamptons, the need for a large yacht, the need for a rare Patek Philippe watch, the need for a multimillion dollar annual bonus. Lax oversight provides the opportunity. Intelligent people with broken moral compasses—*can't they afford new ones?*—provide the rationalizations.

SEC Chairman Cox testified that the SEC was investigating whether there was unlawful manipulation of Bear Stearns's stock that led to a run on the firm. Cox did not refer to earlier statements (early 2007 earnings reports) made by CEOs and CFOs that may have *propped up* stock prices, but he might want to look into it.[11] How do we explain the SEC's poor reaction time to the securitization problems at the investment banks it regulates? *Could the SEC's conflicts of interest have anything to do with it?* Former SEC staffers often seem to land very lucrative jobs working for law firms that represent investment banks, working for law firms seeking expert witnesses to defend investment banks, or working for investment banks needing a new general counsel. Some SEC officials often end up affiliated with a huge private equity fund or start a fund of their own with fundraising help from investment banks. I am sure there are many rationalizations for this.

Warren Buffett is among those that felt the Fed action with respect to Bear Stearns was probably necessary: "Just imagine the thousands of counterparties having to undo contracts."[12] I disagree, but I could be wrong, and there is no way to prove this either way since the bailout already occurred. Banks will bid on all or part of a derivatives book. It is a pain in the neck, but it has been done successfully several times in the past. I agreed with Bernanke when he said in testimony: "Normally the market sorts out which companies survive and which fail, and that is as it should be."[13] I wish Bernanke had stuck to that.

Federal chairmen may not want to bite the hand that may feed them in future. Jeremy Grantham wrote in his April newsletter that a Federal Reserve chairman may find that on the retirement lecture circuit "grateful bailees . . . hire you for $300,000 a pop."[14] Charles I. Plosser, president of the Philadelphia Federal Reserve Bank, and Jeffrey M. Lacker, president of the Richmond Federal Reserve Bank, also expressed concern. Plosser said the Fed might be "sowing the seeds of the next crisis."[15] Lacker said the credit hand-out to financiers "might induce greater risk-taking."[16]

Congress embraced The Emergency Economic Stabilization Act of 2008, the bailout bill proposed by Paulson and Bernanke, with weak oversight and no requirement for using market prices. William Poole, the retired president of the St. Louis Fed, finds it "appalling" that the Fed is "a backstop for the entire financial system."[17]

If the Federal Reserve Bank did not seem like such a pushover, investment banks (and AIG) might have managed their businesses more carefully. Warren pointed out that Wall Street will not worry about the consequences, and I might add that is especially true when an accommodating Fed shelters Wall Street from the consequences of its folly. If Bear Stearns had failed, investment banks, hedge funds and banks might have sat at the table and sorted out their problems.

In September 2008, the Fed let Lehman Brothers (a larger investment bank than Bear Stearns) fail, and helped AIG with a credit line of $85 billion. Were there alternatives? In my view, there were. AIG could have contacted its credit default swap counterparties and asked them for better collateral terms while it was still rated double-A. There is a precedent for this. When ACA, the failed monoline bond insurer (unlike AIG it did not have a diversified business with valuable assets) needed time, its counterparties gave it a six month reprieve. But that was before the Fed bailed out Bear Stearns's creditors. AIG knew it could run to the Fed, and it initially did, even before it approached JPMorgan Chase and Goldman Sachs for a loan. AIG remained in denial for many months. It worked on a strategic plan instead of acting on its problems, Moral hazard creates opportunity costs, because people with a sense of entitlement tend to get complacent about managing complex risk. Taxpayers can only hope that AIG's valuable assets are ultimately enough to cover its liabilities, but it never should have become the problem of U.S. taxpayers. We may have to come up with a new slogan—*no taxation without regulation.*

The Federal Reserve should have saved its fire power, because we have even more serious problems. Warren's Berkshire Hathaway backs Clayton Homes' business. In contrast, Fannie Mae and Freddie Mac are highly (and dangerously) leveraged. They had only a 2 percent core capital requirement; banks hold a minimum of 6 percent in "tier one" capital. The burden of both mortgage giants increased in the past two years. In 2006, they accounted for 33 percent of total mortgage backed securities issuance, and as of the summer of 2008 they accounted for 84 percent. Fannie Mae and Freddie Mac have been pressured to help other lenders out of the mortgage mess. Fannie Mae and Freddie Mac guarantee approximately 40–45 percent of the $11.5 trillion U.S. residential mortgage market. As of March 31, 2008, Fannie Mae and Freddie Mac had combined debt of $1.6 trillion and credit obligations of $3.7 trillion. This is a total of $5.3 trillion, *roughly the same as U.S. government bonds.*[18] The U.S. government took over Fannie Mae and Freddie Mac on September 7, 2007, and this is the problem that will probably cost taxpayers the most. The government is in charge of financing most of the U.S. mortgage market, and the mortgage market is still under-regulated. *U.S. taxpayers have too many sticky bombs.*

The new regulators and the new CEOs do not inspire me with confidence. James Lockhart is the head of the Federal Housing Finance Agency (which will now also oversee the 12 Federal Home Loan Banks) and he was head of the Office of Federal Housing Enterprise Oversight (starting June 15, 2006, just when effective action seemed most needed), the former regulator for Fannie Mae and Freddie Mac. It had over 200 employees and wrote long after-the-fact reports. As Warren put it to CNBC: "You had two of the greatest accounting misstatements in history. You had all kinds of management malfeasance . . . the classic thing was . . . OFHEO wrote a 350–400 page report . . . they blamed [everyone else]."[19] This predated Lockhart, but under Lockhart's watch, things went from bad to conservatorship.

Initially, the mortgage giants charged fees to guarantee prime mortgages (up to a specific size) and borrowers made 20 percent down payments. It was a license to print money, which motivated Warren Buffett to make a large investment in their shares in the first place. It is amazing to me that Fannie, Freddie and OFHEO could screw this up, but over-reaching has that effect. That is what motivated Warren to sell the shares in 2000.

In June 2008 (before the government takeover), former St. Louis Federal Reserve President William Poole, said: "Congress ought to recognize [Fannie Mae and Freddie Mac] are insolvent, that it is continuing to allow these firms to exist as bastions of privilege, financed by the taxpayer."[20] In 2006, U.S. regulators imposed limits on lending for Fannie Mae and Freddie Mac after discovering $11.3 billion of accounting errors. On March 1, 2008, regulators *lifted* those limits. Meanwhile, the FHA, which provides funding for low-income borrowers, is struggling to abolish future no-money-down mortgages.[21, 22]

In July 2008, Treasury Secretary Paulson obtained broad authority to purchase unlimited shares of the stock in the companies,[23] which could mean unlimited tax dollars—*a completely insane and unsound economic policy.* The costs are potentially unlimited, as are the opportunities for looting the treasury by gaming the shares. There is no *quid pro quo* except for a goal of reducing the size of the portfolios over time. Yet there is still little discipline for mortgage brokers and many mortgage lenders. If we want to restore confidence in Fannie Mae and Freddie Mac, we need a two-pronged approach: (1) support the *debt* (not the shares) issued by Fannie Mae and Freddie Mac; and (2) strongly regulate what backs that debt in the first place. In other words, if taxpayer money is used to help, we must enforce sound lending: 20 percent down payments, verified income, low debt loads and more—the traditional standards of sound mortgage lending. There are worse things than renting; for example, piling up crushing debt that forces you into bankruptcy just as the country sinks into stagflation—that is much worse.

The Government Accountability Office (GAO) says we have even greater worries. We are $52.7 trillion in the hole based on our fiscal burdens of social security, Medicare, public debt, and more. That number grows $3 to 4 trillion per year on autopilot. The GAO recommends *tough* budget controls, comprehensive tax reform, reform of social security, and reform of Medicare. The U.S. needs to generate more revenues through growth. In the face of this, the only advice one can give is *don't retire and keep saving.*[24] On August 21, 2008, Warren appeared in the documentary on our growing debt burden *I.O.U.S.A.,* a scarier summer thriller than *JAWS*. Your odds of suffering a shark bite are small, but we are being slowly devoured by our national debt.[25]

🌷 🌷 🌷

On March 13, 2007, while New Century watched its credit lines disappear and faced allegations of fraud, U.S. regulators complained that the United States investment banks lost business to London. Sarbanes-Oxley requirements became the scapegoat. Hank Paulson assembled a panel at Washington's Georgetown University. Paulson invited several notables in the financial markets, and Mr. Buffett went to Washington.[26]

John Thain, then head of the New York Stock Exchange (later the CEO of Merrill Lynch that arranged its sale), said that only two of 25 IPOs in 2006 were made in the United States. The implication seemed to be that Sarbanes-Oxley, inspired by Enron, Worldcom, and other corporate malfeasance, hampers business. The collapse of Enron and WorldCom led to billions of dollars in losses for investors and cost thousands of people their jobs. Adelphia's former CEO, John Rigas, and his son, Timothy Rigas, the chief financial officer, were found guilty of fraud and conspiracy after hiding $2.3 billion in debt. On June 17, 2005, Tyco's L. Dennis Kozlowski and Mark Swartz, charged with stealing $600 million in unapproved compensation and illicit share deals, were found guilty of criminal counts of securities fraud, eight counts of falsifying business records, grand larceny and conspiracy. Ex-waitress Karen Kozlowski filed for divorce in August 2006 and sought to keep booty paid with loans that Tyco later "forgave," including some of hundreds of thousands of dollars in Harry Winston jewelry. She may be disappointed. Businesses will fund business trips, but you might have to reimburse the company if it funds your ego trips.[27, 28, 29]

Warren felt that after such astonishing corporate malfeasance, it is a "question of restoring trust." He added "American business is working pretty darned well." Although compliance with Sarbanes-Oxley cost Berkshire Hathaway tens of millions, he said it might do some good if it restores investors' confidence: "There are worse things than Sarbanes-Oxley."[30] Three years prior to Paulson's meeting, Warren attended a conference at which Mikhail Khodorkovsky, the former

CEO and owner of AOA Yukos Oil Co., asked him if it would be dangerous to bring an IPO in the United States. Three or four months later Khodorkovsky was imprisoned in Siberia. Yukos went belly-up in 2006 and had back-tax claims exceeding $30 billion. Yukos's assets were subsequently bought by Russia's largest oil company, AOA Rosneft at bankruptcy auction.[31] Sarbanes–Oxley requirements seemed to discourage Khodorkovsky from making an initial public offering of Yukos's stock in the United States. We dodged a bullet.

Jeffrey Immelt, chairman and CEO of General Electric Co., also attended Paulson's conference. He complained that regulatory requirements are "just too gosh-darn complex."[32] *As too gosh-darn complex as the subprime-backed investments that later cost GE $300 to $400 million of dollars worth of write-downs?*[33]

In contrast, Warren noted that some of Sarbanes–Oxley requirements promoted transparency, and he eagerly reads financial reports: "like a teenager reading *Playboy*."[34] *Readers of financial reports and Playboy agree that more transparency is desirable.*

Part of the reason we are losing business to London may be that quite a few international investors are concerned about structured financial products they bought from U.S. investment banks. Loans were made to people who would not be able to pay them back, ratings are flawed, and securitization technology is suspect. We are losing business because we were found out. Europeans in particular feel that smart Americans abused securitization technology to fool a lot of people in the short run. In a letter to the *Financial Times* on March 19, 2007, I wrote:

> Wall Street's former standard: "Your word is your bond, did not mean "Your spin is your shield." . . . [I]n areas in which we are lightly regulated, our words are unworthy.[35]

Until recently, I opposed hedge fund regulation. Eric Mindich (formerly of Goldman Sachs) now heads Eton Park Capital Management. When Mindich was assigned to head the President's Working Group Asset Managers Project, I volunteered my perspective: "I am a laissez faire capitalist, and do not believe in protecting consenting adults from making informed decisions, even if that decision is to make a blind bet." That was in September 2007, but my point of view is changed, since U.S. taxpayers bail out hedge funds creditors.

The hedge fund business is approximately $1.9 trillion in size, and 87 percent of the money is controlled by fewer than 10 percent of the hedge funds. The larger hedge funds have a lot of clout. Large hedge funds act as if they are investment banks. Often they accumulate large trades—taking the other side of an investment bank's trade—then call up the investment bank and ask them if they would like to negotiate to close out the transaction. *In other words, for some types of transactions a hedge fund is the other side of an illiquid market.*

Furthermore, when investment banks bail out hedge funds (and structured investment vehicles), these entities are not truly off balance sheet. For example, Citigroup took around $9 billion of assets on balance sheet from Old Lane Partners, the former hedge fund of its CEO, Vikram Pandit.[36] Bear Stearns bailed out creditors of two of BSAM's hedge funds, and Bear Stearns was subsequently purchased by JPMorgan Chase with help from the Fed. Since the Federal Reserve Bank supplies liquidity to the banking system, and since the SEC regulates investment banks, hedge funds should be regulated.

Bank problems could get even worse. Banks moved assets off their balance sheet using structured finance. They set up off balance sheet entities that owned the assets and issued debt. Now the banks may have to take *$5 trillion* in assets back on balance sheet as if they had never been moved.[37] Although the vehicles currently pay for themselves (their assets meet their debt payments), if the assets' quality falls into doubt, banks might have to bail them out (as Bear Stearns bailed out the creditors in the hedge funds). The banks would have to borrow more money from the Fed. Even if that does not happen, banks' debt to equity ratios will increase, and banks will be less willing to lend *you* money.

We have too many ineffective regulators: the OCC, Fed, OTC, FHFA, SEC, FDIC, and more. Watching the regulatory system is like watching bad doubles tennis players. No one hits the ball thinking the *other guy* will get it. Investment banks are not suffering from too much regulation. The global capital markets are suffering from too little competent regulation where it counts most.

The Fed, Congress, the Treasury, and the Bush administration wanted you to believe they have solved the "regulatory problems." On March 31, 2008, a couple of weeks after the Bear Stearns deal, Treasury Secretary Hank Paulson rolled out the "Blueprint for a Modernized

Financial Regulatory Structure." The draft of this report was prepared in November 2006, when the Treasury alleged excessive regulation caused the U.S. financial markets to lose its competitive edge to
London in the global financial markets. In other words, it called for *less
regulation,* not more.[38]

At its core, the mortgage lending crisis is no more sophisticated than
a schoolyard swindle, and the SEC is the principal. Economists and pundits unhelpfully—and conveniently—focused on the Federal Reserve
Bank and retired Chairman Alan Greenspan. Others blame the rating
agencies. Yet neither the Federal Reserve Bank nor the rating agencies
regulate the securities industry. That job belongs to the SEC. The SEC
has broad authority over banks, too. The Office of the Comptroller, the
OCC, examines the risk management of the capital markets areas of
banks. The Federal Reserve Bank primarily looks at banks at the holding company level. The SEC has broader authority than either the OCC
or the Fed for publicly traded companies. It is *deceptive securitization practices* at the root of the mortgage bubble, and the SEC had the authority
to stop Hurricane Ponzi. Instead, it slumbered.

Wall Street acts fast, and its regulators move at glacial speed. In
other words, the existing regulation—even if it demonstrated the will
to be proactive, which it did not—is too slow. The system is doomed to
repeat its failures, because as Benjamin Graham observed, when things
are going well in the financial markets, there is "a strong temptation
toward imprudent action."[39]

As long as Wall Street enhances revenues with leverage to prop
up kingly bonuses, as long as there are few personal consequences
for CEOs (and board members and other top executives) for shoddy
risk management, as long as CEOs are allowed to walk away with
millions, nothing will change. The fact that shareholders are wiped out
is no deterrent, and moral hazard will live on. I see nothing that will
change that in the future. In fact, just the opposite. We have handed out
hundreds of billions of dollars in taxpayer dollars and have put hundreds of billions more at risk without demanding effective conditions.

Our bailout bills are mounting. The treasury has extended more
"temporary" credit lines to the 12 Federal Home Loan Banks, and the
government has an additional $90 billion in exposure to the FHA. A new
housing bill created a $4 billion fund for local governments to buy
foreclosed homes, a $7,500 tax break for first-time home buyers, and a

$300 billion insurance fund for refinanced mortgages (but no clear way on how to control the risk of the new mortgages). As of July, there is an 18 month line of credit for Fannie and Freddie to borrow from the Fed, and Bazooka Hank has authority to purchase shares. The FDIC has taken on $39.3 billion of failed bank assets (as of September 2008, and there is more to come). The Fed created various special financing programs amounting to hundreds of billions of dollars. The Fed took $29 billion (after using up JPMorgan's $1 billion on the original $30 billion) of exposure to Bear Stearns's assets and gave an $85 billion credit line to AIG. If that were not alarming enough, the Fed relaxed its borrowing standards to allow borrowers to present equities as collateral. Benjamin Graham cautioned that if you have common stocks you "must expect to see them fluctuate in value."[40] *You* now means the U.S. taxpayer.

The Treasury issues new debt to fund the Fed's liquidity bailouts along with the hundreds of billions (perhaps running into the trillions) of dollars called for by The Emergency Economic Stabilization Act of 2008 (the Paulson Plan). In other words, the government is printing money like crazy. That is inflationary, and inflation weakens the dollar.

The United States is a nation at war. A handful of financial institutions are chiefly responsible for roiling the housing market, the municipal bond markets, the economy, and the dollar. Yet, executives may still earn tens of millions of dollars through stock awards. The Paulson Plan does not require market prices for the assets our Treasury may buy or for the trading books of the institutions it is bailing out. Warren and I proposed that market prices (to restore confidence) should be required along with new capital, but someone else gave Congress a bad education. Wall Street is getting what it wants, and U.S. taxpayers are underrepresented in Congress. Thomas Jefferson warned: "A government big enough to give you everything you want is strong enough to take everything you have."

The policies of Washington and Wall Street have weakened the dollar. It is unclear whether the United States has the will to pull the dollar up from its tailspin. The United States dollar is less secure in 2008 than it was 10 years ago, and it is weaker than it was 10 years ago. Warren sometimes takes currency positions to hedge this risk. He currently seeks good foreign companies to add operating earnings in foreign currencies. If you know of a good foreign company (understandable business, sound management, favorable prospects, fair price) that is $1 billion or more in size—$5 billion would be even better—please call Warren.

Chapter 13

The Fogs of War, Religion, and Politics

What would happen if Internet communications were disrupted, how would we trade?

—Warren Buffett
to Janet Tavakoli, August 25, 2005

While the rest of the world seemed bent on mutually assured destruction—pursuing wealth through leveraged mortgage loan products, hedge funds, and leveraged buyouts—Warren had already taken steps to do something about the weakening dollar problem for Berkshire Hathaway shareholders. He used derivatives to take positions in the relative strength of foreign currencies, and he looked abroad for well-run companies that earn money in foreign currencies.

On October 25, 2005, Warren received a letter from Eitan Wertheimer, chairman of Israel's ISCAR Metalworking, saying: "Berkshire Hathaway would be the ideal home for ISCAR."[1] On May 5, 2006, Berkshire Hathaway used *Business Wire* to announce it had agreed to acquire 80 percent of the tool-cutting company. Two months later on July 5, 2006, the acquisition was completed. Berkshire Hathaway paid $4 billion.[2]

ISCAR's main plant is located in Israel's Galilee around 7.5 miles south of Israel's border with Lebanon. It does business in more than 60 countries, has a good source of foreign revenues (a hedge against a weakening dollar), and it is a business with products the world needs: cutting tools used with machine tools. The management is in place, and the family is dedicated to the business.

Eitan Wertheimer is the chairman of ISCAR, and 20 percent of the stock remains in the Wertheimer family. Michael Federmann, the Chairman of Elbit Systems Ltd., a Haifa-based electronic defense company, knows Stef "Steffie" Wertheimer, Eitan Wertheimer's father. "Steffie," he later told me, "is the entrepreneur who built the company. Eitan is an administrator and a good steward of the legacy." Stef Wertheimer started in a backyard shed with no funds and worked his way up from there. Michael's enthusiasm inspired me to read more about Stef, and I learned that he was expelled from formal education at age 14 for "slugging a teacher who harassed a female classmate."[3]

On May 8, 2007, three days after the Berkshire Hathaway annual meeting, I attended a dinner sponsored by the Jewish American Chamber of Commerce at Chicago's Conrad Hilton Hotel in honor of Eitan Wertheimer. Ralph Gidwitz, a Managing Partner of Capital Results LLC, asked if I would invite Warren, and I did, but he had to decline. Warren attends only one function per year for his senior managers and he had already committed to support one of Eitan's Canadian charities.

I sat at the same table with Eitan and Ariel Wertheimer. Ariel explained that Eitan's father, Steffie, settled in Israel after fleeing Nazi Germany as a 10-year-old boy. Stef Wertheimer seems to focus on hope and how he can improve the lot of others. The company he founded is a large employer of Arab Israelis, and Ariel said it provides intensive training and good working conditions. Ariel's account of Stef reminded me of one of Winston Churchill's maxims: "Live dangerously; take things as they come; dread naught, all will be well."[4]

Eitan Wertheimer gave a speech detailing his vision for a Middle East renaissance including Arabs in Israel and neighboring Arab countries. Like his father, his belief is that wealth distribution via economic growth is the only viable avenue to produce lasting peace in Israel and the Middle East. His contribution is the stewardship of ISCAR and the creation of a pleasant work environment for the large number of Arab Israelis he employs. Eitan talked of the goal of lasting peace, but when Warren had announced the acquisition, we were oblivious that in two months Israel would be embroiled in a bloody conflict with Lebanon.

It was not as if tensions were not a concern, but Warren publicly stated that the world in general was a dangerous place and that in the absence of war: "Most of the time Israel is no more dangerous than the U.S."[5] Berkshire Hathaway's headquarters is located in the Midwest as is Oklahoma City, the site of the deadliest home-grown domestic terrorist attack in U.S. history. In 1995, Timothy McVeigh's bomb attack killed 168 people and injured more than 800 others.[6]

🙲 🙲 🙲

Israel during peace time is as safe as the United States, but Israel has tensions with Palestine's Hamas Movement as well as Lebanon's Hezbollah. Iran and Syria back Lebanon's Hezbollah terrorist organization, and although Iran does not actively support Palestine's Hamas (as far as I know), it is sympathetic with its thinking. On June 6, 2006, shortly after dinner with the Wertheimers, but before the war, I sent Warren an e-mail about a Web site (http://iranvajahan.net/english) with a summary in English about international news about Iran. I noted it draws on media sources in English, German, French, and Farsi: "Print media compilations cannot compete with a well-designed Internet compilation."

On June 14, 2006, I sent Warren a commentary I had written about our growing tensions with Iran. The U.S. media seem fixated on Iran's President Mahmoud Ahmadinejad, but he does not control Iran, and he does not have a job for life. Iran's president serves at the pleasure of the

Ayatollah. Ayatollah Ali Khameni is the supreme leader of Iran, and his control in Iran is close to absolute. He controls the media, the judiciary, the military, and he effectively controls the legislature.

Iran has been deeply suspicious of the United States ever since we deposed its first democratically elected government. Iran elected Prime Minister Mussaddiq in the summer of 1953. One of his first acts was to force into exile the young Reza Pahlavi, son of a self-proclaimed Shah, a brutal despot and a commoner of nonroyal origins. Mussaddiq wanted to nationalize the British Anglo-Iranian oil company because Iranians were not getting a fair share of the profits. The United States CIA and the UK's MI5 deposed Mussaddiq and reinstalled the young Shah, a foreign-educated dictator who now owed allegiance to both Britain and the United States. At the time, Eisenhower was president of the United States. John Foster Dulles was Secretary of State, and his brother, Allen Dulles, was Director of Central Intelligence. The Dulles brothers were alumni of law firm Sullivan and Cromwell, whose prestigious clients included the British Anglo-Iranian Oil Company.

On June 20, 2006, I sent Warren my concerns about Iran's potential treatment of Israel based on my first-hand experiences living in Iran at the time of the Shah's overthrow and Khomeini's return. At a party shortly after the Shah was deposed, a couple announced they were moving to Canada. My then husband, a Moslem in name only, observed that the wife was wise to leave because her grandfather is Jewish. Her *grandfather*? He insisted it might become a problem. As it turned out, he was probably right.

In the summer of 1978, when midday temperatures exceeded 100°F, I met Habib Elghanian at the Shahanshahi Club, where Iranian waiters dispensed pastel-colored iced melon drinks to foreign businessmen and captains of Iranian industry. Elghanian, a pleasant man pushing late middle age, was the third richest man in Iran and a leader in the thriving Iranian Jewish community. He and his two brothers accumulated most of their wealth in Iran during World War II, and one of his brothers had settled in Israel. Among other things, Elghanian owned a manufacturing company that produced refrigerators. His factories created jobs in Iran and were a major contributor to the Iran's modest industrial progress. My ex-father-in-law imported refrigerators, freezers, stereos, and various luxuries for sale in Iran, and Elghanian occasionally visited his stores to examine the displays of foreign appliances and glean ideas for improvements of his own products.

In May 1979, I remembered Habib Elghanian's pleasant smile with deepening sadness and horror as I watched his televised kangaroo court trial. Facial bruises and swelling showed through heavy makeup. Bearded mullahs dressed in dark cloaks spat questions at him. Before he could answer, a mullah answered the question for him and twisted it into an accusation. Elghanian had no defense counsel and seemed disoriented and unsteady in his chair. He had been accused of being a Zionist spy, and the mock trial served as a warning to those who wanted to oppose the clerics. If this could happen to Habib Elghanian, any Iranian could be arrested for being a collaborator with the Shah, and any foreigner could be accused of spying. The next morning, the newspapers printed a photograph of Habib Elghanian's corpse. He was naked from the waist up and lay on his back in the courtyard of the prison. His execution as a spy was the pretext clerics used to seize his property for the benefit of the Islamic revolution. The Shahanshahi Club was renamed the Revolutionary Club.

In mid-June 2006, Warren recommended I see *The Fog of War*, a movie about Robert Strange McNamara's role in the Vietnam War and the United States' military industrial complex. The Middle East is unstable, and one of the challenges of having a large military industrial complex with powerful lobbyists in Washington is that it tends to find a reason for growing, namely a war. I ordered an old VHS copy that arrived in early July, and wrote Warren on July 14, 2006, two days after the war began. McNamara seemed to admit to having floundered his way through the Vietnam conflict.

> Thank you for your recommendation [to see] *The Fog of War*. I watched it twice back-to-back, and I will watch it again in the near future. I was fascinated by Robert S. McNamara's view of himself, and I was startled by what he felt were revelations. I agree that war is chaotic. But in the epic battle, I'd rather have

been one of the hundreds of Roman legionnaires than one of
the tens of thousands of Queen Boudica's Iceni. I am fond of a
good plan.

Israel is always in need of a good plan. The 33-day war with
Lebanon began on July 12, 2006, when Lebanese Hezbollah, a terrorist organization backed by Iran, shelled Israel's border and attacked two
Humvees, killing seven soldiers including those killed in a subsequent
failed rescue attempt of the two Israeli soldiers captured and spirited
into Lebanon. Rockets landed in the ISCAR main plant's industrial
park. The plant shut down for several days, but there was no major
damage, and business continued as usual after the war. Israel's forceful response included massive air strikes, the invasion of ground forces,
and the crippling of Lebanon's Rafic Hariri Airport and other parts of
the country's infrastructure. As in Turkey's conflict in the 1990s with
Kurdish insurgents belonging to the PKK (for Kurdistan Workers Party),
in which tens of thousands of Kurds were killed, Lebanese casualties
were many times the number of Israeli casualties. There were up to
1,000 civilian casualties. The casualties got much more media attention
than the much deadlier Turkish conflict with the PKK, perhaps because
the Lebanese conflict was between different religious groups. (The
media seems to relatively ignore the misery in Darfur, where Moslems
are killing hundreds of thousands of Moslems and displacing millions.[7])

By August 11, 2006, the United Nations Security Council approved
Resolution 1701. Both Lebanon and Israel agreed to the resolution,
which included troop withdrawals and, among other things, the disarma-
ment of Hezbollah. Predictably, Hezbollah has not disarmed. Just because
you negotiate an "agreement" and obtain a paper with dried ink signatures, it does not mean you necessarily have a deal in the Middle East.

🌑 🌑 🌑

Meanwhile, the dollar is being weakened by the expense of our poorly
planned ongoing Iraq War. However one wants to debate how we
got there, one of the reasons we may be quick to enter into a war is
because we have the military industrial complex to wage it.

On December 8, 2006, I wrote Warren a note about *The Iraq Study Group Report*. Despite the fact that we waged war in Iraq for more than three and a half years (at the time), we had recruited few Arab speakers, and we hadn't trained people to speak Arabic. Only *six* of the 1,000 embassy staff in Iraq spoke Arabic fluently, and only 33 in total spoke any Arabic at all. There were "fewer than 10 analysts on the job at the Defense Intelligence Agency who have more than two years' experience in analyzing the insurgency,"[8] and the report didn't make clear if any of them were fluent in Arabic, the language of the people they are trying to understand. Our costs were around $8 billion per month for this war, and we had spent a total of $400 billion.

The ultimate dollar cost of the Iraq War might reach $2 trillion in addition to lives lost—thousands of Americans, and tens of thousands injured or killed Iraqis. In January 2007, I wrote Warren about another movie, *Why We Fight,* a warning about the unchecked growth of a military industrial complex enabled by lobbyists and Washington think tanks. The Iraq war has been mismanaged. Besides possible overcharging by Halliburton, there were many reasons to investigate mismanagement of the war. For example, $12 billion, about half of Ambassador Paul Bremer's budget for rebuilding Iraq, simply disappeared. I had to add a Bremer amendment to my theory of everything in finance: *What is the probability you have someone handing out shrink wrapped bags of money that disappear from your organization?* I doubt Berkshire Hathaway will be tapping Bremer's management expertise any time soon.[9]

In April 2007, I wrote Warren and sent him a link to an article that appeared in the *Washington Post*:

> When I lived in London, I joined . . . the American Women's Club . . . [T]hey made it their mission to coax me to use my vacation days for bridge, hiking, lectures, short trips to the continent, language lessons and a variety of other activities they creatively planned. They called the club their Disney Land for women.
>
> Among the members was Peggy Sheehan . . . John J. Sheehan, Peggy's husband, turned down the "War Czar" job and stated his reasons in a *Washington Post* article.

John Sheehan is a retired Marine Corps general. He turned down the job as White House implementation manager for the Iraq and Afghanistan wars because he thought there is no consensus in Washington on strategy. He was also concerned about Iran as "an ideological and destabilizing threat to its neighbors and, more important, to U.S. interests."[10] Most important, he felt that Washington lacks "a broader view of the region and how the parts fit together strategically."[11]

Some pundits feel that pulling out of Iraq would allow Al Qaeda to flourish, but Al Qaeda is almost completely made up of Sunnis. The government of Iraq's 25 million people is dominated by Shiites. Shia Moslems make up around 55 percent of Iraq's population, and Sunnis make up most of the other 45 percent.

Iran already has a foothold in Iraq, and Iran would probably help eliminate the influence of Al Qaeda Sunnis. Shiites in Iraq and Iran have strong ties even though they have ethnic and language differences. Khomeini temporarily hid in Iraq when the Shah ousted him, and Shia Moslems make up around 90 percent of Iran's population of 68 million people. The greater threat might be that Hezbollah, an enemy of Israel, would find more support if we withdrew from Iraq.

It sometimes seems to me that Moslems would get along much more easily with Warren Buffett, a good-hearted atheist, than with members of a different faction of Islam. For centuries, the various factions of Islam have quarreled and, at times, have even gone to war.

The birthplace of Mohammed, the founder of the Islam, is Medina, located in Saudi Arabia. Shiites believe that Ali, Mohammed's son-in-law, is his successor. The Sunnis believe the Caliphs are Mohammed's successors. All Moslems have ties to Saudi Arabia. Devout Moslems believe that the *hajj,* a pilgrimage to Mecca in Saudi Arabia, is required at least once in one's lifetime. Performing the *hajj* is one of the five pillars of Islam. The other four are professing one's faith, praying in Arabic five times per day, giving alms to the poor, and fasting during Ramadan.

One would think those similarities would be enough for people to get along, but Islam is divided among itself, sometimes with snobbery that makes a British royal appear egalitarian. Most Iraqis are Arabs, but some are Kurds. Kurds consider themselves to be racially distinct from Arabs.

Minority populations of nomadic Kurds also live in neighboring countries. Iraqis chiefly speak Arabic, but regional minority languages include Kurdish and Turkmen. Iranians, formerly known as Persians, consider themselves Aryans, but many Persians appear to look Arabic.

When I lived in Iran, an Iranian friend joked that 40 percent of Iranians may have Arabic blood, and 100 percent of them will deny it. Nose jobs are a brisk business among Iranians living in foreign countries. Yet, many Iranians claim they are descended from the prophet Mohammed, who was an Arab. My Iranian ex-husband, who earned his Ph.D. in chemical engineering, had no problem performing the required mental gymnastics to live with this contradiction. This is not that unusual, either. Having been born and raised a U.S. Catholic, I know a few who cannot accept that Jesus was Jewish. Many who do accept it believe he looked like the blond blue-eyed actor Jeffrey Hunter in the *King of Kings*.

Iran's official language is Farsi (or Persian). It is an Indo-European language (most Westerners find Farsi much easier to master than Arabic), yet it uses Arabic script. All Iranian Moslems pray in Arabic, even if they do not understand the language. (Catholics recite Latin prayers without fully understanding them.) Iran has a small Arab minority and one of its neighbors is Arab-speaking Iraq. The United States has a much bigger language barrier in Iraq than Iran has. Given the large population of Shia Moslems in both Iraq and Iran, and given their common economic interest in oil, it is easy to see why Iran's influence is rapidly growing in Iraq. What that would mean for Israel is unclear, but it is a concern.

Warren invested in ISCAR with his eyes wide open, and he is a long-term investor. One of my British friends complained that Warren's investment in Israel is highly risky. I responded that financial risk is relative, and I saw people making much riskier bets in the mortgage market and in hedge funds for the promise of much less return.

Warren does not ignore risk, but he has a unique perspective. When we first met, Warren asked me what I thought the greatest global risks and surprises might be, and if I think of anything else later, to let him know. He asked what might happen if, for example, global computer communication were knocked out. How would we track trades? I responded that we might exhibit ingenuity. I recall that in *Apollo 13,* stranded astronauts and their Houston-based colleagues reached for *pencils* and *slide rules.* We sent men to the moon before computers were in every middle-class home. It is an unwelcome thought that we would go back to those days, but Warren tries to consider all angles.

While the 33-day Lebanese-Israeli war was still waging, on August 1, 2006, Bear Stearns Asset Management launched the Bear Stearns High Grade Structured Credit Strategies Enhanced Leverage fund. The fund invited investors with comforting words like "high grade" and "enhanced," and the investors seemed to be persuaded that they were getting a relatively safe and rewarding investment. Yet a terrorist attack would have posed less risk to their investment. Within a year, Bear Stearns told the fund's investors they would probably get nothing. Had the investors put their money in Berkshire Hathaway instead, they would have had more than $1.2 million for every $1 million they invested. Furthermore, the hapless investors in the hedge fund will have no peace. They hired lawyers.

Warren looks for companies that create value for consumers. ISCAR continues to thrive, and once he finds value, Warren's favorite holding period is forever. As a result, Berkshire Hathaway still owns the major part of a company that creates economic opportunity for both Jews and Arabs in Israel. Perhaps one day, it will be part of a Middle East renaissance. I like to think that Warren's investment has a chance to make the world a better place.

Chapter 14

Finding Value

[T]here was an absolutely open-ended, no-score-kept generosity of ideas, time, and spirit.

—Warren Buffett
on Benjamin Graham, 1976

After I met Warren for lunch, I began spending more time on my personal ideas of value. I bought energy and energy-related stocks, a potash manufacturer ripe for takeover, metals stocks, and some value stocks. I kept my Berkshire Hathaway holdings, of course.

I could write a long book on valuing Berkshire Hathaway. Instead I will offer you *my completely unauthorized and lazy shortcut to understanding the value of Berkshire Hathaway.* You can play around with balance sheets, discount rates, multiples, and the like; but basically Berkshire Hathaway invests in sound business that will stick around, and the businesses it owns have growing earnings.

A thorough analysis is hard, but understanding that there is a lot of value in the stock is easy. Getting the annual report brings a smile to my face and I dive in and get right to the action. Warren wrote in the 2007 shareholder letter that investments (about 40 percent financed by insurance float) are worth $90,600 per share. Now you add to that the value of $4,093 per share of a growing stream of earnings from the non-insurance operating businesses. As a long-term investor, you might use a 10-times multiple to earnings (as some long-term investors do) for a combined value—including investments—of $131,530. If you apply a 15 times earnings multiple (as other long-term investors do), you get a value of $151,995. No one knows what may happen in the super-cat insurance business managed by Ajit Jain who runs Berkshire Hathaway's reinsurance business, and I did not factor that into the numbers. 2006 was a lucky year and the super-cat insurance business went from red to very black. 2007 was a good year, too. No one can predict what will happen, but the premiums are well invested, and this is only a part of the overall business.

Obviously, this is a gross oversimplification. My point is there is substance behind the numbers. First and second quarter 2008 earnings were down, but Berkshire Hathaway's businesses continued and will continue to generate earnings. As noted before, there was an unrealized loss on derivatives, but shareholders know it is unlikely a payment will ever be due, Berkshire Hathaway has wisely invested the premium income, and Berkshire Hathaway is not leveraged and has lots of cash. This is why Warren Buffett and Charlie Munger are right to call this fluctuation meaningless. Meanwhile, the operating businesses generate earnings, and Warren is on the hunt for more good companies to grow operating revenues.

Intelligent investors revisit the stocks they own periodically, especially as market conditions change, but they do not overreact to a change in market prices. Although one's favorite holding period may be forever, you do not have to hold stocks you no longer favor. If you are a value investor, you won't have to check your portfolio every day, but you should periodically reevaluate your decisions.

Berkshire Hathaway may never match the stellar returns of its early years, but it is likely to remain a great steady performer returning 10 percent to 15 percent over a five-year period. Even if a prolonged recession hurts returns, I am still likely to be much better off than the rest of the market. Berkshire Hathaway's companies make things people use, want, and need. While results may not be as exciting as they were in previous decades, they are likely to be satisfactory in the long run. You will not gasp with delight one day only to gasp for air the next. It is not my only holding, but it is one I do not worry about.

When we had lunch, Warren encouraged me to use what I know, so I fell back on my engineering background to look for opportunities. For example, in the late spring of 2006, it seemed to me oil pipe replacement orders were not keeping up with stress corrosion cracking and ordinary corrosion. A pipeline at Alaska's North Slope proved the point by leaking oil through a corroded pipe shortly after I bought steel shares. The smaller steel companies were ripe for takeover and produced gains of more than 30 percent.

In December 2006, I wrote Warren that I had rejected a pitch by a California-based hedge fund manager that did not seem to offer anything new and demonstrated some inconsistencies. They strongly believed in the housing bubble, so they did not own their own homes. Yet this strength of conviction did not extend to their personal transportation. They strongly believed energy prices (and gasoline prices) would explode; yet they drove gas guzzling sports cars (except for the salesman, who seemed smug because he said he drives a hybrid). I was already long energy and oil-related stocks. I had bought shares in two steel companies, which produced gains of more than 30 percent when they were acquired by larger companies, and I profited when my shares in a small potash company was acquired by a large chemical company, and I do not charge myself high fees. Warren Buffett takes advantage of these kinds of market opportunities when he finds them. These are called *merger and acquisition* (M&A) opportunities, and they are sometimes loosely (and not technically correctly) called merger "arbitrage" opportunities. These are not meant to be long-term holdings, but are a way of taking advantage of a good opportunity when it seems to fall in your lap. Sometimes, however, you can be wrong (it is not a genuine arbitrage) and you fall off your chair. The other problem with merger and acquisition opportunities is that once the acquisition occurs and one pockets a gain (currently a short-term gain is taxed higher than a long-term gain and often these are short-term opportunities), one has to reinvest. *What next?* It can be exhausting, so I am trying to find more value stocks as long-term holdings.

When I sent Warren my old copy of *The Intelligent Investor* to sign, he returned it with an inscription: "To Janet – With personal & professional admiration."[1] He may write that inscription for everyone but I glowed the entire day anyway. In August 2007, during one of several minor market upsets, I wrote Warren: "I've been recommending *The Intelligent Investor* for those swimming for the lifeboats."[2]

Warren could have invented the maxim "ponder, and then *act*." His investment style allows him to remain unflappable despite Mr. Market's manic depressive fluctuations. While the asset bubble expanded and exploded, Warren made time for old and new friends.

Warren wrote me at the end of May 2006: "I am swamped at present. You will see why in a little while…."[3] Even though he was terribly busy, he made time for me. I called Warren in June 2006 to ask his thoughts on my nephew selling his business. It is a business too small for Warren (but very substantial), and my nephew is a young man. While Warren's advice was the same as mine, Warren agreed my nephew would more readily accept advice from "the voice of authority."[4] The prospect of getting a large upfront payment was very enticing to my nephew, but he loved running his business. Would he rather spend his money beating back tropical vegetation from a Caribbean estate, or would he rather invest his cash in a growing business that he finds rewarding to manage? Warren said he envied him having a business he loved (but only because my nephew was in his early 30s). I wrote Warren on June 20, 2006:

> Tony was very surprised that you would spend even a picosecond considering his dilemma and was curious about my impressions about how you spend your money, meaning whether or

not it was spent in a way that impresses people. I responded that most of your wealth growth occurred after age 65, and you spent your wealth reinvesting in good businesses. It struck me that you lived how and where you wanted and didn't waste a moment's thought on how others might assume you should live. Yet, you are still the kind of man who would spend time considering someone else's problems, even when there was nothing immediately in it for you. I was deeply impressed. What could be more impressive?[5]

On June 22, 2006, Warren wrote back and mentioned Tony: "Tell him I wish him the best."[6] Not only did I tell Tony, I gave him a copy of Warren's letter. Tony did not sell his business. My nephew probably would have come to this decision himself, but it helps to have a sounding board. My nephew was floored that he called to ask me about this and I was able to have a conversation with Warren and get back to him with Warren's opinion in the same afternoon. Warren must have known the effect this would have. At the time of our conversation, I had no idea Warren was in the middle of finalizing his arrangements to leave the major part of his wealth to the Gates Foundation. On June 26, 2006, Warren made the announcement with Bill and Melinda Gates in New York.

I responded: "In my June 20 letter I asked: 'What could be more impressive?' Your answer is magnificent."[7]

Value isn't just about money, but value investing may give you more time for the other things you value in your life.

When I think back to my unanswered invitation, I cannot explain what took me so long to answer. It seemed to me Warren did not just invite me to lunch. He invited me to come around (even more) to his way of thinking. Benjamin Graham wrote about the pretensions of stock market pundits: "The farther one gets away from Wall Street, the more skepticism one will find."[8] Graham might have said the same things about the social pretensions of the Maserati drivers of Wall Street. Warren had written me that he thought Tony was "better off for having the experience of thinking through what he truly wants to do in his life."[9] At the time Warren had already given a lot of thought about his legacy, and it seemed to me that everyone benefits from the experience of thinking through what is really valuable to us in life. There is something to be said for moving 1,269 miles away from Wall Street in one's mind. One gets a clearer view.

Value investing principles can also help you think clearly in the face of scary financial turmoil. Warren proposed a fix for the economy that added protection for U.S. taxpayers, but the bailout bill did not include it.[10] Warren will try to profit from the folly. In September 2008, Berkshire invested $5 billion in Goldman Sachs' perpetual preferred shares paying a 10% dividend (plus warrants). By then Goldman was a bank holding company and the government had committed to massive bailouts.[11]

The U.S. stock market became increasingly volatile and fell thousands of points in the fall of 2008. Warren's personal account held only U.S. government bonds, and he began buying stocks. Warren feels the market will probably move higher, perhaps much higher before the economy improves again: "So if you wait for the robins, spring will be over."[12]

Warren Buffett may be my benchmark for sanity in the global financial markets (and how to conduct one's life), but he is not perfect and is not above using statistics to his advantage. At his annual meeting he joked that he (at 77) and Charlie Munger (at 84) have an average age of 80. They are aging by 1.25 percent per year, whereas 50-year-old executives are aging around 2 percent per year. According to these statistics, I am aging around 60 percent faster than Warren.

I really must write him about that.

Notes

Preface

1. Josh Hamilton and Dan Reichl, "Buffett Has $2.1 Million Lunch Date with Hedge-Fund Manager," *Bloomberg News,* 28 June 2008.
2. Steven F. Hayward, *Churchill on Leadership* (Rocklin, CA: Forum, 1997), 3.

Chapter 1: An Unanswered Invitation

1. Warren Buffett to Janet Tavakoli, letter, 6 June 2005.
2. Ann C. Logue, "The Cassandra of Credit Derivatives," *Business Week Chicago,* 28 January 2008.
3. Warren Buffett, "Shareholder Letter," *Berkshire Hathaway 2002 Annual Report,* 14.
4. Ibid., 11.
5. Ibid., 13.
6. Ibid., 14.
7. Ibid., 15.

Chapter 2: Lunch with Warren

1. Katherine Graham, *Personal History* (New York: Random House, 1997), 534.
2. Ibid., 531.

3. Taesu Bynun, "IMDb Mini Biography for Dustin Hoffman," *Mndb.com*, 2008.

4. Carol J. Loomis, "The Jones Nobody Keeps Up With," *Fortune*, April 1966.

5. Benjamin Graham, *The Intelligent Investor* (New York: Harper & Row, 1973), 108.

6. Benoit Mandelbrot and Richard L. Hudson, *The (Mis)Behavior of Markets* (New York: Basic Books, 2004), 261.

7. Based on the Yale Endowment Updates 1993–2007 and Berkshire Hathaway historical daily share price data from Yahoo! Finance.

8. Benjamin Graham, *The Intelligent Investor* (New York: Harper & Row, 1973), 277.

9. Ibid., 103.

10. Cifuentes Arturo, "CDOs and Their Ratings: Chronicle of a Foretold Disaster," *Total Securitization*, 4 June 2007.

11. Brooke Masters, "Former Reagan Aide Charged with Fraud," *Financial Times*, 26 March 2007.

12. Warren Buffett to Janet Tavakoli, e-mail correspondence, 27 August 2007.

Chapter 3: The Prairie Princes versus the Princes of Darkness

1. *Berkshire Hathaway 2007 Annual Report*, 15.

2. Julie Rannazzisi, "Coca-Cola to Expense Stock Options," *CBS Marketwatch .com*, 14 July 2002.

3. Tom McGinty, "Fewer Investors Back Plans to Weigh in Executive Compensation," *Wall Street Journal*, 22 May 2008.

4. Janet Tavakoli, "FASB in Error on Options Valuation," *Financial Times*, 5 April 2004.

5. Warren Buffett, "Fuzzy Math and Stock Options," *Washington Post*, 6 July 2004.

6. Mark Maremont, "Authorities Probe Improper Backdating of Options— Practice Allows Executives to Bolster Their Stock Gains; A Highly Beneficial Pattern, *Wall Street Journal*, 11 November 2005.

7. Charles Forelle and James Bandler, "The Perfect Payday—Some CEOs Reap Millions by Landing Stock Options When They Are Most Valuable; Luck—or Something Else?" *Wall Street Journal*, 18 March 2006.

8. "Perfect Payday: Options Scorecard," *Wall Street Journal*, 4 September 2007.

9. Kip Hagopian, "Point of View: Expensing Employee Stock Options is Improper Accounting," *California Management Review* 48 no. 4 (Summer 2006): 136–156.

10. Holman W. Jenkins, Jr., "Stock Option Fiends Revealed," *Wall Street Journal*, 30 August 2006.

11. Janet Tavakoli, "The Golden Fleece Award for Optional Integrity," Tavakoli Structured Finance, Inc. (client note), September 6, 2006.

12. Janet Tavakoli, "The Golden Fleece Award for Optional Integrity," *Lipper HedgeWorld,* October 2, 2006 (printed with permission of Tavakoli Structured Finance, Inc., which retains the copyright).

13. Warren Buffett to Janet Tavakoli, e-mail correspondence, 2 October 2006.

14. Kevin Allisonin, "HP's Dunn Charged With Conspiracy," *Financial Times,* 5 October 2006.

15. Warren Buffett, memo of September 27 was published in the *Financial Times* on October 9, 2008. It was sent to me six days after Buffett sent it to his managers.

16. Ibid.

17. Floyd Norris, "The 1994 Honor Roll (of Sorts)," *New York Times,* 25 December 1994.

18. Benjamin Graham, *The Intelligent Investor* (New York: Harper & Row, 1973), 96.

Chapter 4: The Insatiable Curiosity to Know Nothing Worth Knowing (Oscar Wilde Was Right)

1. Anita Raghavan and Mitchell Pacelle, "Buffett Has Renewed His Talks to Acquire Long-Term Capital," *Wall Street Journal,* 27 October 1998.

2. Roger Lowenstein, *When Genius Failed* (New York: HarperCollins, 2002), 128–129, 224–225.

3. Claudia H. Deutsch, "Edson Mitchell Dies at 47, Executive of Deutsche Bank," *New York Times,* 26 December 2001. Edson Mitchell died in 2001 at the age of 47, after the twin-engine Beechcraft flying him to Rangeley, Maine to join his ex-wife and his children for the holidays, crashed into a mountain. He had left Merrill Lynch in 1995 to run global markets at Deutsche Bank.

4. Anita Raghavan, "Long-Term Capital's Partners Got Big Loans to Invest in Fund," *Wall Street Journal,* 6 October 1998.

5. "A Top Trader Quits Salomon," *New York Times,* 22 December 1994. Hufschmid was head of Foreign Exchange at Salomon in 1993; his foreign exchange trading group reportedly made more than $200 million.

6. Edward Wyatt, "Profits of Hedge Fund Insiders Appear to Be Off but Still Big," *New York Times,* 26 September 1998.

7. Sandra Hernandez, "Two-Year Notes Have Biggest Weekly Decline in 2008 on Fed Cut," *Bloomberg News,* 21 March 2008.

8. Gregory Zuckerman, "Shakeout Roils Hedge-Fund World," *Wall Street Journal,* 17 June 2008. Estimates varied from as low as 6,000 to 8,500 globally,

depending on who was counting. That number does not include managed offshore entities that looked a lot like hedge funds but are called by a variety of structured finance labels, *structured investment vehicles* (SIVs), and *special purpose acquisition vehicles* (SPACs). Many of them invest in leveraged bets on tranches of collateralized debt obligations.

9. Gregory Zuckerman, "Shakeout Roils Hedge-Fund World," *Wall Street Journal,* 17 June 2008.

10. Josh Hamilton, "Warren Buffett's Berkshire Salary Remains $100,000," *Bloomberg News,* 17 March 2008.

11. Jenny Strasburg, "Tudor Investors Pull More than $1 Billion from Raptor," *Bloomberg News,* 14 December 2007.

12. Carrick Mollenkamp and Ian McDonald, "SEC Plumbs Money Firm's Files," *Wall Street Journal,* 24 March 2006.

13. *Kenneth M. Krys and Christopher Stride, et. al. v. Christopher Sugrue, Mark Kavanagh, et al.* Supreme Court of the State of New York, County of New York, Index No. 08600653, filed May 5, 2008.

14. Greg Newton, "Serve Him Right: SPhinX Liquidators Sue Angolan Resident," *Naked Shorts,* 3 April 2008.

15. See note 13 in Chapter 3.

16. W. W. Meissner, S.J., M.D. *Ignatius of Loyola: The Psychology of a Saint* (New Haven: Yale University Press, 1992), 26.

17. Gary Belsky, and Thomas Gilovich, *Why Smart People Make Big Money Mistakes and How to Correct Them* (New York: Fireside, 1999), 118.

18. Lowenstein, *When Genius Failed,* 123.

19. *Berkshire Hathaway 2007 Annual Report.* 17.

20. Nassim Taleb, *Fooled by Randomness* (New York: Random House, 2001) xxvi. Emphasis in original.

21. Janet Tavakoli, "Dead Man's Curve," *Client Note,* 21 September 2006. A longer version of this client note was published in *HedgeWorld.com,* 22 September 2006 (printed with permission of TSF, which retains the copyright). The following is an excerpt for those interested in more detail:

> If we use the model for a normal (Gaussian) distribution, a five-standard deviation credit event should only happen once in every 7,000 years. But in the market place, we see this happen once or twice in a decade. Amaranth was short fall natural gas futures contracts and long winter natural gas futures contracts in sequential years from 2006 through 2009, among other trades. But just as too much money flowing into these trades can collapse spreads in the treasury market, too much leveraged money flowing into the much thinner

commodities market undid Amaranth's trades. Spreads tightened by five to ten standard deviations in the September/December natural gas spreads depending on which time period you use for your data. In September, Amaranth lost more than half of its value, skidding from $9 billion to only $3 billion in assets (according to the *Wall Street Journal*) having put on the classic "Dead Man's Curve" trade. These trades don't follow a normal curve or even a historical spread pattern, and even if historical patterns eventually return, in the meantime, one is merely "dead" right.

22. Warren Buffett to Janet Tavakoli, e-mail correspondence, 27 September 2006.

23. Ianthe Jeanne Dugan, "Failed Hedge Fund Haunts Celebrities," *Wall Street Journal,* 22 August 2006.

24. Richard Esposito, "Police Investigating Possible Suicide by Hedge Fund Cheat," *ABC News,* 9 June 2008.

25. Ibid.

26. Greg Newton, "Surfacing Scammy," *Naked Shorts,* 10 June 2008.

27. Ianthe Jeanne Dugan, "Manhunt is Launched for Trader in Big Fraud," *Wall Street Journal,* 11 June, 2008.

28. Ibid.

29. Greg Newton, "Show Me the Corpse!" *Naked Shorts,* 9 June 2008.

30. Carlyn Kolker and David Glovin, "Bayou's Samuel Israel to Forfeit Bail, Begins 20-Year Sentence, *Bloomberg News,* 3 July 2008.

31. Christian Boone and Bill Rankin, "Marietta Man in Hedge Fund Fraud Commits Suicide," *Atlanta Journal-Constitution,* 25 May 2008.

32. D. H. Lawrence, "The Rocking Horse Winner," in *The Woman who Rode Away and Other Stories* (1928), edited by Dieter Mehl and Christa Jansohn (Cambridge, U.K.: Cambridge University Press, 1995) 230–243.

33. Benjamin Graham, *The Intelligent Investor* New York: Harper & Row, 1973), 98.

34. Richard Heckinger to Janet Tavakoli, e-mail correspondence, 22 August 2006. Heckinger is now the senior policy advisor in the Financial Markets Group of the Federal Reserve Bank of Chicago.

35. Gregory Zuckerman, "Shakeout Roils Hedge-Fund World," *Wall Street Journal,* 17 June 2008. The calculations on the number of hedge funds controlling assets is from Tavakoli Structured Finance Inc. based on market share data from Hedge Fund Research, Inc. sourced in this article.

36. Tom Cahill, "HFR Hedge Fund Index Rebounds in April after Decline in March," *Bloomberg News,* 30 April 2008.

37. Matthew Lynn, "Hedge Funds Come Unstuck on Truth-Twisting, Lies," *Bloomberg News,* 9 April 2008.

38. Tom Cahill, "Hedge Fund Outlook Is 'Much Worse' Than 1998, LTCM Veteran Says," *Bloomberg News,* 8 August 2008. Hans Hufschmid became the chief executive officer of GlobeOp Financial Services LP.

39. Neil Weinberg and Bernard Condon, "The Sleaziest Show on Earth," *Forbes,* 24 May 2004.

40. Ibid.

41. Ralph Cioffi (former managing director of Bear Stearns Asset Management) in a conversation with author, 30 March 2006. (This is not proprietary information).

42. *Berkshire Hathaway Inc. 2007 Annual Report,* 17.

43. Carol J. Loomis, "Buffett's Big Bet," *Fortune/CNNMoney.com,* 9 June 2008.

Chapter 5: MAD Mortgages—The "Great" Against the Powerless

1. *Berkshire Hathaway 2003 Annual Report,* 5.

2. *OHC Liquidation Trust, et al v. Credit Suisse First Boston et al.,* U.S. Bankruptcy Court, Delaware. Civil Action No. 07–799 JJF (Chapter 11 Case No. 02–13396) Memorandum Opinion June 9, 2008. (Partial Summary Judgment) Oakwood provided both mortgage loans and retail installment sales contracts (RICs) to buyers of its homes. Credit Suisse First Boston and subsidiaries (CSFB) provided Oakwood with a warehouse facility. CSFB received a warrant to purchase just under 20 percent of Oakwood's common stock and earned fees for the warehouse facility and for structuring real estate mortgage investment trusts (REMICs) backed by Oakwood's loans. CSFB was also the underwriter and marketer. CSFB bought the REMIC Certificates and sold them to investors. On November 15, 2002, Oakwood filed for protection under Chapter 11 of the Bankruptcy Code. From 1994 to 2002, CSFB underwrote $7.5 billion of Oakwood's securitizations, of which $1.3 billion were done in 2001–2002. In 2001–2002 alone CSFB earned around $21 million in fees. Oakwood's liquidator wanted $50 million for the decline in its value while it was sinking and to get back $21 million in fees it paid in 2001–2002 to Credit Suisse. In 1999, one of CSFB's credit officers had written that Oakwood posted "real/immediate bankruptcy risk issues/concerns," and that Oakwood "is the weakest company in its [industry]" 5. Oakwood's liquidator was unsuccessful in its claim. What applied here is *in pari delicto potior est condition defendentis.* It is an equitable defense barring someone from profiting from his own wrong.

3. *Berkshire Hathaway 2003 Annual Report,* 5.

4. Housing Vacancies and Homeownership (CPS/HVS), U.S. Census Bureau. In 2002, 67.8 million U.S. (and region) residents owned homes; in 2004, 68.6 million

owned homes; in the first quarter of 2008 the number of homeowners was back down to 67.8 million, and at 68.1 million in the second quarter of 2008.

5. Eliot Spitzer, "Predatory Lenders' Partner in Crime," *Washington Post,* 14 February 2008.

6. "Roland E. Arnall, 68; Founded High-Risk Lender Ameriquest," *Washington Post,* 20 March 2008. Roland E. Arnall died in March 2008.

7. Gerri Willis discussed 2007 foreclosures during an interview with Jon Stewart on Comedy Central's *The Daily Show* on January 30, 2008.

8. Gerri Willis, Andy Serwer, Paul Krugman, Janet Tavakoli, and Peter Dunay, "Busted! Mortgage Meltdown," CNN, March 28, 2008 (first airing).

9. Ibid.

10. Aaron Krowne, entrepreneur and head of Planet Math, started this website (http://ml-implode.com) in late 2006 to chronicle unfolding events in the troubled US mortgage lending market.

11. "New Century Financial Corporation to Restate Financial Statements for the Quarters Ended March 31, June 30 and September 30, 2006," *PR Newswire,* 7 February 2007.

12. Amanda Beck, "KPMG allowed fraud at New Century, report says," *Reuters,* March 27, 2008.

13. Vikas Bajaj and Christine Haugney, "Tremors at the Door," *New York Times,* 26 January 2007.

14. Warren Buffett's to Liz Clayman, CNBC interview,13 March 2007.

15. Tom Hudson and Janet Tavakoli, "Fed's Role in the Subprime Meltdown," *First Business Morning News,* 19 March 2007.

16. *Berkshire Hathaway 2003 Annual Report,* 5.

17. Floyd Norris, "Color-Blind Merrill in a Sea of Red Flags," *New York Times,* 16 May 2008.

18. Ibid.

19. "Subprime Winners and Losers," *Squawk Box,* CNBC, 3 August 2007. Segment with Janet Tavakoli, Joe Kernen, and Becky Quick.

20. Antonin Scalia to Leslie Stahl, *60 Minutes,* CBS, 27 April 2008.

21. David Enrich, "Banks Find New Ways to Ease Pain of Bad Loans," *Wall Street Journal,* 19 June 2008. Thrift holding company Astoria Financial Corp's non-performing loans were $106 million at the end of 2007, but the following quarter, it changed its internal policy to define "non performing" loans as missing *three* payments instead of *two.* Wachovia and Washington Mutual started using OFHEO data for first quarter results.

22. Betsy McKay, Wells Fargo's Net is Better Than Expected, Earnings Decline But Beat Estimates; Stock Rallies 33%," *Wall Street Journal,* 17 July 2008.

23. Robin Sidel, "Banking's Winners and Sinners Part Ways," *Wall Street Journal,* 19 July 2008.

24. "Remarks by Chairman Alan Greenspan, *Consumer Finance,*" at the Federal Reserve System's Fourth Annual Community Affairs Research Conference, Washington, D.C. April 8, 2005. Greenspan said the following:

   > With these advances in technology, lenders have taken advantage of credit-scoring models and other techniques for efficiently extending credit to a broader spectrum of consumers. . . . Where once more-marginal applicants would simply have been denied credit, lenders are now able to quite efficiently judge the risk posed by individual applicants and to price that risk appropriately. These improvements have led to rapid growth in subprime mortgage lending.

   The full text is available at http://www.federalreserve.gov/BoardDocs/speeches/2005/20050408/default.htm.

25. Janet Tavakoli and Thalia Assuras, "Making the Most of the Market," *CBS Evening News,* 4 August, 2007.

26. Janet Tavakoli to Warren Buffet, e-mail correspondence, 15 August 2007. The following is the gist of my remarks:

   > Asset-backed conduits that issue commercial paper have been investing in very risky credit linked notes (CLNs). The risk is linked to leveraged structured products including subprime and other mortgage loan debt. Some are also linked to corporate leveraged loans (private equity buyout debt and other debt). The credit linked notes employ credit derivatives technology. [This is related to my comments about super senior mark-to-market manipulation. Many firms put leveraged super senior linked notes (CLNs) in the conduits to avoid the unpleasantness of marking them to market.] . . . Investors can be left holding the bag, because entities that provide the liquidity facilities sometimes refuse to buy the paper based on "technicalities (foreseen technicalities)." Nice kids. I call this the "Wiffelwaferdooper Exception." It appears in many forms in many documents. This is what seems to be happening right now in Canada.

27. "Bracing for Regulation," CNBC, 13 August 2007. Segment with Steve Forbes, Janet Tavakoli, Carl Quintanilla, and Eugene Ludwig,

28. Becky Quick, "Buffett Eyes Countrywide," CNBC, 21 August 2007.

29. Katherine Graham, *Personal History* (New York: Random House, 1997), 534.

30. Harlan Levy, "The Finger Is Pointing toward the Underwriters," *Journal Inquirer* (Connecticut), 9 October 2007.

31. E. Scott Reckard, "Countrywide Financial Chairman Angelo Mozilo's e-mail sets off a furor," *Los Angeles Times,* 21 May 2008.

32. James R. Hagerty, "Rainmaker Mozilo Exits under a Cloud," *Wall Street Journal,* 28 June 2008.

33. David Wighton, "Reputations to Restore at Unforgiving Merrill," *Financial Times,* 10 October 2007.

34. Janet Tavakoli, "Subprime Mortgages: The Predator's Fall," *GARP Risk Review,* no. 35 (March–April 2007). This article was published on April 13, 2007. I wrote the original draft in February 2007.

35. "Inside Merrill Lynch," *Squawk Box,* CNBC, 24 October 2008. Segment with Janet Tavakoli, Joe Kernan, Jack Welch, and Charlie Gasparino,

36. Stan O'Neal, "Risky Business," *Wall Street Journal,* 24 April 2003.

37. "More than 400 Defendants Charged for Roles in Mortgage Fraud Schemes as Part of Operation 'Malicious Mortgage' Federal Bureau of Investigation Press Release, Washington, 19 June 2008.

38. Ruth Simon, "Countrywide's Pressures Mount," *Wall Street Journal,* 26 June 2008.

39. Andrew Harris, "Countrywide Sued by Florida Over 'Deceptive' Loans," *Bloomberg News,* 1 July 2008.

40. Illinois Attorney General Lisa Madigan made these comments when Tom Hudson interviewed her for a segment, "Countrywide in the Crosshairs," on *First Business Morning News,* which aired June 25, 2008.

41. Ruth Simon, "Countrywide's Pressures Mount," *Wall Street Journal,* 26 June 2008.

42. Damian Paletta and David Enrich," Crisis Deepens as Big Bank Fails," *Wall Street Journal,* 12 July 2008. Senator Charles Schumer (D. N.Y.) had written to the Office of Thrift Supervision about IndyMac's solvency and depositors withdrew around $1.3 billion in following 11 days. The largest two bank failures before 2008 were Continental Illinois National Bank and Trust (Chicago) in 1984; it had $40 billion in assets, and First Republic Bank (Dallas) in 1988; it had $32.5 billion in assets.

43. Michelle A. Danis and Anthony Pennington-Cross, "The Delinquency of Subprime Mortgages," Federal Reserve Bank of St. Louis (Working Paper 2005–022A), March 2005, 15.

44. AP New York, "S&P: Subprime delinquencies continue to climb," 22 May 2008.

45. James Tyson, "Fannie, Freddie Surplus Capital Requirement Is Eased," *Bloomberg News,* 19 March 2008.

46. James R. Hagerty, Ruth Simon, and Damian Paletta, "U.S. Seizes Mortgage Giants," *Wall Street Journal,* 8 September 2008.

47. Dan Levy, "U.S. Foreclosures Hit Record in August as Housing Prices Fell," *Bloomberg News,* 12 September 2008.

48. Gretchen Morgenson and Charles Duhigg, "Loan Giant Overstated the Size of Its Capital Base," *New York Times,* 7 September 2008.

49. Caroline Baum, "No Limit to Greenspan's Once-In-A-Century Events: Caroline Baum," *Bloomberg News,* 18 August, 2008.

50. *Berkshire Hathaway 1999 Annual Report.* 15.

51. *Berkshire Hathaway 2000 Annual Report.* 12.

52. *Berkshire Hathaway 2003 Annual Report,* 5.

53. Ibid.

Chapter 6: Shell Games (Beware of Geeks Bearing Grifts)

1. Matthew Goldstein, "Bear Stearns Shakes the CDO Honey Pot," *TheStreet .com,* 5 August 2005.

2. Ibid.

3. Elizabeth MacDonald, *"Did the SEC Miss Warning Signs at Bear Stearns?" FoxBusiness.com,* 23 June 2008.

4. Floyd Norris, "A Lesson in Fraud for Chris Cox," *New York Times,* 29 July 2005.

5. Ibid.

6. Ibid.

7. Aaron Johnson, "TABS CDO Auction Recoups Just 3% of Total Debt," *Securitization News,* 4 April 2008.

8. Michael Mackenzie, "Credit Vehicle Defaults Reach $170 billion," *Financial Times,* 24 April 2008.

9. Jody Shenn, "State Street, BlackRock Manage Some CDOs in Default," *Bloomberg News,* January 4, 2008. This is excerpted from the Tavakoli Structured Finance, Inc. client note of December 7, 2007.

> Adams Square Funding I had collateral consisting of both cash and synthetic (pay-as-you-go credit default swaps) of ABS CDOs on mezzanine subprime among other items. The conflicts of interest between the collateral manager, Credit Suisse Alternative Capital (CSAC), and other affiliated entities, including the Leveraged Investment Group (LIG) of Credit Suisse Securities (CSS) are [disclosed in the prospectus]. This is the kind of moral hazard from which I stated investors should walk briskly away [See p. 194 *Collateralized Debt Obligations* (John Wiley & Sons, 2003).] Rating agencies models do not capture the risks of moral hazard, and the rating agencies even failed to capture the obvious magnitude of

the collateral risks. . . . Monolines rated "AAA" are not laughing, however, nor are the lower rated monolines. Writing guarantees on super-senior tranches seemed fine according to generic models, but many of these tranches have substantial principal risk. . . . [and] would require substantial capital increases.

10. Prospectus for Adams Square Funding I, Ltd. CreditSuisse offering memorandum, January 22, 2007, 34, 35.

11. Carrick Mollenkamp and Serena Ng, "Wall Street Wizardry Amplified the Credit Crisis," *Wall Street Journal,* 27 December 2007.

12. Ibid.

13. Janet Tavakoli, "Dead Calm: No One Trusts You: A Letter to Certain Banks and CDO Managers," Tavakoli Structured Finance, Inc. 30 July 2008. The following is an excerpt:

> Some market pundits say that 'disclosure' is the answer to the "dead calm" of a securitization market adrift in the doldrums. That is not it guys. It is one thing to have documents that disclose risks—many of the documents of death spiral collateralized debt obligations (CDOs backed by private-label residential mortgage backed securities) in 2007 disclosed eye-popping risks—it is quite another to bring deals to market that you knew or should have known were overrated and deeply troubled the day the deal closed.
>
> The real issue is timely, complete and continuing disclosure. If you knew or should have known your "triple-A" tranches deserved a junk rating on the day the deal closed, that should have been specifically disclosed, no matter what the rating agencies, or your attorneys, said. As the investment bank securitizing the deal and selling the securities, it was down to you. You thought the disclaimers in the documents protected you—well how is that working out? You are now suffering some of the consequences. The SEC may say you were within the "rules" (let's see what happens), but the market is holding you responsible. Investors shun you.
>
> The reason no one trusts securitizations is not "disclosure" of loan data. The reason is that you, the securitization departments of several investment banks and the "friendly" CDO "managers," that "managed" their death spiral CDOs, have no credibility. If securitization professionals failed to perform appropriate due diligence, they have a problem. If they performed due diligence, but suppressed the reports, they also have a problem. Going forward, investors may not even trust "disclosures" of due diligence, because loan data can be manipulated. Your current lack of credibility means your former customers will be reluctant to believe your data and your documents in future.

So, how did the CDOs that Merrill Lynch brought to market in 2007 perform? All of the deals I captured are in serious trouble at the "triple-A" level. [The deal names are: Lexington Cap Fundg III; Port Jackson CDO 2007–1; Highridge ABS CDO I; Maxim High Grade CDO I; Broderick CDO 3; Kleros Real Estate CDO IV; Norma CDO I; Maxim High Grade CDO II; Newbury Street CDO Ltd.; South Coast Funding IX; Euler ABS CDO I; Glacier V; Lexington Capital Funding V; Libertas Preferred Funding IV; Silver Marlin; Kleros Preferred Funding VII; NEO CDO 2007–1; Forge ABS High Grade CDO I; IMAC CDO 2007–2; Mars CDO I; Brookville CDO I; Fourth Street Funding Ltd.; Wester Springs CDO; Jupiter High Grade CDO VI; Tazlina Funding II; West Trade Funding CDO III; Robeco HG CDO I; Durant CDO 2007–1; Biltmore CDO 2007–1; Bernoulli High Grade CDO II]. All have one or more originally "triple-A" rated tranches downgraded below investment grade (junk) by one or more rating agencies. Of the 30 CDOs, 27 have even the topmost original "triple-A" tranche now ranked as junk by one or more rating agencies.

As of June 10, 2008, of 30 CDOs totaling more than $32 billion in notional amount, 19 have declared an event of default, are in acceleration, or have been liquidated. Ten others are "toast," as evidenced by downgrades of their "triple A" tranches to junk status, yet I could find no record of a declared event of default (EOD). The remaining CDO has "triple-A" tranches downgraded to junk, but the two topmost tranches are still rated investment grade (the topmost is Aa1 neg/ AAA neg and the formerly "triple-A" tranche below that is Baa2 neg/ BBB+ neg). The EOD may be undeclared due to documents that avoid that declaration so that investors cannot trigger acceleration or liquidation (or the declaration may be pending).

Merrill had pieces of other investment banks' deals embedded in many of the CDOs, and likewise other investment banks had pieces of Merrill's CDOs in their deals. And, of course, their credit derivatives desks bought and sold protection on each others CDOs.

As far as I can tell, disclosing loan data is not the problem. The problem is that investment banks knew or should have known they packaged damaged product to sell to unwary investors.

Granted, some of these investors were sophisticated and should have known better; investment banks and "sophisticated" investors, like the bond insurers can slug it out with each other. But there is a difference between an account with a lot of money and a "sophisticated" investor. Many smaller municipalities and other retail-like accounts may have been saddled with dodgy products.

Investment banks and the rings of highly paid managers, securitization professionals, and lax CDO managers have an enormous amount of responsibility for the collateral damage done to the U.S. housing market and "insured" bond markets.

One can argue that the bond insurers were willing victims, but municipalities paying higher funding costs were not. One can argue that some homeowners knowingly overextended themselves, but many others were victims of predatory lending practices. U.S. taxpayers are unwilling victims, paying either directly or indirectly for housing market assistance, turmoil in municipal bond markets, frozen auction rate securities, and bailouts of errant mortgage lenders and investment banks.

The Federal Reserve Bank is now providing liquidity for many investment banks either directly or indirectly. Investment banks may not be "borrowing," but the Fed's willingness to accept "AAA" assets in exchange for treasuries is a back-door bailout.

14. Elinor Comlay, "Merrill Lynch 2007 CDOs under water-consultant," *Reuters,* 31 July 2008.

15. Greg Newton, "Thos 2007 Merrill CDOs in Foole," *Seeking Alpha,* 31 July 2008.

16. Yalman Onaran, "Banks Hide $35 Billion in Writedowns From Income, Filings Show," *Bloomberg News,* 19 May 2008.

17. Yalman Onaran, "Subprime Losses Top $396 Billion on Brokers' Writedowns: Table," *Bloomberg News,* 18 June 2008.

18. Yalman Onaran and Dave Pierson, "Banks' Subprime Market-Related Losses, Capital Raised," *Bloomberg News,* 16 October 2008.

19. Huw Jones, "IMF sticks by $1 trillion U.S. subprime fallout," *Reuters,* 16 July 2008.

20. Warren Buffett to Janet Tavakoli, private conversation, 10 January 2008.

21. Benjamin Graham, *The Intelligent Investor* (New York: Harper & Row, 1973), 300.

Chapter 7: Financial Astrology: AAA Falling Stars

1. Based on data from Berkshire Hathaway annual reports for 2002 to 2007.

2. Aline van Duyn and Francesco Guerrera, "Wall St. Banks Face $10bn Cost," Financial Times, 11 June 2008.

3. Jo Johnson, "Questions Raised over Fitch's Credibility," *Financial Times,* 20 July 2003.

4. Ibid.

5. Warren Buffett, memo dated September 27, 2006, *Financial Times* 9 October 2008.

6. Ibid.

7. Arturo Cifuentes, "CDOs and Their Ratings: Chronicle of a Foretold Disaster," *Total Securitization,* 4 June 2007.

8. Charles Bachelor, "Agencies Under Fresh Pressure on Rating Worth" *Financial Times,* 23 December 2003.

9. Ibid.

10. Janet Tavakoli, "Investors Are the Gullible Ones if They Rely on Ratings as Indicators of Financial Robustness," *Financial Times,* 29 December 2003; and Janet Tavakoli, *Collateralized Debt Obligations & Structured Finance* (Hoboken, N.J.: John Wiley & Sons, 2008), 386–388.

11. Paul J Davies, "Questions Lie Behind CPDO Hype," *Financial Times,* 14 November 2006.

12. Sam Jones, Gillian Tett and Paul J. Davies, "Moody's Error Gave Top Ratings to Debt Products," *Financial Times,* 20 May 2008.

13. Ibid.

14. Karen Richardson, Kara Scannell, and Aaron Lucchetti, "The Hits Keep on Coming at Moody's," *Wall Street Journal (Deal Journal),* 23 May 2008.

15. Neil Unmack, "CPDO Investors May Lose 90% as ABN Funds Unwind," *Bloomberg News,* 25 January 2008.

16. Aline van Duyn and Joanna Chung, "S&P Discloses Errors in Rating Models," *Financial Times,* 13 June 2008.

17. Gyan Sinha and Karan Chabba, "Sell on the Rumor, Buy on the News," Bear Stearns, 12 February 2007.

18. Janet Tavakoli, "Comments on SEC Proposed Rules on Rating Agencies," 13 February 2007.

19. "Fed & Sub-Prime Loans," CNBC, 20 February, 2007. Segement with Susan Bies, Steve Liesman, and Gyan Sinha.

20. Bethany McLean, "The Dangers of Investing in Subprime Debt," *Fortune,* 19 March 2008.

21. Ibid.

22. Mark Pittman, "Moody's, S&P Defer Cuts on AAA Subprime, Hiding Loss," *Bloomberg News,* 11 March 2008.

23. Eric Gelman, "Fear of a Black Swan," *Fortune,* 14 April 2008.

24. Benjamin Graham, *The Intelligent Investor* (New York: Harper & Row, 1973), 110.

25. Ibid. 98.

26. Craig Karmin, "Springfield, Mass., Takes Aim at Merrill over Subprime Losses," *Wall Street Journal,* 19 January 2008.

27. Vickie Tillman, "The Truth about Triple-A Ratings," *Financial Times,* 20 March 2008.

28. Aaron Lucchetti, "S&P Email: 'We Should Not Be Rating It'," *Wall Street Journal,* 2 August 2008.

29. David Scheer and Karen Freifeld, "Citigroup to Unfreeze $29.5 Billion of Auction Debt," *Bloomberg News,* 7 August 2008.

30. Karen Freifeld and Michael McDonald, "Morgan, JPMorgan Settle Auction-Rate Probe, Pay Fines," *Bloomberg News* 14 August, 2008.

31. Robert Frank and Liz Rappaport, "Big Boys Face 'Auction' Monster Alone: Settlement Excludes 4Kids, Other firms; Battle with Lehman" 29 August 2008.

32. Karen Richardson, Kara Scannell, and Aaron Lucchetti, "The Hits Keep on Coming at Moody's."

Chapter 8: Bear Market (I'd Like a Review of the Bidding)

1. "U.S. Housing and the Gamble of Subprime Loans," CNBC 30 January 2007. Segment with Diana Olick, Jim Melcher, and Janet Tavakoli.

2. David Evans, "Florida Got Lehman Help Before Run on School's Funds," *Bloomberg News,* 18 December 2007. This article gives a subprime chronicle of events in 2007 including information on New Century and HSBC.

3. Gyan Sinha and Karan Chabba, "Sell on the Rumor, Buy on the News," Bear Stearns, 12 February 2007.

4. Steven Church and Bradley Keoun, "ResMae Collapse May Signal More Subprime Bankruptcies," *Bloomberg News,* 23 February 2007.

5. Gretchen Morgenson, "Crisis Looms in Mortgages," *New York Times,* 11 March 2007.

6. Randall Smith and Susan Pulliam, "As Funds Leverage Up, Fears of Reckoning Rise," *Wall Street Journal,* 30 April 2007.

7. Ibid.

8. Richard Beales, "NY Fed Warns on Hedge Fund Risk," *Financial Times,* 3 May 2007.

9. James Mackintosh, "Hedge Funds Survey Reveals Lower Gearing," *Financial Times,* 1 May 2007.

10. Janet Tavakoli, "Letter: Greater Global Risk Now than at Time of LTCM," *Financial Times,* 7 May 2007.

11. Serena Ng and Emily Barrett, "Fed Turns Focus to Derivatives Market, Wants Improved Infrastructure Soon," *Wall Street Journal,* 10 June 2008.

12. Everquest Financial Ltd., Form S-1 Registration Statement under the Securities Act of 1933, 9 May 2007.

13. Offering Circular for Octonion I CDO, Ltc. Octonion I CDO Corp., March 16, 2007. Most of Everquest's assets were priced as of December 31, 2006, but there were some 2007 additions to the portfolio. For example, it owned some of the "first loss" equity risk of a CDO named Octonion I CDO (Octonion), a deal underwritten by Citigroup in March 2007. If the IPO came to market, some of the proceeds from Everquest would pay down Citigroup's $200 million credit line. Octonion's prospectus disclosed an inexperienced CDO

manager with conflicts of interest with the CDO investors. It used 95 percent credit default swaps referencing BBB rated asset-backed securities including subprime assets. This CDO appeared to be a very risky investment for investors in the AAA or AA rated tranches. The equity, 48 percent of which was owned by Everquest, may have been entitled to the residual cash flow of the deal. Even if they did not, the tranches looked high risk, undeserving of an investment grade rating. Time proved my concerns warranted since Octonion triggered an event of default in February 2008, at which time even the original seniormost AAA tranche was downgraded to CCC by S&P (it was still AAA by Moody's). By the summer of 2008, the seniormost AAA had been downgraded to Caa3 by Moody's and CCC- by S&P.

14. The information about the underwriters (UBS, Citigroup, Merrill and others) is not listed in the registration statement, but can be found by cross referencing the listed CDO with the information in each of the prospectuses. Everquest also invested in mezzanine tranches that were problematic as well since the amount of protection underneath them can be too slender for assets backed by risky mortgage loans. These tranches were already trading at wide spreads—lower prices—in the secondary market.

15. Everquest Financial Ltd., Form S-1, p. 48. It is impossible to calculate a precise number without more information, but it can be ball-parked from the S-1. It showed 16.2 percent of non–Parapet (a CDO-squared) assets were ABS/CDOs. There was more subprime exposure in a CDO-squared called Parapet, the initial deal backed by assets coming from the two hedge funds managed by BSAM. Parapet accounted for 53 percent of the CDO assets. Included in Parapet were mezzanine tranches that were 38.6 percent of the CDO assets, of which it appeared that a high percentage were subprime. Furthermore, 42.8 percent of the Parapet equity was backed by ABS/CDOs, most of which according to the S-1 was subprime. As a rough estimation subprime exposure was 40 percent to 50 percent of the collateral. That seemed substantial to me. As for the hedges, the document said that on May 8, 2007, the two hedge funds had transferred their interest on credit default swaps that referenced 48 tranches of ABS securities held by the CDOs with a notional amount of $201 million and stated: "The hedges will not cover all our exposure to RMBS held by our CDOs that are backed primarily by subprime residential mortgage loans. Our CDOs may experience negative credit events relating to RMBS tranches that are not hedged." The hedges may or may not have done the trick. There was no indication of when the hedges were actually put on, only that they were transferred on May 8, 2007. Single name ABS/CDO credit derivatives had become very expensive and were no longer very good hedges, so the timing was important.

16. Peter Eavis, "Freddie Mac Report Soft-Pedals Thorny Case," The Street. com, Real Money, 24 July 2003. According to a report by Freddie Mac's then regulator, the Office of Federal Housing Enterprise Oversight (OFHEO),

Freddie Mac's officers decided that volatility calculated based on the then current market prices did not reflect fair value. Instead, Freddie Mac used historic prices as the basis on which to calculate volatility when it revalued its options. This one assumption change alone eliminated $731 million from Freddie's 2001 accounting transition adjustment gain (through adoption of a new accounting rule, SFAS133).

17. Office of Federal Housing Enterprise Oversight, *Report of the Special Examination of Freddie Mac,* December 2003, 134–135.

18. Everquest IPO. Everquest's managers would get an annualized base fee of 1.75 percent of the company's net assets up to $2 billion decreasing on a sliding scale until they reached only 1 percent on net assets over $4 billion. If Everquest returned more than 8 percent, as computed by the managers that stood to benefit, the managers would get 25 percent of the upside, and that seemed high by industry standards for a fund that managed assets originally transferred by funds already managed by BSAM. Cioffi later said Everquest's employees had an asset management agreement with BSAM and Stone Tower and that asset management fees that BSAM received for managing Everquest were rebated back to the hedge funds.

19. Everquest IPO,"Table of Contents." ii.

20. Matthew Goldstein: "The Everquest IPO: Buyer Beware," revised title "Bear Stearns' Subprime IPO," *BusinessWeek,* 11 May 2007. The article quoted me as saying there was moral hazard with BSAM providing the valuations and surveillance on the CDO equity, and why would a customer want to buy "if it is trying to get CDO equity off of its balance sheet, incur the costs of securitization, and sell the risk without arm's length valuation." I had been clear that the assets were coming from the hedge funds, not Bear Stearns's balance sheet, but the quote seemed to imply otherwise, and elsewhere in the article, it implied the assets were coming from Bear Stearns, instead of the hedge funds managed by BSAM, an affiliate of Bear Stearns, although the conflicts with the assets coming from the BSAM managed hedge funds seemed worse.

21. Jody Shenn, "Bear Stearns Funds to Transfer Subprime-Mortgage Risk with IPO," *Bloomberg News,* 11 May 2007.

22. Cioffi had said he was "short sub prime thru the ABS CDS market . . . the 2006 vintage exposure the market value totals only about $70M, against which I have shorted $340M Baa2 and Baa3 sub prime names thru the single name ABS CDS market. We determined these to be the weakest of the 2006 deals." The Everquest IPO states: "The hedges will not cover all our exposure to RMBS held by our CDOs that are backed primarily by sub-prime residential mortgage loans" (p. 55).

23. Kurdas, Chidem, Levered Bear Funds: A Peek into the Black Box," *HedgeWorld,* 26 June 2007.

24. Matthew Goldstein, "Bear's Big Loss Arouses SEC Interest," *BusinessWeek,* 25 June, 2007.

25. Kate Kelly and Serena Ng, "Bear Stearns Bails out Fund with Capital Injection," *Wall Street Journal,* 23 June 2007.

26. Kate Kelly, and Serena Ng, "The Sure Bet Turns Bad," *Wall Street Journal,* 7 June 2007.

27. Kate Kelly and Serena Ng, "Bear Stearns Bails out Fund with Capital Injection."

28. Janet Tavakoli, *Credit Derivatives & Synthetic Structures* (New York: John Wiley & Sons, 1998). I wrote about Askin's problems: "The investment banks were eager to extend financing because they wanted to get rid of the "nuclear waste" tranches of collateralized mortgage obligations ("CMO's"). Once the risky piece was sold, investment banks could underwrite more transactions and book attractive underwriting fees. When liquidity for these instruments dried up, risk managers started asking tough questions, but much too late

29. Laura Jereski, "Wall Street Firms Profited by Ravaging Askin's Holdings," *Wall Street Journal,* 22 April 1996. In 1995, Askin settled charges with the SEC that he mismarked bonds at misled investors. He paid a $50,000 fine and agreed to a two-year ban from association with any investment advisor.

30. Ibid.

31. Ibid.

32. Jeffrey B. Lane left JPMorgan/Bear Stearns and became CEO of Modern Bank on July 1, 2008. (PR Newswire, "Modern Bank Appoints Jeffrey B. Lane as CEO," June 24, 2008.)

33. Jody Shenn, "FGIC Sees No Need to Honor Agreement with IKB, Calyon," *Bloomberg News,* 26 March 2008.

34. Kate Kelly and Serena Ng, "Bear Stearns Fund Hurt by Subprime Loans," *Wall Street Journal,* 12 June 2007.

35. "Bear CDO Lists Total at Least $1.44 Bln – Sources," *Reuters,* 20 June 2007.

36. Michael Mackenzie, "Credit Vehicle Defaults Reach $170 billion," *Financial Times,* 24 April, 2008.

37. Kara Scannell, Siobhan Hughes, and David Reilly, "SEC Probes CDOs and Bear Funds, *Wall Street Journal,* 27 June 2007.

38. Kate Kelly and Serena Ng, "Bear Stearns Bails out Fund with Capital Injection."

39. Kate Kelly, Serena Ng, and David Reilly, "Two Big Funds at Bear Stearns Face Shutdown," *Wall Street Journal,* 20 June 2007.

40. Eric Martin, "U.S. Stocks Retreat, Led by Financials; Bear Stearns Tumbles" *Bloomberg News,* 10 March 2008.

41. Charlie Corbett, "Bear Stearns Lied To Us, Fund Says Sub-prime Exposure Underplayed," *Investor Daily,* 8 October 2007.

42. Yalman Onaran, "Spector Ousted by Cayne Over Too Much Bridge, Money," *Bloomberg News,* 3 October 2007.

43. *United States of America against Ralph Cioffi and Matthew Tannin,* CR 08 415. f.#2007R01328, filed June 18, 2008.

44. Patricia Hurtado and David Scheer, "Former Bear Stearns Fund Managers Arrested by FBI," *Bloomberg News,* 19 June 2008.

45. Landon Thomas Jr., "Prosecutors Build Bear Stearns Case on E-Mails," *New York Times,* 20 June 2008.

Chapter 9: Dead Man's Curve

1. Benjamin Graham, *The Intelligent Investor* (New York: Harper & Row, 1973), 95.

2. Ibid.

3. Nikki Tait, "The Joyti De-Laurey Case: Queen of Deceit Duped City High-Flyers," *Financial Times,* 21 April 2004.

4. James Mackintosh "Wheels Come Off as Crunch Hits Peloton," *FT.com* [*Financial Times*], 29 February 2008.

5. Cassell Bryan-Low, Carrick Mollenkamp, and Gregory Zuckerman, "Peloton Few High, Fell Fast," *Wall Street Journal,* 12 May 2008.

6. Emiliya Mychasuk and Emiko Terazono, "Hedgie Heroes," *Financial Times,* 29 January 2008.

7. Cassell Bryan-Low, Carrick Mollenkamp, and Gregory Zuckerman, "Peloton Few High, Fell Fast."

8. James Mackintosh, "Peloton Partners in $2 billion Assets Sale, *Financial Times,* 28 February 2008.

9. Cassell Bryan-Low, Carrick Mollenkamp, and Gregory Zuckerman, "Peloton Few High, Fell Fast."

10. Ibid.

11. James Mackintosh, and Daniel Thomas, "Peloton Puts Office on Market," *FT.com* [*Financial Times*], 9 March 2008.

12. Cassell Bryan-Low, Carrick Mollenkamp, and Gregory Zuckerman, "Peloton Few High, Fell Fast."

13. James Mackintosh and Gillian Tett, "Peloton Fund Fall Highlights Danger of Overreaching, *Financial Times,* 4 March 2008.

14. The Carlyle Group, "Firm Profile," www.carlyle.com/company (14 June 2008).

15. "Carlyle's Debt Team Is a Secret Weapon" *Investment Dealers' Digest,* 29 September 2003.

16. Ed Vulliamy, "Dark Heart of the American Dream" *The Observer,* 16 June 2002.

17. "Carlyle Capital's Troubles Since IPO: Timeline," *CNBC.com,* 13 March 2008.

18. Peter Lattman, Randall Smith, and Jenny Strasburg, "Carlyle Fund on Ropes as Banks Get Nervous" *Wall Street Journal,* 17 March 2008.

19. "Carlyle Capital's Troubles Since IPO: Timeline."

20. Ibid.

21. Edward Evans, "Carlyle Capital Nears Collapse as Rescue Talks Fail, *Bloomberg News,* 13 March 2008.

22. Roddy Boyd, "The Last Days of Bear Stearns" *Fortune,* 28 March 2008.

23. Kate Kelly, "Fear, Rumors Touched Off Fatal Run on Bear Stearns," *Wall Street Journal,* 28 May 2008. Alan Schwartz left Bear Stearns two months after the sale of Bear Stearns to JPMorgan Chase was completed.

24. Mark Pittman, "Moody's, S&P Defer Cuts on AAA Subprime, Hiding Loss," *Bloomberg News,* 11 March 2008.

25. Kate Kelly and Serena Ng, "The Sure Bet Turns Bad," *Wall Street Journal,* 7 June 2007.

26. "Testimony, Ben S. Bernanke, *Developments in the financial markets:* Before the Committee on Banking, Housing, and Urban Affairs, U.S. Senate, April 3, 2008, Federal Reserve press release. See http://www.federalreserve.gov/newsevents/testimony/bernanke20080403a.htm.

27. "Financials Lead Sell-Off After Carlyle News," *CNBC.com,* 13 March 2008.

28. Ibid.

29. Carlyle Group, "The Carlyle Group Issues Additional Statement on CCC," Carlyle Group Press Release #2008–025, March 13, 2008.

30. James Tyson, "Freddie Mac has 1st-Quarter Net Loss of $211 Million," *Bloomberg News,* 14 June 2008. This article referenced remarks made on June 11, 2008 by James Lockhart, director of the Office of Federal Housing Enterprise Oversight, in which he said Freddie Mac and Fannie Mae owned $170 billion in subprime mortgage-backed securities rated AAA.

31. Peter Lattman, Randall Smith, and Jenny Strasburg, "Carlyle Fund on Ropes As Banks Get Nervous."

32. Ibid.

33. Ibid.

34. "SEC, CFTC Formalize Cooperation Agreement," *CNBC.com,* 11 March 2008.

35. Roddy Boyd, "The Last Days of Bear Stearns," *Fortune,* 28 March 2008.

36. Kate Kelly, "Fear, Rumors Touched off Fatal Run on Bear Stearns," *Wall Street Journal,* 28 May 2008.

37. Roddy Boyd, "The Last Days of Bear Stearns," *Fortune,* 28 March 2008.

38. Alan Schwartz and David Faber, "Bear Stearns CEO," *Squawk on the Street,* CNBC, 12 March 2008.

39. Ibid.

40. Ibid.

41. Serena Ng and Randall Smith, "Another Source of Quick Cash Dries Up," *Wall Street Journal,* 17 March 2008.

42. Lester Pimentel, "Fed's Action May Have Hastened Bear Stearns' Decline, UBS Says," *Bloomberg News],* 17 March 2008.

43. Kevin O'Leary's comments were made on Canada's Business News Network, BNN's "Squeeze Play," March 14, 2008.

44. Roddy Boyd, "The Last Days of Bear Stearns," *Fortune,* 28 March 2008.

45. My comments were made on Bloomberg TV and Canada's Business News Network, BNN's "Squeeze Play," March 14, 2008. Bruce Foerster's comments were made on Bloomberg TV.

46. Bruce Foerster's comments were made during the segment referred to in endnote 45 in which we appeared together on Bloomberg TV, March 14, 2008.

47. Jim Rogers has made these comments on Bloomberg TV and CNBC several times in the past several months. Rogers made these particular comments from Singapore during a segment that aired June 5, 2008.

48. Josh P. Hamilton and Erik Holm, "Buffett Castigates Wall Street, Bankers on Blunders," *Bloomberg News,* 5 May 2008.

49. Kate Kelly, "Bear Stearns Neared Collapse Twice in Frenzied Last Days," *Wall Street Journal,* 29 May 2008.

50. Kate Kelly, "Lost Opportunities Haunt Final Days of Bear Stearns," *Wall Street Journal,* 27 May 2008.

51. U.S. Senate Committee on Banking, Housing, and Urban Affairs, "Testimony of Jamie Dimon Before the Senate Committee on Banking, Housing, and Urban Affairs," April 3, 2008.

52. Ibid.

53. Stephen Labaton, "Testimony Offers Details of Bear Stearns Deal," *New York Times,* 4 April 2008. Jamie Dimon repeated the comment in an interview with Charlie Rose on July 8, 2008.

54. Alistair Barr, "Bear Portfolio Worth $28.9 Billion, Fed Says," *Market Watch,* 3 July 2008. The revaluation mentioned in the title already represents a loss

of $100 million for the Fed and it is not even based on market prices (which would have resulted in a greater stated loss); the Fed admitted it priced the securities based on its notion of an "orderly market."

55. Ben White, "Bear Stearns Passes into Wall Street History," *Financial Times,* 29 May 2008.

56. Kate Kelly, "Bear Stearns Neared Collapse Twice in Frenzied Last Days."

57. Ibid.

58. Herbert Lash, "JPMorgan's Bear Takeover Not Looking Good: Analyst," *Reuters.com,* 9 June 2008.

59. "JPMorgan Chase: We Got Bear Stearns on the Cheap," CNBC, 17 June 2008.

60. Landon Thomas Jr., "Buffett Said to Consider Bear Stake," *New York Times,* 27 September 2007.

61. CNBC aired several segments on September 27, 2007, including: "Bear Hunting," "Buffett Bearish?," "Buffett Buzz Buoys Bear," "Buffett Bear Hunting?," and "Buffett Buying Bear?"

Chapter 10: Bazooka Hank and Dread Reckoning

1. "Risky Business," *Squawk Box,* CNBC, 8 August 2007.

2. AIG, "Residential Mortgage Presentation (Financial Figures are as of June 30, 2007)," 9 August 2007. The CDO consisted of BBB tranches with an average of 29 percent subprime in the original residential mortgage-backed securities portfolios. AIG claimed most of this was 2005 vintage and therefore not as suspect as loans originated in 2006 and 2007. Even though the super senior originally had a 36 percent cushion, a significant portion of the cushion could be eaten through (in some of my probable scenarios and in other scenarios, all of it) and that should have been reflected in an accounting loss. Even if AIG did not believe that there would be any ultimate principal loss, the price what it protected had declined which should have shown up in a mark-to-market loss. By August 2007, the prices of BBB rated tranches of residential mortgage backed securities deals tanked. Since AIG was writing protection on the super senior (ultimately backed by that collateral), it would have shown a loss.

3. U.S. Department of Justice, "Former Gen Re and AIG Executives Found Guilty on All counts of Fraudulent Manipulation Scheme," Press Release #80–141:02–25–08.

4. David Reilly, "In Subprime, AIG Sees Small Risk; Others See More," *Wall Street Journal,* 13 August 2007. AIG is a multinational conglomerate doing business in aroudn 130 countries. AIG has insurance operations (life, property, casualty, retirement products, commercial), and manages investments related

to its insurance obligations. The insurance business is supposed to be separate and regulated (by state regulators), but at one point, AIG (at the holding company) was given permission to have its insurance operations provide a bridge loan to AIG's financial products operations—another unprecedented move by regulators. AIG's finacial operations act as a credit derivatives counterparty (primarily selling protection) on mortgage products, corporate risk and other assets. AIG also has assests such as International Lease Finance Corporation (ILFC, which leases aircraft), among other valuable assets.

5. Ibid

6. Amir Efrati and Liam Plevin, "SEC, Justice Scrutinize AIG on Swaps Accounting," *Wall Street Journal,* 6 June 2008.

7. Liam Plevin, "AIG's Board Now Comes Under Fire of Dissidents (online title: "AIG Holders Add Change in the Board to Demands")" *Wall Street Journal,* 12 June 2008.

8. Amir Efrati and Liam Plevin, "SEC, Justice Scrutinize AIG on Swaps Accounting."

9. Charles Duhigg, "At Freddie Mac, Chief Discarded Warning Signs," *New York Times,* 5 August 2008.

10. Gretchen Morgenson and Charles Duhigg, "Loan Giant Overstated the Size of Its Capital Base," *New York Times,* 7 September 2008.

11. Mark Gilbert, "I Spy More Road Kill on the Credit-Crunch Highway: Mark Gilbert," *Bloomberg News,* 21 August 2008.

12. Jay Yarrow, "Bill Gross Cashes in on Fannie Freddie Bailout," *The Business Sheet,* 9 September 2008. The Pimco Total Return Fund had over $130 billion in assets at the end of June 2008.

13. "Fannie Mae and Freddie Mac removed from S&P 500," *Associated Press,* 9 September 2008.

14. James R. Hagerty, Ruth Simon, and Damian Paletta, "U.S. Seizes Mortgage Giants," *Wall Street Journal,* 8 September 2008. (Mr. Moffett's affiliation with the Carlyle Group was not reported in this article but was available on the Carlyle Group's Web site www.carlyle.com with his biography as one of the Carlyle team.) Richard Syron's Freddie Mac exit package was estimated at up to $15 million; Daniel Mudd's Fannie Mae exit package was estimated at up to $14 million.

15. Gregory Mott, "Dodd Plans Senate Hearing on Fannie, Freddie Takeover," *Bloomberg News,* 8 September 2008.

16. Hugh Son and Shannon D. Harrington, "AIG May Disclose Its Strategic Review Before Sept. 25 Deadline," 13 September 2008.

17. Hugh Son, "AIG Seeks Loan from Goldman, JPMorgan as Fed Resists," *Bloomberg News,* 15 September 2008.

18. Christine Harper, "Goldman Net Drops 70% as Merger Advice, Trading Slow," *Bloomberg News,* 16 September 2008.

19. Erik Holm and Christine Richard, "AIG's Collapse Would Have Impact Around the Globe," *Bloomberg News,* 16 September 2008.

20. Matthew Karnitschnig, Deborah Solomon, and Liam Pleven, "U.S. Plans Rescue of AIG to Halt Crisis; Central Banks Inject Cash as Credit Dries Up," *Wall Street Journal,* 16 September 2008.

21. Federal Reserve (press release), 16 September 2008 (9:00 p.m. EDT). The (up to) $85 billion AIG facility has a 24-month term and will accrue interest at three month Libor plus 850 basis points.

22. Miles Weiss, "Gross's Fund Guaranteed $760 Million of AIG Debt Through Swaps," *Bloomberg News,* 16 September 2008.

23. Caroline Baum, "No Limit to Greenspan's Once-in-a-Century Events: Caroline Baum," *Bloomberg News,* 18 August 2008.

24. Hugh Son and Eric Holm, "Fed Said to Reverse Stance, Consider AIG Loan Package," *Bloomberg News,* 16 September 2008.

25. Nicholas Varchaver, "What Warren Thinks . . .," *Fortune,* 28 April 2008, p. 62.

26. Benjamin Graham, *The Intelligent Investor* (New York: Harper & Row, 1973), 315, 316.

27. McSheehy and Hugh Son, "AIG Chief Sullivan Seeks to Ease Rules on Writedowns" *Bloomberg News,* 18 March 2008.

28. Ibid.

29. Warren Buffett, "Shareholders Letter," *Berkshire Hathaway 2002 Annual Report,* 14.

30. Telos Demos, Nina Easton, Adam Lashinsky, Eugenia Levenson, Carol Loomis, Brian O'Keefe, Patricia Sellers, and David Stires, "Crisis Council," *Fortune,* 3 September 2007. 60.

31. Division of Corporate Finance, "Sample Letter Sent to Public Companies on MD&A Disclosure Regarding the Application of SFAS 157 (Fair Value Measurements)," U.S. Securities and Exchange Commission, March 31, 2008, http://www.sec.gov/divisions/corpfin/guidance/fairvalueltr0308. htm. The letter concerned Management's Discussion and Analysis for their upcoming quarterly reports on Form 10-Q. Excerpt: "Current market conditions may require you to use valuation models that require significant unobservable inputs for some of your assets and liabilities. As a consequence, as of January 1, 2008, you will classify these assets and liabilities as Level 3."

32. Ibid.

33. Joyce Moullakis, "Merrill Says Level 3 Assets Jump 70% in First Quarter," *Bloomberg News,* 6 May 2008.

34. Bradley Keoun, "Merrill to Pay Ex-Goldman Trader Montag $40 Million," *Bloomberg News,* 2 May 2008. Thain compensated Montag for $50 million in equity awards he would leave behind. He also agreed to pay him a $39.4 year bonus for 2008, even though the announcement was made in *May* 2008. In addition, Montag would get a $600,000 salary for a total of $40 million.

35. Susanne Craig and Tom Lauricella, "Big Loss at Lehman Intensifies Crisis Jitters," *Wall Street Journal,* 10 June 2008.

36. Ken Auletta, *Greed and Glory on Wall Street: The Fall of the House of Lehman* (New York: Random House, 1986), 158.

37. Ibid.

38. Ibid.

39. Jesse Westbrook, "SEC to Make Wall Street Banks Reveal Capital, Liquidity Levels," *Bloomberg News,* 7 May 2008.

40. David Reilly and Karen Richardson, "For Financial Stocks, Is It Another False Bottom?" 16 Janaury 2008.

41. In a client note I observed that the difference between my numbers and Citi's numbers are due to a combination of assumptions, and there is a lot of leeway in how one can account for structured products: "What's a few billion anyway (except when one is trying to attract capital)? Since when do shareholders shrug off a 10% dilution in shareholder equity? It would be nice to have heard something along the lines of 'We know what went wrong (and here it is. . . .), and we know exactly what to do about it (other than pass the hat)."

42. Lewis, Michael, "The Rise and Rise of Analyst Meredith Whitney," *Bloomberg News,* 9 April 2008.

43. Yalman Onaran and Dave Pierson, "Banks' Subprime Market-Related Losses 91 Capital Raised," *Bloomberg News,* 16 October 2008.

44. David Enrich and Jenny Strasburg, "Citigroup to Close Hedge Fund; Blow to CEO," *Wall Street Journal,* 12 June 2008; and Joyce Moullakis and Josh Fineman, "Citigroup Shuts Down Old Lane, Co-Founded by Pandit," *Bloomberg News,* 12 June 2008.

45. David Einhorn, "Accounting Ingenuity," remarks at the Ira W. Sohn Investment Research Conference, 21 May 2008. David Einhorn thought Lehman's 1Q 2008 writedowns on its commercial mortgages were insufficient given the AAA commercial mortgage backed securities (CMBS) index fell 10 percent. According to Einhorn, Lehman had $39 billion in exposure to lower rated assets, yet it took a write down of only 3 percent. He questioned Lehman's accounting for its share of KSK Energy Ventures. When he challenged Lehman's statements, the stories changed (this happened more than once). He noted Lehman's SunCal (California land developer) investment did not have a material charge unlike other home builders that took huge writedowns.

46. Alan Sloan and Roddy Boyd, "The Lehman Lesson," *Fortune,* 13 September 2008.

47. Jason Kelly and Jonathan Keehner, "Lehman's Survival Hinges on Fuld's Reluctant Sale of Fund Unit," *Bloomberg News,* 11 September 2008.

48. Carrick Mollenkamp, Susanne Craig, Sernea Ng and Aaron Lucchetti, "Lehman Files for Bankruptcy, Merrill Sold, AIG Seeks Cash," *Wall Street Journal,* 16 September 2008. Lehman filed for protection under Chapter 11 of the U.S. Bankruptcy Code. This is an attempt to ensure an orderly liquidation. Lehman said the filing did not include broker-dealer subsidiaries (or other LBHI subsidiaries or Neuberger Berman Holdings LLC). Neuberger Berman is operating as usual. Its assets are segregated from Lehman Brothers.

49. Bank of America press release, "Bank of America Buys Merrill Lynch Creating Unique Financial Services Firm," 15 September 2008. Bank of America will exchange .8595 shares of Bank of America common stock for one Merrill Lynch common share.

50. Nicholas Varchaver, "What Warren Thinks…" *Fortune,* 28 April 2008, p. 59.

51. Bradley Keoun, "Accounting Rule Defying Common Sense," *Bloomberg News,* 8 June 2008. If accounting weren't bizarre enough, as of January 1, 2008, firms can record an increase in revenue when the price of their own bonds declines, and this "revenue" has been used to net off against losses, so the losses reported by investment banks and monoline insurance companies look less damaging than they would have otherwise appeared.

52. Yalman Onaran, "Banks Keep $35 Billion Markdown Off Income Statements," *Bloomberg News,* 19 May 2008. By May 2008, *Bloomberg* estimated that tens of billions more in writedowns would have shown up on balance sheets if the losses had not been offset by the decline in the price of investment banks' debt. The theory is that if the bonds are redeemed at a lower price, it is a net benefit to the company. That is only true, however if a firm has the ability to buy the bonds due to an increase in revenues or other means without strain in some other area. If you want to report the maximum revenues due to a decline in the value or your debt, go into bankruptcy. Now your debt will only be worth your recovery value, if any.

53. Warren Buffett has long been a critic of pension rate assumptions, and he made similar comments on CNBC March 3, 2008. Even pension fund accounting can be very misleading. Often rates used by pension funds are mandated, and Warren thinks they are too high. Berkshire Hathaway owns some public utilities, and although he would like to use a lower rate for pension fund assumptions, the lowest rate is 6.5 percent. At least that is lower than the 8 percent rate much of the rest of the financial world uses. The rate difference may not seem that much at first glance, but for long term funds like pension funds, it is an enormous difference. For example, $100,000 compounded

at an annual rate of 6.5 percent for 30 years is $661,436, but compounded at 8 percent, it is $1,006,265. If Warren Buffett thinks 6.5 percent is too much to promise—meaning pension funds are not kicking in enough to make their future payments—do you think the rest of the world will do a better job using an assumed rate of 8 percent?

54. *Berkshire Hathaway 1990 Annual Report* 3.

55. Josh Hamilton and Erik Holm, "Buffett's Berkshire Says Net Declines on Insurance, Derivatives," *Bloomberg News,* 3 May 2008.

56. *Berkshire Hathaway 2007 Annual Report,* 16.

57. Ibid.

Chapter 11: Bond Insurance Burns Main Street

1. Jody Shenn, "FGIC Sees No Need to Honor Agreement with IKB, Calyon," *Bloomberg News,* 26 March 2008. On March 12, FGIC, a bond insurer, filed a lawsuit in the New York Supreme Court against Calyon, a French investment bank, and IKB, the German-owned state bank. Calyon had arranged a deal for IKB, and FGIC was nullifying a $1.9 billion guarantee on a portfolio of mortgage-backed securities. At the start of 2008, FGIC was still rated AAA, but that day Fitch downgraded the bond insurer to BBB, the lowest investment grade rating. It now struggles for survival with a junk rating.

2. Traditionally, the main line of business of monoline insurance companies, or *monolines,* was to provide bond insurance. Bond insurers (or monolines) provided *credit wraps,* which are *financial guarantees,* and under New York law, home of the largest U.S. investment banks, monolines are the only entities allowed to provide financial guarantees. Many of the bond insurers bought subprime-related CDOs including, in some cases, risky CDO-squared products.

3. Michael McDonald, "Auction-Bond Failures Deplete New Hampshire Fund," *Bloomberg News,* 17 March 2008.

4. Darrell Preston, "Banks Say Auction-Rate Investors Can't Have Money," *Bloomberg News,* 6 June, 2008.

5. Michael McDonald, "UBS E-Mails Show Conflicts With Auction-Rate Customers in Suit," *Bloomberg News,* 27 June 2008.

6. Karen Freifield and Michael McDonald, "Morgan, JPMorgan Settle Auction-Rate Probe, Pay Fines," *Bloomberg News,* 14 August 2008.

7. David Scheer and Karen Freifeld, "Citigroup to Unfreeze $19.5 Billion of Auction Debt," *Bloomberg News,* 7 August 2008. Closed end funds issued preferred auction-rate securities which were not included in these buy-back settlements.

8. Robert Frank and Liz Rappaport, "Big Boys Face 'Auction' Monster Alone," *Wall Street Journal,* 29 August 2008.

9. Moody's Investors Service, Global Credit Research Announcement:, Moody's Announces Rating Actions on Financial Guarantors, 14 December 2007. Moody's had a stable outlook when it affirmed the ratings of Ambac (Aaa). Fitch placed the AAA ratings of Ambac, MBIA, and FGIC on review for possible downgrade. XL Capital Assurance was put under review, and Fitch said it needed to raise $2 billion. Fitch indicated Ambac and MBIA would be cut to AA+.

10. Aaron Lucchetti, "CDO Battles: Royal Pain Over Who Gets What," *Wall Street Journal,* 17 December 2007. Analysts seemed to have just noticed details like unwind triggers, including market value triggers for shaky *structured investment vehicles* (SIVs) that issued short-term debt to fund risky longer-term higher yielding assets—similar to Countrywide's problem in August, but the Fed was not bailing out the structured investment vehicles. For example, in November 2007, MBIA Inc., the largest bond insurer, sold assets to bond-holders of its Hudson Thames Capital SIV. It wound down from $2 billion to $400 million after announcing that it had failed to find investors since August in the asset-backed commercial debt issued by this vehicle. MBIA waged a legal battle with Deutsche Bank, Wachovia Corp., and UBS over the cash flows of Sagittarius CDO I, a constellation CDO. In November 2007, it triggered an event of default leading to an unwind. MBIA seemed to think it had a traditional deal entitling it to the remaining cash flows—*did it ever read a prospectus?* LaCrosse Financial Products LLC, an MBIA affiliate, had done a credit derivatives transaction on the seniormost tranche. The unnecessarily complicated prospectus language made it difficult for the trustee to determine which investor had payment priority. As was typical of these deals, there is an interest-only class. If the deal went into liquidation as other CDOs had done, the fight could be over less cash. On December 17, 2007, I told the *Wall Street Journal:* "If you liquidate a lot of assets at once, you don't always get the best price." More than that, the structure disadvantaged naïve senior note-holders. The equity holder seemed to benefit at their expense. The equity is like the blow and burn in the arms trade, the detonator of whatever you are pedaling. It marks you as a pro, since you can profit even when a deal goes bad, and this CDO was scheduled for a meltdown the day it closed. I pitied any investor in the AAA or AA rated tranches of the CDO.

11. "Shorting Bond Insurers for Charity," *New York Times DealBook, dealbook.blogs.nytimes.com,* 28 November 2007.

12. Janet Tavakoli, "Dicey Deals Done Dirt Cheap," Tavakoli Structured Finance, Inc., 3 January 2008. No model is required to grasp the problem. In December 2007, Standard & Poor's stress test estimated that monoline financial guarantors have $10.7 billion in potential aggregate losses, but S&P's *stress*

case for losses was below my *base* case. S&P assumed stress case losses of only 15.5 percent. For 2006 vintage first lien subprime loans, I used a 30 percent default rate and a 70 percent loss rate. *My net base case losses were 21 percent.* Moody's base case used an 11 percent loss assumption for 2006 vintage first lien subprime loans. Moody's stress case loss of 19 percent for subprime loans was near my base case of 21 percent and well below my stress case of 30 percent for 2006 originated subprime loans. To achieve the triple-A (Aaa) rating, Moody's looks for an insurer with capital equal to 130 percent times base case losses and 100 percent times stress case losses. Using my base case assumptions for subprime losses and Moody's base case capital criteria, *five of the seven triple-A-rated financial guarantors did not merit their high ratings.* In the late 1990s, when CapMAC Holdings Inc., was in trouble (CapMAC merged with MBIA in 1998), it was given a minimal grace period to raise capital before losing its top rating; there was no kidding around. But now the rating agencies reeked of desperation. Several bond insurers were given more than a month to raise more money. Moody's had nearly 90,000 politically charged public finance deals on negative watch for downgrades—due to the potential downgrades of two of the smaller bond insurers (FGIC and XL) alone.

13. Ibid. In December 2007, Standard & Poor's affirmed the ratings for Ambac Assurance Corp, CFIG's entities, MBIA Insurance Corp., and Security Capital Assurance (XL Capital Assurance Inc. and XL Financial Assurance Ltd. (XL)) with a negative outlook. Financial Guaranty Insurance Corporation (FGIC) was rated AAA but was on negative watch. ACA Financial Guaranty Corp. had been recently downgraded from A to CCC with CreditWatch Developing, but the downgrade was long overdue. Moody's put the triple-A ratings of FGIC and XL on review for possible downgrade. It affirmed the triple-A ratings of MBIA and CIFG, but with a negative outlook. Financial Guaranty Insurance Corporation (FGIC), MBIA Inc. (MBIA) and Security Capital Assurance (XL Capital Assurance Inc. and XL Financial Assurance Ltd. (XL) merited immediate multi-notch—in some cases multi-grade—downgrades. Ambac Financial Group Inc. (Ambac) and CIFG were stronger yet not sufficiently strong to merit the triple-A rating, and only Financial Security Assurance Inc. (FSA), and Assured Guaranty Corp. (AGC) seemed eligible to retain a "triple-A" rating (based on subprime exposure). Unfortunately, the latter two were relatively small (with FSA being the larger) so the problems of the larger players had a huge market impact. Stress test scenarios were even worse. If one considered that an increase in capital cushion might also be required to support other business lines, the situation was desperate. Canadian Imperial Bank of Commerce (CIBC) had already announced $2 billion in write-downs, and Merrill had billions more related to ACA.

14. Becky Quick, Janet Tavakoli, David Kotok, "Backing up the Bond," CNBC, January 7, 2008 (video segment).

15. Ibid.

16. Ibid.

17. Saskia Scholtes, "MBIA in $1bn Deal to Retain Rating," *Financial Times,* 11 January 2008.

18. Janet Tavakoli, Matthew Fabian, Charles Gasparino, "Bond Insurance: The Bigger Problem," *Squawk Box,* CNBC, 25 January 2008.

19. Ibid.

20. Ibid.

21. Liz Rappaport and Serena Ng, "Bond Insurers Inflict Further Pain on Market," *Wall Street Journal,* 21 June 2008. By the end of June 2008, formerly triple-A bond insurers FGIC, CFIG and XL were all below investment grade, and MBIA and Ambac lost their triple-A ratings. They were already downgraded two notches to AA by S&P and were under review for a further downgrade. Bond insurers had several lawsuits or other investigations underway challenging the validity of the credit derivatives contracts related to subprime backed securitizations with their investment banking counterparties.

22. Jeremy R. Cooke and Darrell Preston, "Moody's Loses Credibility; Muni Ranks Mean No Savings," *Bloomberg News,* 11 September 2008.

23. Benjamin Franklin, *The Autobiography of Benjamin Franklin* (1868; reprint, Mineola, N.Y.: Dover, 1996), 75, 81, 82.

24. "The Quotable Franklin," *The Electric Ben Franklin,* http://www.ushistory .org/franklin/quotable/index.htm.

25. Andrew Tobias, *The Invisible Bankers* (New York: Washington Square Press, 1982), 15, 94.

26. *Berkshire Hathaway 1987 Annual Report.* The chairman's letter containing this quote is posted on the Berkshire Hathaway Web site (www.berkshirehathaway .com/letters) without page numbers.

27. Jonathan Stempel, "Buffett Poised to Cash in on Bond Insurer Woes," *Reuters .com,* 30 January 2008.

28. Ibid.

29. Martin Z. Braun, "Auction-Bond Failures Roil Munis, Pushing Bond Rates Up," *Bloomberg News,* 13 February 2008. The tender option bond market, which relies on periodic auctions to set the reinvestment yield, failed the second week in February. Bonds sold by the Port Authority of New York and New Jersey could not attract bidders at reasonable rates, and yields popped up to 20 percent from 4.3 percent the previous week. The U.S. Treasury's 10-year bond yields traded at less than 3.7 percent, yet the supposedly triple-A-rated tender option bonds traded at a yield of 20 percent.

30. John Glover, "Auction-Rate Bonds Lure Investors with 20% Interest," *Bloomberg News,* 18 February 2008.

31. Vikas Bajaj, "Buffett Offers to Reinsure Bonds," *New York Times,* 12 February 2008. On February 6, 2008, Mr. Buffett offered a better deal, but it was a package deal for around $800 billion in municipal bonds. The bond insurers had to first accept the offer. Then they would have 30 days to shop the offer. If they found a better deal, they would pay a 1.5 percent kill fee to Berkshire Hathaway Assurance. He proposed to reinsure the bonds for a premium equal to 1.5 times the remaining premium left over the life of the bond, which is the original premium less the amount proportionally earned up until then. This solution would allow $800 billion of municipal bonds to keep a solid and dependable AAA rating. The solution was elegant. Even if the monolines lost their AAA ratings, the municipal bond markets would maintain AAA ratings with the assurance of Berkshire Hathaway Assurance's AAA backstop. The financial guarantors would release regulatory capital equal to the premium they would pay Berkshire Hathaway Assurance, so they could continue doing business. The monolines turned him down.

32. Warren Buffett made this comment about the 206 transactions during a March 3, 2008, interview on CNBC.

Chapter 12: Money, Money, Money (Warren and Washington)

1. Erik Kirschbaum, "Buffett Sees 'Long, Deep' U.S. Recession," *Reuters.com,* 24 May 2008.

2 Benjamin Graham, *The Intelligent Investor* (New York: Harper & Row, 1973), 101.

3. Eliot Spitzer, "Predatory Lenders' Partner in Crime," *Washington Post,* 14 February 2008.

4 Alan Feuer and Ian Urbina, "Affidavit: Client 9 and Room 871," *New York Times,* 11 March 2008.

5. Eliot Spitzer, "Full Text of Spitzer Resignation," *New York Times,* 12 March 2008.

6. David Koceiniewski and Danny Hakim, "Felled by Scandal, Spitzer Says Focus Is on His Family," *New York Times,* 13 March 2008.

7. "Testimony, Ben S. Bernanke, *Developments in the financial markets:* Before the Committee on Banking, Housing, and Urban Affairs, U.S. Senate, April 3, 2008, Federal Reserve press release. See http://www.federalreserve.gov/newsevents/testimony/bernanke20080403a.htm.

8. Alistair Barr, "Bear Portfolio Worth $28.9 Billion, Fed Says," *Market Watch,* 3 July 2008.

9. Jim Rogers has made these comments on Bloomberg TV and CNBC several times in the past several months. Rogers made these particular comments from Singapore during a segment that aired on Bloomberg Television June 5, 2008.

10. Josh P. Hamilton and Erik Holm, "Buffett Castigates Wall Street, Bankers on Blunders," *Bloomberg News,* 5 May 2008.

11. Kara Scannell, "SEC Role Is Scrutinized in Light of Bear Woes" *Wall Street Journal,* 27 March 2008.

12. Jonathan Stempel, Buffett Backs Fed Over Bear Stearns," *Reuters.com,* 4 May 2008.

13. "Testimony, Ben S. Bernanke, *Developments in the financial markets,* before the Committee on Banking, Housing, and Urban Affairs, U.S. Senate, April 3, 2008.

14. Jeremy Grantham, "Immoral Hazard," *GMO Quarterly Letter,* April 2008.

15. Bloomberg News, "Two Fed Bank Presidents Warn About Lending to Securities Firms," *New York Times,* 6 June, 2008.

16. Jeffrey M. Lacker "Financial Stability and Central Banks," speech presented by the president of the Federal Reserve Bank of Richmond, London, June 5, 2008.

17. Craig Torres, "Fed 'Rogue Operation' Spurs Further Bailout Calls," *Bloomberg News,* 2 May 2008.

18. Krishna Guha, Saskia Scholtes and James Politi, "Saviours of the Suburbs," *Financial Times,* 4 June 2008.

19. Warren Buffett during a televised CNBC interview with Becky Quick, *Squawk Box,* 22 August, 2008.

20. Dawn Kopecki, "Fannie, Freddie 'Insolvent' After Losses, Poole Says," *Bloomberg News,* 10 July 2008.

21. Jody Shenn and James Tyson, "Fannie Mae, Freddie Mac Portfolio Caps Will Be Lifted," *Bloomberg News,* 27 February 2008.

22. Nick Timiraos, "U.S.-Backed Mortgage Program Fuels Risks: FHA Struggles to Eliminate Loans for Zero Down," *Wall Street Journal,* 24 June 2008.

23. Sannon D. Harrinton and Abigail Moses, "Company Bond Risk Rises as Bank Concerns Offset Fannie Rally," *Bloomberg News,* 14 July 2008.

24. David M. Walker, *Saving Our Future Requires Tough Choices Today,* a presentation given by the former Comptroller General as part of the Fiscal Wake-Up Tour at Haas School of Business, University of California–Berkeley, Berkeley, California, March 5, 2008, U.S. Government Accountability Office document GAO-08–583CG.

25. Creadon, Patrick, dir. *I.O.U.S.A.* Documentary. Agora Entertainment, 2008. After the August 21, 2008 debut, Warren Buffett, CEO of Berkshire Hathaway; William Niskanen, Chairman of the CATO Institute; Bill Novelli, CEO of AARP; Pete Peterson, Senior Chairman of The Blackstone Group and Chairman of the Peter G. Peterson Foundation; and Dave Walker,

President & CEO of the Peter G. Peterson Foundation and former U.S. Comptroller General participated in a live discussion broadcast to the movie viewers.

26. Stephen Labaton, "Paulson, at Talks on Regulation, Suggests Pendulum Has Swung Too Far," *New York Times,* 13 March 2007.

27. Laurel Brubaker Calkins, "Enron's Skilling Asks Appeals Court for Reversals," *Bloomberg News,* April 2, 2008.

28. Bob Ivy, "John Rigas's 'Taj Mahal' Sold to Illinois Firm for $3.5 Million," *Bloomberg News,* 7 April 2008.

29. Christopher Bowe, "Kozlowski's Wife Begins Divorce Action," *Financial Times,* 16 August 2006.

30. Warren Buffett to Liz Clayman, CNBC interview at Georgetown, March 13, 2007.

31. Lucian Kim, "Rosneft Profit Rises Fivefold on Yukos Acquisitions," *Blomberg .com,* 8 April 2008.

32. Deborah Solomon, "A Summit on U.S. Rules: 'Too Gosh-Darn Complex,'" *Wall Street Journal,* 14 March 2007.

33. Wall Street Journal Research, "Subpar Earnings: Companies Blame Housing, Credit Problems for Weakness," *Wall Street Journal,* 5 October 2007.

34. Warren Buffett to Liz Clayman.

35. Janet Tavakoli, "Subprime Lending Excesses Have Damaged US's Standing as Global Leader in Finance," *Financial Times,* 19 March 2007.

36. Francesco Guerrera, "Citigroup Takes $9bn Assets in Old Lane Move," *Financial Times,* 13 June 2008.

37. Paul J. Davies and Jennifer Hughes, "US Banks Fear Being Forced to Take $5,000bn Back on Balance Sheets," *Financial Times,* 4 June 2008.

38. U.S. Department of Treasury, *The Department of the Treasury Blueprint for a Modernized Financial Regulatory Structure,* March 2008, http://treas.gov/press/releases/reports/Blueprint.pdf.

39. Benjamin Graham, *The Intelligent Investor* (New York: Harper & Row, 1973), 101.

40. Benjamin Graham. 100.

Chapter 13: The Fogs of War, Religion and Politics

1. Berkshire Hathaway Inc.,"Berkshire Hathaway to Acquire Iscar Metalworking Companies," *Business Wire,* 5 May 2006. Text of ISCAR Ltd. Joint News Release.

2. *Berkshire Hathaway 2006 Annual Report,* 5.

3. Amy Teibel, "Buffett's Israeli Acquisition Born in Shed," *Washington Post,* 8 May 2008.

4. Steven F. Hayward, *Churchill on Leadership,* Forum (an imprint of Prima Publishing, Rocklin, CA 1997, 1998. 129.

5. Neil Sandler, "Buffett Tours Plant in War-scarred Tefen," *BusinessWeek,* 18 September 2006.

6. "Oklahoma Mourns Those Lost in Bombing," *United Press International,* 20 April 2008. McVeigh was executed in 2001.

7. Gideon Rachman, "Death, Double Standards and the Battle for the Moral High Ground," *Financial Times,* 8 August 2008.

8. The Iraq Study Group, James A. Baker III and Lee H. Hamilton co-chairs, *The Iraq Study Group Report: The Way Forward—A New Approach,* Washington D.C., December 6, 2006.

9. Jay Newton-Small, "Waxman Probes Iraq Contracting, Missing $12 Billion," *Bloomberg News,* 6 February 2007.

10. John J. Sheehan, 'Why I Declined to Serve," *Washingtonpost.com,* 16 April 2007.

11. Ibid.

Chapter 14: Finding Value

1. Warren Buffett to Janet Tavakoli, inscription note, 18 February 2006.

2. Janet Tavakoli to Warren Buffett, e-mail correspondence, 16 August 2007.

3. Warren Buffett to Janet Tavakoli, handwritten note, 30 May 2006.

4. Warren Buffett to Janet Tavakoli, telephone conversation, mid June 2006.

5. Janet Tavakoli to Warren Buffett, letter, 20 June 2006.

6. Warren Buffett to Janet Tavakoli, letter, 22 June 2006.

7. Janet Tavakoli to Warren Buffett, letter, 26 June 2006.

8. Benjamin Graham, *The Intelligent Investor* (New York: Harper & Row, 1973), 96.

9. Warren Buffett to Janet Tavakoli, letter, 22 June 2006.

10. Chris Isidore, "Buffett: My Fix for the Economy," CNNMoney.com, 2 October 2008. Warren proposed private investors put up 20 percent cash for asset purchases. The Treasury would finance the other 80 percent in exchange for getting paid principal back first, interest payments, and a share of the upside. This would force the use of market prices.

11. Christine Harper, "Goldman Raises $10 Billion From Bullet, Public Sale." *Bloomberg News,* 24 September 2008. Buffett's preferred shares have a 10 percent redemption premium. Warrants allow Berkshire to buy $5 billion worth of common shares at $115 any time in five years. Goldman raised $5 billion more in the market and the Treasury injected another $10 billion in capital.

12. Warren E. Buffett, "Buy American. I Am." *New York Times,* 17 October 2008.

Bibliography

Auletta, Ken. *Greed and Glory on Wall Street: The Fall of the House of Lehman.* New York: Random House, 1986.

Beales, Richard, and Guerra, Francesco. "Buffett Orders Crackdown on Unethical Practices," *Financial Times,* 9 October 2008.

Belsky, Gary, and Gilovich, Thomas. *Why Smart People Make Big Money Mistakes and How to Correct Them,* Fireside, New York, NY, 1999.

Berkshire Hathaway Inc. *Annual and Interim Reports 1995–2008.* http://www.berkshirehathaway.com/reports.

Bernanke, Ben S. "Testimony, Ben S. Bernanke, *Developments in the financial markets:* Before the Committee on Banking, Housing, and Urban Affairs, U.S. Senate," April 3, 2008. http://www.federalreserve.gov/newsevents/testimony/bernanke 20080403a.htm.

Blackstone, Brian. "U.S. Moves to Bolster Fed Balance Sheet," *Wall Street Journal,* 18 September, 2008.

Boyd, Roddy. "The Last Days of Bear Stearns" *Fortune,* 28 March 2008.

Buffett, Howard G., and Brokaw, Tom. *Tapestry of Life.* BioImages/World Vision, 2001.

Buffett, Warren E. *Berkshire Hathaway, Inc. Shareholder Letters 1977–2007.* http://www.berkshirehathaway.com/letters/letters.html.

————. "Full text of Warren Buffett's September 27 memo," *Financial Times*, 9 October 2008.

————. "Fuzzy Math and Stock Options," *Washington Post*, 6 July 2004. Burden, Matthew Currier. *The Blog of War: Front-Line Dispatches from Soldiers in Iraq and Afghanistan*. New York: Simon & Schuster, 2006.

Cahill, Tom, and Moullakis, Joyce. "Lehman Prime Brokerage Assets Won't Soon Be Returned," *Bloomberg News*, 17 September 2008.

"Carlyle's Debt Team Is a Secret Weapon," *Investment Dealers' Digest*, September 29, 2003.

Camerer, Colin, Loewenstein, George, and Prelec, Drazen. "Neuroeconomics: How Neuroscience Can Inform Economics" *Journal of Economic Literature*, March 2005.

Cialdini, Robert B., Ph.D. *Influence* New York: Quill, 1984.

Cifuentes, Arturo. "CDOs and Their Ratings: Chronicle of a Foretold Disaster," *Total Securitization*, 4 June 2007.

CNBC. "Backing up the Bond," 7 January 2008. Video segment with Becky Quick, Janet Tavakoli, and David Kotok.

————. "Risky Business," *Squawk Box*, 8 August 2007. Segment with Becky Quick and Janet Tavakoli.

————. "U.S. Housing and the Gamble of Subprime Loans," 30 January 2007. Segment with Diana Olick, Jim Melcher, and Janet Tavakoli.

————. "Bond Insurance: The Bigger Problem," *Squawk Box*, 25 January 2008. Segement with Janet Tavakoli, Matthew Fabian, and Charles Gasparino.

Danis, Michelle A., and Pennington-Cross, Anthony. "The Delinquency of Subprime Mortgages," Working Paper 2005-022A, Federal Reserve Bank of St. Louis, March 2005.

Efrati, Amir, and Pleven, Liam. "SEC, Justice Scrutinize AIG on Swaps Accounting," *Wall Street Journal*, 6 June 2008.

Einhorn, David. "Private Profits and Socialized Risk," *Greenlight Capital Letter*, 8 April 2008.

Einhorn, David. "Accounting Ingenuity," remarks at the Ira W. Sohn Investment Research Conference, 21 May 2008.

Erdman, Paul. *Tug of War*. New York: St. Martin's Press, 1996.

Evans, David. "Florida Got Lehman Help Before Run on School's Funds, *Bloomberg News*, 18 December 2007.

Everquest Financial Ltd. Form S-1 Registration Statement Under the Securities Act of 1933, 9 May 2007.

Federal Housing Finance Agency. "Statement of FHFA Director James B. Lockhart," 7 September 2008.

Franklin, Benjamin. *The Autobiography of Benjamin Franklin.* Reprint, Mineola, N.Y.: Dover, 1996.

Glassman, James K. "Big Deals: David Rubenstein and His Partners Have Made Billions With the Carlyle Group," *Washingtonian,* June 2006.

Glover, John. "Pimco, Vanguard Are Biggest Lehman Bond Fund Losers," *Bloomberg News,* 15 September 2008.

Goldstein, Matthew, and Henry, David. "Bears' Hocus Pocus [cover story]: Bear Bets Wrong," *Business Week,* 22 October 2007.

Goldstein, Matthew. "The Everquest IPO: Buyer Beware" [revised title "Bear Stearns' Subprime IPO"], *Business Week,* May 11, 2007.

Graham, Benjamin. *The Intelligent Investor.* New York: Harper & Row, 1986. This edition include a preface written by Warren Buffett in tribute to Benjamin Graham reprinted from the *Financial Analysts Journal,* November/December 1976. It also includes an edited transcript of a talk Warren Buffett gave in 1984 at Columbia University: "The Superinvestors of Graham-and-Doddsville."

Graham, Benjamin, and Dodd, David L. *Security Analysis.* New York: McGraw, 1951.

Graham, Katherine. *Personal History.* New York: Random House, 1997.

Grant, Audrey, Prociuk, Paula, and Carruthers, John Grant. *Ex-Etiquette: The Etiquette of Separation, Divorce and Remarriage.* Scarborough, Ont., Canada: Prentice Hall, 1988.

Grantham, Jeremy. "Immoral Hazard," *GMO Quarterly Letter,* April 2008.

Greenspan, Alan, "Remarks by Chairman Alan Greenspan, *Consumer Finance.*" Federal Reserve System's Fourth Annual Community Affairs Research Conference, Washington, D.C., April 8, 2005.

Gross, Bill. "Looking for Contagion in All the Wrong Places," *PIMCO Investment Outlook,* July 2007.

Hagopian, Kip. "Point of View: Expensing Employee Stock Options is Improper Accounting," *California Management Review 48,* no. 4 (Summer 2006): 136–156.

Hayward, Steven F. *Churchill on Leadership.* Forum. Rocklin, California: Forum, 1998.

Hilsenrath, Jon, and Reddy, Sudeep. "Fed Plans Expanded Lending Facilities, *Wall Street Journal,* 15 September 2008.

Hockenberry, John. "In Iraq for 365," *Wired.com,* 23 June 2005.

Holm, Erick, and Richard, Christine, "AIG's Collapse Would Have Impact Around the Globe," *Bloomberg News,* 16 September, 2008.

Johnson, Jo. "Fimalac Chief Under Governance Pressure," *Financial Times,* 30 July 2003.

Jones, Alfred Winslow. "Fashions in Forecasting," *Fortune,* March 1949.

Kahneman, Daniel, Slovic, Paul, and Tversky, Amos (eds.). *Judgment Under Uncertainty: Heuristics and Biases.* Cambridge, UK: Cambridge University Press, 1982.

Karnitschnig, Matthew, Solomon, Deborah, and Pleven, Liam. "U.S. Plans Rescue of AIG to Halt Crisis; Central Banks Inject Cash as Credit Dries Up," *Wall Street Journal,* 16 September 2008.

Keenan, Matthew. "Gross's Total Return Falls the Most in Three Years," *Bloomberg News,* 17 September 2008.

Kelly, Kate. "Bear Stearns Neared Collapse Twice in Frenzied Last Days," *Wall Street Journal,* 29 May 2008.

———. "Fear, Rumors Touched off Fatal Run on Bear Stearns," *Wall Street Journal,* 28 May, 2008.

———. "Lost Opportunities Haunt Final Days of Bear Stearns," *Wall Street Journal,* 27 May 2008.

Kelly, Kate and Serena Ng. "Bear Stearns Bails out Fund with Capital Injection," *Wall Street Journal, 23* June 2007.

Kenneth M. Crys, and Christopher Stride, et al. v. Christopher Sugrue; Mark Kavanagh, et al. Supreme Court of the State of New York, County of New York, Index No. 08600653, filed May 5, 2008.

Lacker, Jeffrey, M. "Financial Stability and Central Banks," speech presented by the president of the Federal Reserve Bank of Richmond, London, June 5, 2008.

Lauricella, Tom, Rappaprot, Liz, and Lobb, Annelena. "Mounting Fears Shake World Markets As Banking Giants Rush to Raise Capital," *Wall Street Journal,* 18 September 2008.

Lawrence, D. H. "The Rocking Horse Winner," in *The Woman who Rode Away and Other Stories* (1928), edited by Dieter Mehl and Christa Jansohn. Cambridge, UK: Cambridge University Press, 1995. 230–243.

Lewis, Michael. *Liar's Poker.* New York: W. W. Norton, 1989.

Lowenstein, Roger. *When Genius Failed.* New York: HarperCollins, 2002.

Lucchetti, Aaron, Smith, Randall, and Strassburg, Jenny. "Morgan Stanley in Talks with Wachovia, Others," *Wall Street Journal,* 18 September 2008.

Mandelbrot, Benoit, and Hudson, Richard L. *The (Mis)Behavior of Markets* New York: Basic Books, 2004.

Martin, Judith. *Miss Manners' Guide to Excruciatingly Correct Behavior.* New York: W. W. Norton, 2005.

McGinty, Tom. "Fewer Investors Back Plans to Weigh in Executive Compensation," *Wall Street Journal,* 22 May 2008.

Meissner, W. W., S.J., M.D. *Ignatius of Loyola: The Psychology of a Saint.* New Haven: Yale University Press, 1992.

Mollenkamp, Carrick, and Ng, Serena. "Wall Street Wizardry Amplified Credit Crisis," *Wall Street Journal,* 27 December, 2007.

Moody, Emma. "Moody's Says Some Employees Breached Code of Conduct," *Bloomberg News,* 1 July 2008.

Moody's Investors Service, "Global Credit Research Announcement: Moody's Announces Rating Actions on Financial Guarantors," 14 December 2007.

Munger, Charles T. *Poor Charlie's Almanack: The Wit and Wisdom of Charles T. Munger.* The Donning Publishers, 2005.

Newton, Greg. "So Help Us, God," *NakedShorts,* 1 August 2005.

Office of Federal Housing Enterprise Oversight. *Report of the Special Examination of Freddie Mac,* December 2003.

OHC Liquidation Trust, et al v. Credit Suisse First Boston et al., U.S. Bankruptcy Court, Delaware. Civil Action No. 07-799 JJF (Chapter 11 Case No. 02-13396) Memorandum Opinion. June 9, 2008.

Onaran, Yalman. "Banks Keep $35 Billion Markdown Off Income Statements," *Bloomberg News,* 19 May 2008.

———. "Spector Ousted by Cayne Over Too Much Bridge, Money," *Bloomberg,* 3 October, 2007.

Paulos, John Allen. *Innumeracy: Mathematical Illiteracy and Its Consequences.* New York: Hill and Wang, 1989.

Pittman, Mark. "Moody's, S&P Defer Cuts on AAA Subprime, Hiding Loss," *Bloomberg News,* 11 March 2008.

Reckard, Scott E. "Atty. Gen. Jerry Brown rejects probe of Sen. Charles Schumer in IndyMac Failure," *Los Angeles Times,* 23 August 2008.

Reilly, David. "In Subprime, AIG Sees Small Risk; Others See More," *Wall Street Journal,* 13 August 2007.

Rosch, John. "Alaska Oil Spill Fuels Concerns Over Arctic Wildlife, Future Drilling," *National Geographic News,* 20 March 2006.

Savage, Sam. "The Flaw of Averages," *San Jose Mercury News,* 2000.

Shenn, Jody. "Bear Stearns Funds to Transfer Subprime-Mortgage Risk with IPO," *Bloomberg News,* May 11, 2007.

Shenn, Jody, and Tyson, James. "Fannie Mae, Freddie Mac Portfolio Caps Will Be Lifted," *Bloomberg News,* 27 February 2008.

Sinha, Gyan, and Chabba, Karan. "Sell on the Rumor, Buy on the News," Bear Stearns, 12 February 2007.

Solomon, Deborah, Corkery, Michael, and Rappaport, Liz. "Mortgage Bailout Is Greeted with Relief, Fresh Questions," *Wall Street Journal,* 9 September 2008.

Spence, Jonathan D. *The Memory Palace of Matteo Ricci.* New York: Penguin Books, 1985.

Spitzer, Eliot. "Full Text of Spitzer Resignation," *New York Times,* 12 March 2008.

————. "Predatory Lenders' Partner in Crime" *Washington Post, 14* February 2008.

Swensen, David F. *Unconventional Success: A Fundamental Approach to Personal Investment.* New York: New York, 2005.

Sykes, Christopher. *No Ordinary Genius: The Illustrated Richard Feynman.* New York: W.W. Norton & Company, 1995.

Taleb, Nassim. *Fooled by Randomness.* New York: Random House, 2001.

Tavakoli, Janet. "Are You Sure You Made a Fortune Shorting the ABX (or TABX)?" [Commentary], *LIPPER HedgeWorld,* 5 December 2007.

————. "Bear's Bailout [of BSAM's hedge funds] A Bad Idea," *LIPPER HedgeWorld,* 27 June, 2007.

————. "Best Practices Among CDO Mangers," *Asset Securitization* (Conference Daily), 7 November, 2006.

————. "CDOs: Caveat Emptor," *GARP Risk Review,* Issue 26 (September–October 2005).

————. *Collateralized Debt Obligations & Structured Finance.* New York: John Wiley & Sons, 2003.

————. "Comments on SEC Proposed Rules on Rating Agencies," 13 February 2007.

————. *Credit Derivatives & Synthetic Structures,* 2nd ed. New York: John Wiley & Sons, 2001.

————. "Dicey Deals Done Dirt Cheap," Tavakoli Structured Finance, Inc., 3 January 2008.

————. "The Elusive Income of Synthetic CDOs," *Journal of Structured Finance,* Winter 2006.

————. "The Golden Fleece Award for Optional Integrity," *HedgeWorld.com,* 2 October 2006.

————. "My Favorite Hedge Fund: Part II," *HedgeWorld.com,* October 24, 2005.

————. "Invisible Hedge Funds," *GARP Risk Review,* Issue 19 (July–August 2004).

————. "Misfortune's Formula: Structured Credit Ratings (Commentary), *HedgeWorld.com,* 19 September 2007.

———. "Oil and Power: Iran Approach Must Avoid Past Mistakes," *HedgeWorld. com,* 14 June 2006.

———. "Rating the Rating Agencies," *GARP Risk Review,* Issue 22 (January– February 2005).

———. "Structured Finance: Challenges for Supervision and Regulation (Presentation to the International Monetary Fund)," 19 April 2005.

———. *Structured Finance & Collateralized Debt Obligations,* 2nd ed. Hoboken, N.J.: John Wiley & Sons, 2008.

———. "Subprime Mortgages: The Predators' Fall," *Global Association of Risk Professionals,* March–April 2007.

The Federal Reserve Board. "Minutes of the Federal Open Market Committee," 7 August 2007.

Tobias, Andrew. *The Invisible Bankers.* New York: Washington Square Press, 1982.

U.S. Department of Treasury, *The Department of the Treasury Blueprint for a Modernized Financial Regulatory Structure,* March 2008, http://treas.gov/press/ releases/reports/Blueprint.pdf.

U.S. Securities and Exchange Commission, Division of Corporate Finance. "Sample Letter Sent to Public Companies on MD&A Disclosure Regarding the Application of SFAS 157 (Fair Value Measurements)," March 31, 2008. http://www.sec.gov/divisions/corpfin/guidance/fairvalueltr0308.htm.

U.S. Senate Committee on Banking, Housing, and Urban Affairs. "Testimony of Jamie Dimon Before the Senate Committee on Banking, Housing, and Urban Affairs," April 3, 2008.

United States of America against Ralph Cioffi and Matthew Tannin, CR 08 415, f.#2007R01328, filed June 18, 2008.

Vulliamy, Ed, "Dark Heart of the American Dream," *The Observer,* 16 June 2002.

Walker, David M. *Saving Our Future Requires Tough Choices Today.* Presentation for the Fiscal Wake-Up Tour at Haas School of Business, University of California–Berkeley, Berkeley, California, March 5, 2008. U.S. Government Accountability Office document GAO-08-583CG.

Wall Street Journal Research. "Subpar Earnings: Companies Blame Housing, Credit Problems for Weakness," *Wall Street Journal,* 5 October 2007.

Weinberg, Neil, and Condon, Bernard. "The Sleaziest Show on Earth," *Forbes,* 24 May 2004.

Williams, John Burr. *The Theory of Investment Value.* 1938. Reprint, New York: Fraser, 1997.

Index